# DIVERGENT THINKING

# Creativity Research

## Mark A. Runco, *Series Editor*

*Counseling Gifted and Talented Children*, edited by Roberta M. Milgram
*Divergent Thinking*, by Mark A. Runco

### In Preparation:

*Achieving Extraordinary Ends: An Essay on Creativity*, by Sharon Bailin
*Perspectives on Creativity: The Biographical Method*, by John E. Gedo and
    Mary M. Gedo
*More Ways Than One: Fostering Creativity*, by Arthur J. Cropley
*Creative Thinking: Problem Solving and the Arts Orientation*,
    by John Wakefield
*Genius Revisited: High IQ Children Grown Up*, by Rena Subotnik,
    Lee Kassan, Ellen Summers, and Alan Wasser
*Creativity in Government*, by Thomas Heinzen
*Problem Finding, Problem Solving, and Creativity*, edited by Mark A. Runco
*Creativity and Affect*, edited by Melvin Shaw and Klaus Hoppe
*Understanding and Recognizing Creativity: Emergence of a Discipline*,
    *Volume 1*, edited by Scott G. Isaksen, Mary C. Murdock, Roger L.
    Firestien, and Donald J. Treffinger
*Nurturing and Developing Creativity: Emergence of a Discipline, Volume 2*,
    edited by Scott G. Isaksen, Mary C. Murdock, Roger L. Firestien, and
    Donald J. Treffinger
*Contexts of Creativity*, by Leonora Cohen, Amit Goswami, Shawn Boels,
    and Richard Chaney
*Creativity: Theories, Themes and Issues*, by Mark A. Runco

# DIVERGENT THINKING

## Mark A. Runco

**California State University, Fullerton**

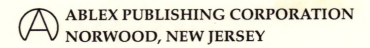

ABLEX PUBLISHING CORPORATION
NORWOOD, NEW JERSEY

**Library of Congress Cataloging-in-Publication Data**

Runco, Mark A
     Divergent thinking / Mark A. Runco
       p.     cm.
     Includes bibliographical references.
     ISBN 0-89391-700-1 (cloth)
     1. Divergent thinking. 2. Creative thinking. I. Title
     BF441.R86  1989
     155.4'1342—dc20                89-27528
                                     CIP

Ablex Publishing Corporation
355 Chestnut St.
Norwood, NJ 07648

# Dedication

For my parents, Ray and Ann, and their parents,
Joseph and Mary, and Richard and Olga.

# Contents

# Preface

Divergent thinking tests are probably the most commonly used measure of children's potential for creative thinking. Divergent thinking is not synonymous with creative thinking, but the research presented in this volume suggests that divergent thinking is an important component of the creative process. This research also suggests that divergent thinking tests are not perfect measures (just as IQ tests are not perfect measures of intelligence), but they are useful estimates of the potential for creative thought.

This view of divergent thinking reflects a type of synthesis. Indeed, looking back, the research on tests of creative thinking can be described as following a dialectical path, with the "thesis" introduced by J. P. Guilford. In Guilford's terms, the "divergent production" of ideas is one facet of the human intellect, and is distinct from the "convergent production" of ideas (i.e., thinking which converges on correct or conventional ideas) tapped by IQ and most other conventional tests. Guilford's theory was enthusiastically received, probably because divergent thinking tests offered an alternative (or complement) to IQ tests. This early enthusiasm probably also reflected the ostensible association of divergent thinking and creativity.

An anthetical phase of research followed, and the divergent thinking model received some very pointed criticism. Much of this criticism was directed at Guilford's methodology—particularly his factor analytic procedures for demonstrating the orthogonality of the different faces of the intellect. Additional criticism was directed at the marginal predictive and discriminant validity of divergent thinking tests. Many educators and researchers were disappointed that divergent thinking was not more highly correlated with creative performance.

At present, the divergent thinking model is in the midst of a "synthesis." Divergent thinking is no longer equated with creativity; but tests of divergent thinking have proven their usefulness as estimates of the potential for creative ideation. Divergent thinking appears to be a very important component of the creative process. There are a number of unanswered questions about children's divergent thinking and creativity. Several of these are addressed throughout this book, and may be identified as themes in the research.

One of the themes in this book is that the capacity for divergent thinking may not be normally distributed across all levels of ability. This is an important theme, and apposite to many areas of research. Robert Albert presented a compelling developmental explanation for the non-normal distribution of creative ability. He is conducting a longitudinal investigation on exceptionally gifted children, and one of his premises is that very few individuals experience the two developmental "transformations" that are necessary for exceptionality to manifest itself (see Chapter 1). A second relevant premise in this longitudinal study is that creative abilities are not evenly distributed across domains of performance and achievement (see Chapter 13). For this reason, Albert is comparing exceptionally gifted, conventionally gifted, and nongifted children, with one sample of subjects demonstrating extraordinary talents in mathematics and science, and a second sample identified based on their extremely high general ability (the IQ). I am fortunate to be able to present several samples of Albert's work in the present book.

There are several concerns one must recognize when conducting or evaluating the empirical research on the distribution of creativity. The sampling of subjects, for example, often reflects a restricted range of scores. When one sample is compared to another, the variability within one frequently differs from the variability within the other. This can influence reliability and validity coefficients, and groups with more variability will tend to have higher reliability and validity coefficients. Another potential concern is that differences in test performance may reflect more than cognitive ability per se. I suggest throughout this book that divergent thinking and creativity are partly cognitive and partly strategic, or "metacognitive." Individual differences probably reflect metacognitive skills in addition to ideational skills.

My research addresses the distribution issue in its demonstrating that ideational originality and flexibility are more reliable and valid in gifted children than nongifted children. These differences are apparent even after restricted range of scores and metacognitive components are taken into account. Gifted children consistently and spontaneously think divergently; nongifted children do not. Nongifted children may be occasionally creative, but their divergent thinking is not reliable enough to indicate that they have the same intellectual and strategic skills as the gifted children. Clearly, the research on creative and divergent thinking has implications for our conception and definition of "giftedness."

A second theme in this book was introduced in Wallach and Kogan's *Modes of Thinking in Young Children*. Wallach and Kogan suggested that divergent thinking is influenced by the conditions under which it is assessed. For example, when divergent thinking tasks are described as "tests" and administered with time limits, examinees appear to concentrate on correct answers and grades and may not think as divergently as they might under more flexible and playful conditions. Recent research on consequences and intrinsic motivation supports this view. Some have recently argued that divergent thinking is not influenced by administration procedures, and this may be accurate in terms of the general testing atmosphere. However, there can be little doubt that divergent thinking is influenced by a number of extracognitive factors. For instance, examinees' task perception dramatically influences divergent thinking (see Chapter 6).

A third theme of this book is methodological. Chapter 5, for example, describes the Social Validation procedures. These were adapted from the behavioral assessment paradigm and used to complement existing psychometric evaluations of divergent thinking tests. Chapters 14 and 15 demonstrate a second methodological technique, namely the testing of interactions in predictive validation equations. These interactions offer a critical test of the theory of ideational creativity. Torrance, for example, suggested that creative thinking involves the ability to generate ideas, and the ability to use a variety of ideas, and the ability to find original ideas. The research herein indicates that the interaction between ideational fluency, flexibility, and originality has predictive validity. The interactions between intelligence and divergent thinking, on the other hand, do not contribute to creative performance. This may be because both interact with motivation, and motivation was not examined. Most contemporary theories of creative achievement predict an interaction between intelligence, creativity, and motivation (see Chapter 15).

A final theme is that divergent thinking is important for both "basic" and "applied" research. From the perspective of basic research, the divergent thinking model offers an empirically supported view of a cognitive process (i.e., ideation). From the applied perspective, divergent thinking can be viewed as one component of giftedness and predictive of several expressions of real-world creativity. The basic and applied perspectives are apparent in each of the four sections of this book. The first section examines Developmental research; the second examines Educational research; the third looks at the research on the Dimensions of divergent thinking; and the fourth focuses on the Validity of divergent thinking tests.

I would like to acknowledge the support of my colleagues, Drs. Jerry Johnson and William Higa, and the assistance of my collaborators, Robert Albert, Mike Bahleda, Shawn Okuda, Kathy Pezdek, and Becky Thurston.

Mark A. Runco
Hilo, Hawaii
May, 1987

## Section I

# Developmental Issues

The four chapters reported in this Section each address a developmental issue. The first chapter describes the association between parents' divergent thinking and that of their exceptionally gifted boys. This project is from Albert's longitudinal investigation; and as such, one of the important questions addressed deals with differences between subjects gifted in mathematics and science and subjects gifted in general ability (the IQ). The second chapter reports that birth-order and family size are both predictive of a child's divergent thinking. The third chapter in this Section reports that independence training is correlated with divergent thinking. This chapter is also from Albert's longitudinal study. The final chapter in this Section looks to television and radio as potential influences on divergent thinking. The methodology involves a comparison of ideation elicited by an audio message (like a radio) with ideation elicited by a message with both audio and visual information (like that presented on television).

Developmentally, eminence appears to involve two rather broad cognitive and personality "transformations" of a child's early giftedness into a long-standing capacity for cognitive exceptionality and noteworthy performance (Albert, 1980a, 1980b; Albert & Runco, 1986; Helson, 1985). The earliest transformation is one of cognitive giftedness into outstanding creative ability, usually occuring during—but not entirely through—the first two decades of life. It distinguishes the effective person from the equally bright but uncreative one (Gilmore, 1974; MacKinnon, 1983). The second major transformation begins and continues throughout adolescence, and often into early adulthood. This is a transformation of creative ability into a well-integrated set of cognitive skills, career-focused interests and values, specific creative personality dispositions, and moderately high ambitions. It appears that the earlier this second transformation occurs, the more likely higher eminence will be attained (e.g., Darwin, Einstein, Mozart, and Picasso). Moreover, there appears to be a difference between scientifically oriented and artistically oriented youth in this regard (Getzels & Csikszentamihalyi, 1976; Hudson, 1966; Tyler, 1964), with the second transformation completed earlier for scientists-to-be. Regardless of when they end, the result of these transformations is an exceptionally able young adult who is task-oriented, highly committed to his or her field of interest, and extremely motivated to be productive and achieve in the area(s) of interest.

It goes without much argument that most eminent persons are notably talented and cognitively gifted (Chauncey & Hilton, 1965; Cox, 1926; Walberg, Rasher, & Hase, 1978). It also goes without much argument that not all talented and gifted children undergo these transformations; and even among those who do, not all become eminent. One reason for this is that these transformations require rather special early learning circumstances and parental relationships (Albert, 1971, 1978; Bloom, 1982; Helson, 1985; Viernstein & Hogan, 1975).

Developmental transformations are difficult to observe because they occur over a long period of time and in multiple settings. It has never been easy to observe or determine the significant focal relationships (Albert & Runco, 1987) and crystalizing experiences (Walters & Gardner, in press) in the developmental process. For these reasons, some of our fullest, most suggestive evidence comes from detailed biographies such as the monumental *Samuel Johnson* (Bate, 1977), *Charles Darwin* (Brent, 1981), *Beethoven* (Solomon, 1977), and more recently *The Kennedys: An American Drama* (Collier & Horowitz, 1984). Although such works have their limitations, when serious, they are exhaustive in detail and incorporate the results of many investigators, giving comprehensiveness and reliability to their data and interpretations.

Empirical research on the development of exceptional giftedness also has its problems, perhaps the most critical being the reliance upon data from eminent adults. This approach, with its obvious "selection bias," tells us little about those individuals whose potential has gone unfulfilled. Furthermore, these studies often either focus too selectively upon or ignore the family and other potentially significant persons. The multitude of cross-sectional investigations of gifted children are informative, but most of these rely on paper-and-pencil measures, with occasional interviews with parents, teachers, or even the child. While we gain insights from such work into some of the demographic and personological characteristics of gifted children, little is learned about the developmental processes involved.

4

The general objective of our on-going longitudinal research project is to monitor these processes in two groups of exceptionally gifted adolescents and their families (see Subjects section, following). In order to learn more about the developmental transformations that are necessary for the fulfillment of an exceptionally gifted individual's potential, we are (a) monitoring selected aspects of subjects' and parents' cognitive and extracognitive dispositions and behaviors; (b) relating the son's initial level of cognitive and creative abilities to inter- and intrafamily variables; (c) evaluating subjects' career decisions to ascertain if and how these are related to early parental variables and to the early performances and preferences of the children; and lastly, and the crux, (d) defining a set of predictors of high adult achievement from the array of personality, familial, and cognitive variables measured during pre-adolescence and adolescence.

In addition to comparing adolescents at different levels of ability (i.e., exceptionally gifted versus gifted and nongifted adolescents), we are comparing several different domains of exceptionality (i.e., the IQ versus math-science abilities). This interest in domain-specific talent follows from the research which posits that different domains of performance have idiosyncratic developmental histories (Feldman, 1980; Gardner, 1983; Getzels & Csikszentamihalyi, 1976; Hudson, 1966; Tyler, 1964). This hypothesis is also supported by our theoretical model (Albert & Runco, 1986) and our previous empirical investigations (Albert, 1980b; Runco, 1987).

We are approximately half-way into the longitudinal project, and we have previously reported birth-order, education, and personality similarities and differences between two samples of subjects and their families (Albert, 1980a, 1980b; Albert & Runco, 1985; Runco & Albert, 1985, 1986). The present investigation is focused on intrafamilial cognitive resemblance. Because of heredity, child-parent identification, and the selective emphases within families toward preferred forms of cognitive interests and performances, parents and child may come to share important cognitive capacities. How much and in what forms are to be determined. One important and interesting cognitive capacity is "divergent thinking," or the ability to produce numerous and diverse ideas (Guilford, 1968). Divergent thinking is involved in many definitions of giftedness (Renzulli, 1978), and has previously been used for intrafamilial comparisons (Fu, Moran, Sawyers, & Milgram, 1983).

The questions we are addressing here include, "Are both samples of exceptionally gifted children similar to their parents in creative potential? Are the two groups equally similar, or do they differ from one another as to which parent they are most similar? Most importantly, does the parent-child relationship in the two exceptionally gifted samples' creative potential differ from that of nongifted children and their parents?" Based on the work of Bloom (1982), Helson (1985), and Viernstein and Hogan (1975), as well as our own model of the intrafamilial "fit" which is required for the development of giftedness (Albert & Runco, 1986), we hypothesized that the intrafamilial relationships will be stronger in the present sample than in nongifted samples.

5

## Method

**Subjects**

One exceptionally gifted sample consists of 26 boys, aged 12-13 years, and their families. These boys were among the top 40 individuals in a ranking with a composite achievement score. This composite included both scales of the SAT and six tests of mathematical and science abilities (Stanley, George, & Solano, 1977). Their mean SAT math score was 635, and their mean SAT verbal score was 491. Their families averaged 2.5 children, and a SES indicator (Myrianthopoulos & French, 1968) placed these families well in the upper-middle class. The second sample consists of 28 boys of approximately the same age with IQs above 150 (a mean IQ of 158 and a standard deviation of 6.8), and their families. The average number of children in these families was 2.8, and they were also in the upper-middle SES level.

We recognize that there might be some overlap between the two groups. However, Albert and Runco (1987) present a comprehensive argument that these samples represent very distinct populations. For the present, it should suffice to know that the Math-Science group have only moderate verbal SAT scores, while the IQ group have very exceptional verbal skills. Similarly, the IQ group have above average mathematics ability, but they are significantly below the Math-Science group in this aptitude. They are also well below the Math-Science group in their mathematics experience and training, for the Math-Science adolescents were participants in the work of Stanley et al. (1977) on mathematical talent. Both groups are, then, "exceptionally gifted," but they differ in their intellectual foci.

**Measures and Procedure**

Five divergent thinking (DT) tests from the Wallach and Kogan (1965) battery were used: Instances, Similarities, Uses, Pattern-Meanings, and Line-Meanings. Each test had three items. This battery is highly reliable and valid with gifted children (Runco & Albert, 1985, 1986), and was used in earlier work on intrafamilial DT (Fu et al., 1983).

The divergent thinking tests were administered to the subjects and their parents in their homes as one component of a large set of interview/self-report/ability measures. Participants worked alone, and were allowed as much time as they needed. Care was taken to preclude parent-child collusion. After all data were collected, the DT tests were scored for ideational fluency (the number of distinct ideas) and originality (the number of unique ideas). Total verbal DT scores were calculated for fluency and originality by adding together the scores from Instances, Similarities, and Uses, and total figural scores were calculated by adding together the scores of Pattern Meanings and Line Meanings.

## Results

The means and standard deviations for the dependent measures are given in Table 1-1. (Because of absences, these data include 23 fathers for the Math-Science group, and 26 for the IQ group.) Only fluency scores were used because fluency and originality were highly correlated ($r$ = .82 for the figural tests and .76 for the verbal).

Table 1-1

Means and Standard Deviations (in parentheses)
for the Divergent Thinking Test Scores

| Divergent Thinking Test | Group | | |
|---|---|---|---|
| | High IQ | Math-Science | Total |
| | ($n$ = 28) | ($n$ = 26) | ($N$ = 54) |
| Boys' Figural Fluency | 25.3 (16.7) | 24.7 (18.7) | 24.9 (17.5) |
| Boys' Verbal Fluency | 46.6 (25.1) | 45.3 (24.8) | 45.9 (24.7) |
| Mothers' Figural Fluency | 36.3 (12.2) | 32.0 (15.4) | 34.2 (13.9) |
| Mothers' Verbal Fluency | 80.4 (38.1) | 64.4 (26.3) | 72.6 (33.6) |
| Fathers' Figural Fluency | 39.8 (24.1) | 35.3 (18.7) | 37.6 (21.6) |
| Fathers' Verbal Fluency | 88.9 (58.6) | 65.1 (34.6) | 77.7 (49.8) |

The primary hypothesis of this project was first tested with canonical correlational procedures. These procedures evaluate the overall relationship of the parents' DT with the boys' DT. This particular analysis included the four parental DT scores in one set of variables, and the two DT scores of the boys in the other. Results indicated that parental DT scores were significantly related to their sons' DT scores ($R_C$ = .55, $F$ (8,84) = 2.57, $p$ < .02). In order to interpret this, it is helpful to know that the variate of the first set of variables was correlated with mothers' figural DT ($r$ = .72), mothers' verbal DT ($r$ = .48), fathers' figural DT ($r$ = .28), and fathers' verbal DT ($r$ = .56). The second variate was correlated with boys' figural DT ($r$ = .98) and boys' verbal DT ($r$ = .71). A strong canonical relationship was also found within the Math-Science group ($R_C$ = .68) and the Exceptionally High IQ group ($R_C$ = .62).

Pearson correlations were then calculated to assess the intrafamilial relationships of the individual measures. Because the variances of the scores of the two groups were different (see Table 1-1), the DT scores were transformed into z-scores within the two groups, and these z-scores were used in calculating the bivariate correlations. This eliminated the possibility that the coefficients of the two groups were different because of the discrepant variances. Table 1-2 presents the intrafamily coefficients, with the Exceptionally High IQ group above the diagonal of the matrix, and the

Math-Science group below. The coefficients of greatest interest are those in the top two rows and the first two columns of Table 1-2. These reinforce the finding that the DT scores of these exceptionally gifted adolescents are significantly related to the DT scores of their parents. All of these coefficients would be larger if the reliabilties of the tests were taken into account.

The coefficients in Table 1-2 also suggest that the DT scores of the Math-Science boys are only significantly correlated with their mothers' DT scores, while the Exceptionally High IQ boys' DT scores are significantly related to both parents' DT scores. Of course, statistical power is less than desirable with this sample size. However, 95% confidence intervals were calculated for the coefficients of the IQ group (using an r-to-z transformation); and several of the coefficients of the Math-Science group (i.e., boys' verbal DT with fathers' figural DT, fathers' verbal DT, and mothers' verbal DT) were indeed outside of these intervals.

---

Table 1-2

Correlation Matrix of the Divergent Thinking Test Scores

| Divergent Thinking Test | 1 | 2 | 3 | 4 | 5 | 6 |
|---|---|---|---|---|---|---|
| 1. Boys' Figural Fluency | — | 799** | 321* | 149 | 235 | 313 |
| 2. Boys' Verbal Fluency | 497** | — | 450** | 095 | 434** | 473** |
| 3. Mothers' Figural Fluency | 452** | 087 | — | 335* | 492** | 308 |
| 4. Mothers' Verbal Fluency | 431** | 047 | 769 | — | 121 | 194 |
| 5. Fathers' Figural Fluency | 015 | – 086 | 496** | 594** | — | 889** |
| 6. Fathers' Verbal Fluency | 270 | 108 | – 076 | 287 | 412* | — |

Note: Exceptionally High IQ families ($n$ = 28) are above the diagonal and Exceptionally High Math-Science families ($n$ = 26) are below. Decimals have been omitted, and $*p < .05$ and $**p < .01$.

---

## Discussion

The canonical coefficients and the bivariate correlation matrix indicate that there is a moderately strong statistical relationship between the divergent thinking of the exceptionally gifted boys and that of their parents. This is in direct contrast to the intrafamilial divergent thinking of nongifted children and their parents. Fu et al. (1983), for example, reported that the divergent thinking of nongifted children is entirely unrelated to their parents' divergent thinking. Hence, the primary hypothesis of this investigation is supported, and the relationship between parents' and their children's divergent thinking does appear to be a function of level of ability.

The coefficients presented in Table 1-2 suggest that intrafamilial divergent thinking may vary in different domains, as well as at different levels. We should keep in mind that these coefficients are probably attenuated by the reliabilities of the divergent thinking tests, and that the differences between the IQ and the Math-Science groups were only moderate.

Still, the differences between the two exceptionally gifted samples are congruent with other work on domain-specific talent (Feldman, 1980; Gardner, 1983; Getzels & Csikszentamihalyi, 1976; Hudson, 1966; Tyler, 1964). In fact, the direction of the group difference is the same as that which was found with earlier work with these two groups. Albert and Runco (1987), for example, reported that the Math-Science adolescents have more focused or specialized cognitive skills than Exceptionally High IQ adolescents; and here the verbal and figural divergent thinking performances are not as highly correlated in the Math-Science group as in the Exceptionally High IQ group. More importantly, previous comparisons of personality profiles and attitudes about autonomy indicated that the High IQ boys are more similar to both parents than the gifted Math-Science boys (Albert, 1980b; Albert & Runco, 1985, 1986); and this is also true of the present findings. Although further research is needed on this issue, the findings from the present investigation strengthen the argument that the two exceptionally gifted samples are dissimilar in the association between their cognitive abilities and familial background.

While a genetic contribution to intrafamilial divergent thinking ability cannot be entirely dismissed (Goldsmith, 1983; Horn, 1983), the group differences suggest that other powerful processes may play a role in intrafamilial divergent thinking. For instance, selective child-parent identification and social learning (modeling) might be involved in the development of divergent thinking. This is consistent with the explanations given by Helson (1985) and Viernstein and Hogan (1975) for intrafamilial similarity in other gifted and talented samples. They demonstrated that parents' personalities and motivations are significantly related to a gifted child's achievement motivation, adult career choices, and performances. The group differences might also be indicative of the early temperamental tendencies that determine which aspects of the family environment will become aligned with and reinforce the adolescents' internal developmental processes and abilities (Albert & Runco, 1986; Scarr & MacCartney, 1983).

One might think that the parent-child correlations of divergent thinking can be explained in terms of intrafamilial IQ. Divergent thinking is often thought to be related to IQ. However, recent evidence indicates that even in large, heterogeneous samples, divergent thinking and IQ share at most 20% of their variance (Runco & Albert, 1986). Divergent thinking therefore has a large portion of unique variance. Furthermore, the idea that IQ is a moderating variable—with the relationship between parents' and adolescents' divergent thinking resulting from the overlap of parents' and adolescents' IQs—is a much less parsimonious explanation than looking directly to the relationship of parents' and adolescents' divergent thinking.

The primary finding of this study is that the divergent thinking of exceptionally gifted adolescent boys, unlike that of nongifted individuals, is associated with the divergent thinking of their parents. Of course, divergent thinking ability is not synonymous with creativity (Nicholls, 1972), but these tests are reliable and valid (Runco & Albert, 1985), included in many operational definitions of giftedness (Renzulli, 1978), and probably the most commonly used measure of creative potential. Whether or not these tests and these intrafamilial relationships predict subsequent career choices, accomplishments, and performances of the exceptionally gifted adolescents is still under investigation.

## REFERENCES

Albert, R. S. (1971). Cognitive development and parental loss among the gifted, the exceptionally gifted, and the creative. *Psychological Reports, 29,* 19-26.

Albert, R. S. (1975). Toward a behavioral definition of genius. *American Psychologist, 30,* 140-151.

Albert, R. S. (1978). Observations and suggestions regarding giftedness, familial influences and the achievement of eminence. *Gifted Child Quarterly, 22,* 201-211.

Albert, R. S. (1980a). Family position and the attainment of eminence. *Gifted Child Quarterly, 24,* 87-89.

Albert, R. S. (1980b). Exceptionally gifted boys and their parents. *Gifted Child Quarterly, 24,* 174-179.

Albert, R. S., & Runco, M. A. (1985, August). *Family variables and the creative potential of exceptionally gifted boys.* Paper presented at the meeting of the American Psychological Association in Los Angeles, CA.

Albert, R. S., & Runco, M.A. (1986). The achievement of eminence: A model of exceptionally gifted boys and their familes. In R. J. Sternberg & J. E. Davidson (Eds.), *Conceptions of giftedness* (pp. 332-357). New York: Cambridge University Press.

Albert, R. S., & Runco, M. A. (1987). The possible different personality dispositions of scientists and nonscientists. In D. N. Jackson & J. P. Rushton (Eds.), *Scientific excellence: Origins and assessment* (pp. 67-97). Beverly Hills, CA: Sage.

Bate, J. W. (1977). *Samuel Johnson.* New York: Harcourt Brace Janovich.

Bloom, B. S. (1982). The role of gifts and markers in the development of talent. *Exceptional Children, 48,* 520-522.

Brent, P. (1981). *Charles Darwin.* New York: Harper & Row.

Chauncey, H., & Hilton, T. L. (1965). Are aptitude tests valid for the highly able? *Science, 148,* 1297-1304.

Collier, P., & Horowitz, D. (1984). *The Kennedys: An American drama.* New York: Summit Books.

Cox, C. M. (1926). *Genetic studies of genius, Vol. II. The early mental traits of three hundred geniuses.* Stanford, CA: Stanford University Press.

Feldman, D. (1980). *Beyond universals in cognitive development.* Norwood, NJ: Ablex.

Fu, V. R., Moran, J. D., Sawyers, J. K., & Milgram, R. M. (1983). Parental influence on creativity in preschool children. *Journal of Genetic Psychology, 143,* 289-291.

Gardner, H. (1983). *Frames of mind.* New York: Basic Books.

Getzels, J. W., & Csikszentamihalyi, M. (1976). *The creative vision: A longitudinal study of problem finding in art.* New York: Wiley & Sons.

Gilmore, J. V. (1974). *The productive personality.* San Francisco: Albion.

Goldsmith, H. H. (1983). Genetic influences on personality from infancy to adulthood. *Child Development, 54,* 331-355.

Guilford, J. P. (1968). *Creativity, intelligence, and their educational implications.* San Diego, CA: Knapp.

Helson, R. (1985). Which of the young women with creative potential will become productive? Personality in college and characteristics of parents. In R. Hogan & R. Jones (Eds.), *Perspectives in personality* (Vol. 1, pp. 49-90). Greenwich, CT: JAI.

Horn, J. (1983). The Texas adoption project: Adopted children and their intellectual resememblance to biological and adoptive parents. *Child Development, 54,* 268-275.

Hudson, L. (1966). *Contrary imaginations: A psychological study of the young student.* New York: Schocken Books.

MacKinnon, D. W. (1983). The highly effective individual. In R. S. Albert (Ed.), *Genius and eminence: The social psychology of creativity and exceptional achievement* (pp. 114-127). Oxford: Pergamon.

Myrianthopoulos, N. C., & French, K. S. (1968). An application of the U.S. Bureau of Census Socioeconomic Index to a large, diversified patient population. *Social Science and Medicine, 2,* 283-299.

Nicholls, J. G. (1972). Creativity in the person who will never produce anything original or useful. *American Psychologist, 27,* 717-727.

Renzulli, J. S. (1978). What makes giftedness? Reexamining a definition. *Phi Delta Kappan, 60,* 180-184.

Runco, M. A. (1987). The generality of creativity in gifted and nongifted children. *Gifted Child Quarterly.* [Chapter 13]

Runco, M. A., & Albert, R. S. (1985). The reliability and validity of ideational originality in the divergent thinking of academically gifted and nongifted children. *Educational and Psychological Measurement, 45,* 483-501. [Chapter 10]

Runco, M. A., & Albert, R. S. (1986). The threshold theory regarding creativity and intelligence: An empirical test with gifted and nongifted children. *Creative Child and Adult Quarterly, 11,* 212-218. [Chapter 17]

Scarr, S., & McCartney, K. (1983). How people make their environments: A theory of genotype-environment effects. *Child Development, 54,* 424-435.

Simonton, D. K. (1984). *Genius, creativity, and leadership.* Cambridge, MA: Harvard University Press.

Solomon, M. (1977). *Beethoven.* New York: Schirmer Books.

Stanley, J. C., George, W. C., & Solano, C. H. (Eds.). (1977). *The gifted and the creative: A fifty year perspective.* Baltimore: Johns Hopkins University Press.

Tyler, L. E. (1964). The antecedents of two varieties of vocational interests. *Genetic Psychological Monographs, 70,* 177-227.

Viernstein, M. C., & Hogan, R. (1975). Parental personality factors and achievement motivation in talented adolescents. *Journal of Youth and Adolescence, 4,* 183-190.

Walberg, H. S., Rasher, S. P., & Hase, K. (1978). IQ correlates with high eminence. *Gifted Child Quarterly, 22,* 196-200.

Wallach, M. A., & Kogan, N. (1965). *Modes of thinking in young children.* New York: Holt, Rinehart, & Winston.

Walters, J., & Gardner, H. (1986). The crystallizing experience: Discovering an intellectual gift. In R. J. Sternberg & J. E. Davidson (Eds.), *Conceptions of giftedness* (pp. 306-331). New York: Cambridge University Press.

## Chapter 2

# Birth-Order and Family Size

### Abstract[*]

The relationship of birth-order and creativity is not well understood. Findings from previous research are contradictory; however, no study has been conducted with a sample that is heterogeneous with regard to ability. The present investigation was conducted to evaluate the relationship of birth-order and creativity using a large sample of gifted and nongifted children ($N$ = 234), five divergent thinking tests, and multivariate procedures to test birth-order and its interaction with number of siblings, gender, and age. Results indicated that only children had the highest divergent thinking test scores, followed by eldest, youngest, and finally middle children. Age also accounted for a significant amount of the variance in the scores, with older children having higher scores than younger children. Finally, the number of siblings was important, with subjects with more siblings having higher scores than children with one sibling.

[*] Adapted from Runco, M. A., & Bahleda, M. D. (1986). Birth-order and divergent thinking. *Journal of Genetic Psychology, 148,* 119-125. Reprinted with permission of the Helen Dwight Reid Educational Foundation. Published by Heldref Publications, 4000 Albemarle Street, N.W., Washington, D.C. 20016. Copyright 1986.

Birth-order is frequently implicated in the development of intellectual abilities (Albert, 1980; Breland, 1977; Galton, 1874; Marjoribanks, 1979; Zajonc & Markus, 1975). There are, however, three contradictory views about the importance of birth-order specifically for creative abilities. Eisenman (1964), for example, predicted that first-born children are less creative than middle or youngest children. His reasoning was that first-born individuals tend to be more conforming than later-born individuals, and that artistic talent and originality require autonomy rather than conformity. Eisenman (1964) tested this with 20 art students, instructors' ratings of students' creativity, and scores on the *Creativity Design Test*. The results confirmed that the first-born art students in this sample were less creative than middle or youngest children. Similar findings were reported by Staffieri (1970).

The second view is that first-born children are more creative than later-born children. Lichtenwalner and Maxwell (1969) evaluated birth-order in a sample of preschool children. A divergent thinking test scored for fluency was used to estimate creativity. Results indicated that first-born and only children had significantly higher divergent thinking tests scores than later-born children. Additional support for this view is given by Eisenman and Schussel (1970).

The third view is that birth-order is unrelated to creativity. Datta (1968), for example, compared three groups representing three levels of creative potential (with creative potential estimated by qualified scientists) and found that first-born individuals were equally distributed in the high, medium, and low ability groups. Wilks and Thompson (1979) reported that birth-order and creativity were unrelated in elementary school children.

One explanation for the three discrepant theories concerning birth-order and creativity is that the various investigations used different measures. Also, the various investigations relied on different analytical procedures, often nonparametric comparisons, and used different combinations of predictor variables with birth-order (e.g., number of siblings, gender). Most importantly, none of the earlier studies was conducted with a sample that was heterogeneous in terms of ability. This is especially problematic because creativity tests have different psychometric properties at different levels of ability (Runco, 1985; Runco & Albert, 1985), and because the family dynamics of gifted individuals are different from those of nongifted individuals (Albert & Runco, 1986; Simonton, 1984).

The present investigation was designed to clarify the relationship between birth-order and creativity. This investigation is unique in that it involved (a) a sample of subjects representing a very wide range of ability, including gifted and nongifted children; (b) several predictor variables in addition to birth-order (i.e., number of siblings, gender, and age, as well as their interactions); (c) a complete battery of divergent thinking tests; and (d) multivariate analysis of variance rather than a nonparametric procedure. Divergent thinking tests are not perfect measures of creativity; and they were used here simply to allow an interpretation in the light of earlier investigations on birth-order (Eisenman & Schussel, 1970; Lichtenwalner & Maxwell, 1968; Staffieri, 1970). Additionally, divergent thinking is often considered to be an important component of "giftedness" (Albert & Runco, 1986; Renzulli, 1978) and is in this sense important in and of itself.

## Method

### Subjects

The participants of this study were fifth-, sixth-, seventh-, and eighth-grade children. Many of these children were gifted or talented in terms of IQs and scores from the *Teacher Indicator of Potential* (Piper, 1974). The range of IQ was 97 to 165. The fifth- through eighth-grades were fairly equally represented, as were the boys and girls. Income level was very evenly distributed across birth-orders and family sizes.

### Measures and Procedure

Five divergent thinking tests were used in this project. Instances, Uses, and Similarities are verbal tests, and Line-Meanings and Pattern-Meanings are figural or "visual" tests (Wallach & Kogan, 1965). Each test had three items. Average item scores for fluency, flexibility, and originality were calculated separately for the verbal and figural tests. Put briefly, fluency reflects the number of ideas generated; flexibility reflects the number of ideational categories; and originality reflects the number of unusual (statistically infrequent) responses. The tests were administered to the children in their classrooms, and required approximately two hours each day for four days, with work breaks and other tasks interspersed between tests.

### Results

The reliability of these divergent thinking tests is given by Runco and Albert (1985). The first analysis was therefore a 4 (birth-order) $x$ 2 (gender) multivariate analysis of variance (MANOVA). Birth-order was coded as only ($n = 16$), eldest ($n = 74$), middle ($n = 96$), or youngest ($n = 48$) child. The six divergent thinking test scores were the dependent variables, and age (in months) was included as a covariate. Wilks' $\lambda$ was the criterion. Number of siblings was not tested in this first analysis because only children have no siblings, and because middle children have at least two siblings. Therefore an analysis testing both birth-order and number of siblings will have several empty cells. Our strategy was to conduct two analyses, the first with all available data, including only children, and the second testing both birth-order and number of siblings. This strategy has an additional advantage in that the second analysis specifically contrasts eldest, middle, and youngest children.

Results of the first analysis indicated that age accounted for a significant amount of the variance, both in the multivariate test ($R = .42$, $F$ (6,220) $= 7.78$, $p < .001$) and the univariate tests for verbal fluency ($r = .38$, $F$ (1,225) $= 37.19$, $p < .001$), verbal flexibility ($r = .37$, $F$ (1,225) $= 35.06$, $p < .001$), verbal originality ($r = .29$, $F$ (1,225) $= 20.58$, $p < .001$), figural fluency ($r = .15$, $F$ (1,225) $= 5.10$, $p < .05$), and figural originality ($r = .17$, $F$ (1,225) $= 6.49$, $p < .01$). With this variance controlled, birth-order was significant, both in the multivariate test ($R_c = .28$, $F$ (18,623) $= 2.06$, $p < .01$) and the

15

univariate tests for verbal fluency ($F$ (3,225) = 2.88, $p < .05$) and verbal originality ($F$ (3,225) = 3.08, $p < .05$). Gender was not significant, nor was the interaction. Means and standard deviations for the divergent thinking tests are presented in Table 2-1.

The second MANOVA was a 3 (birth-order, with only children excluded) $x$ 3 (number of siblings) analysis with age included as a covariate. The sibling factor was coded to reflect children with one sibling ($n = 91$), two siblings ($n = 76$), or three or more siblings ($n = 49$). Results indicated that after the variance attributable to age was controlled, number of siblings was significant in terms of two orthogonal multivariate functions ($R_C = .27$, $F$ (12,404) = 2.25, $p < .01$, and $R_C = .23$, $F$ (5,202) = 2.27, $p < .05$) and the univariate tests for verbal fluency ($F$ (2,207) = 3.14, $p < .05$), verbal flexibility ($F$ (2,207) = 3.69, $p < .05$), and verbal originality ($F$ (2,207) = 4.84, $p < .01$). Birth-order was not significant in this analysis, nor was the interaction. Means and standard deviations for each of the three sibling groups are presented in Table 2-2.

---

Table 2-1

Means and Standard Deviations (in parentheses)
for the Divergent Thinking Tests

| | Birth-Order | | | | | | |
|---|---|---|---|---|---|---|---|
| | Only ($n = 16$) | | Eldest ($n = 74$) | | Youngest ($n = 96$) | | Middle ($n = 48$) | |
| Verbal Tests | | | | | | | |
| Fluency | 13.9 | (9.5) | 10.2 | (4.5) | 10.1 | (5.3) | 9.5 | (5.5) |
| Flexibility | 5.7 | (2.1) | 5.1 | (1.4) | 5.1 | ( 1.6) | 4.8 | (1.4) |
| Originality | 12.5 | (12.1) | 6.0 | (4.3) | 6.4 | (6.3) | 6.9 | (10.4) |
| Figural Tests | | | | | | | |
| Fluency | 4.7 | (2.5) | 4.3 | (2.2) | 4.1 | (2.6) | 3.6 | (1.5) |
| Flexibility | 10.8 | ( 4.5) | 10.4 | (4.4) | 9.9 | (4.8) | 9.1 | (3.1) |
| Originality | 7.5 | (5.0) | 5.6 | (3.9) | 5.8 | (5.6) | 4.4 | (3.0) |

Table 2-2

Means and Standard Deviations (in parentheses)
for the Divergent Thinking Tests

|  | Number of Siblings | | | | | |
|---|---|---|---|---|---|---|
|  | One (n = 91) | | Two (n = 76) | | Three or More (n = 49) | |
| Verbal Tests |  |  |  |  |  |  |
| Fluency | 9.4 | (4.8) | 10.0 | (4.2) | 10.8 | (5.5) |
| Flexibility | 4.8 | (1.4) | 5.2 | (1.3) | 5.1 | (1.4) |
| Originality | 5.3 | (4.6) | 5.9 | (4.6) | 8.1( | 8.1) |
| Figural Tests |  |  |  |  |  |  |
| Fluency | 4.2 | (2.4) | 4.1 | (2.3) | 4.1 | (1.9) |
| Flexibility | 10.0 | (4.5) | 9.9 | (4.5) | 9.9 | (3.8) |
| Originality | 5.7 | (4.7) | 5.2 | (5.4) | 5.1 | (3.5) |

## Discussion

The primary finding of this project is that birth-order is related to divergent thinking test scores, with only children having significantly higher divergent thinking test scores than children in other family positions. The pattern of results presented in Table 2-1 is especially interesting with only, eldest, youngest, and finally middle children having descending scores. However, contrary to earlier suggestions about multiple "special family positions" (Albert, 1980), the eldest, youngest, and middle children in this investigation did not have significantly different divergent thinking test scores.

There are several explanations for the relationship between birth-order and divergent thinking. For example, perhaps only children tend to develop the personality traits that are important to divergent thinking. This is consistent with Eisenman's (1964) notion about birth-order and autonomy, and is congruent with Adler and Freud on personality development. More recently, Feuerstein (1980) has suggested that parents function as mediators, selecting and structuring the experiences of their children. These "mediated learning experiences" ostensibly result in a learning style that influences children's formal and informal educations. Similarly, Albert (1980) sees birth-order as a "structural" variable, organizing family relationships, and a "processional" variable, determining the quality and tone of family interactions. In this light, our findings suggest that the parental mediation given to an only child is different from that which is given to other children, and that this mediation in some way facilitates divergent thinking.

Because the number of siblings was only significantly related to the verbal divergent thinking tests, one point to emphasize is that the tests used in the present investigation are not related in a linear or curvilinear fashion to verbal ability per se (Runco & Pezdek, 1984). That children with more siblings had higher verbal divergent thinking test scores might appear somewhat inconsistent with the finding that only children (who have no siblings) had the highest scores. This finding might also appear to be inconsistent with Zajonc and Markus (1975) because they reported that children with fewer siblings had higher intellectual test scores than children with more siblings. However, Zajonc and Markus focused on cognitive abilities other than divergent thinking, and they evaluated age differences between siblings. Unfortunately, age differences were not available in the present study. Further, only children were excluded from this particular analysis, and middle children—who had the lowest divergent thinking test scores—have at least two siblings. Although the effect of number of siblings is intriguing, it should be investigated further before conclusions are drawn.

Future research should also investigate parental divergent thinking skills (Albert & Runco, 1985), family income (Lichtenwalner & Maxwell, 1969), and ethnicity (Majoribanks, 1979; Munroe & Munroe, 1983) in order to build a more comprehensive model of the development of divergent thinking ability. An especially promising avenue for future research is given by Baskett (1984) and Grenier (1985), for they present two methods for monitoring parent-child and child-sibling interactions. Such techniques might further our understanding of the "processional" aspect of birth-order variables. Given the relationship of birth-order and number of siblings with divergent thinking, we should continue to investigate familial factors in the development of creativity.

## REFERENCES

Albert, R. S. (1980). Family position and the attainment of eminence: A study of special family positions and special family experiences. *Gifted Child Quarterly, 24,* 87-95.

Albert, R. S., & Runco, M. A. (1986). Achievement of eminence: A model of exceptionally gifted boys and their families. In R. J. Sternberg & J. E. Davidson (Eds.), *Conceptions of giftedness* (pp. 332-357). New York: Cambridge University Press.

Albert, R. S., & Runco, M. A. (1987). Exceptional giftedness in early adolescence and intrafamilial divergent thinking. *Journal of Youth and Adolescence, 15,* 335-344. [Chapter 1]

Baskett, L. M. (1984). Ordinal position differences in children's family interactions. *Developmental Psychology, 20,* 1026-1031.

Breland, H. M. (1977). Family configuration and intellectual development. *Journal of Individual Psychology, 33,* 86-96.

Datta, L. (1968). Birth order and potential scientific creativity. *Sociometry, 31,* 76-88.

Eisenman, R. (1964). Birth order and artistic creativity. *Journal of Individual Psychology, 20,* 183-185.

Eisenman, R., & Schussel, N. (1970). Creativity, birth-order, and preference for symmetry. *Journal of Consulting and Clinical Psychology, 34*, 275-280.

Feuerstein, R. (1980). *Instrumental enrichment: An intervention program for cognitive modifiability.* Baltimore: University Park Press.

Galton, F. (1874). *English men of science: Their nature and nurture.* London: Macmillan.

Grenier, M. E. (1985). Gifted children and other siblings. *Gifted Child Quarterly, 29*, 164-167.

Guilford, J. P. (1968). *Intelligence, creativity, and their educational implications.* San Diego, CA: Knapp.

Lichtenwalner, J. S., & Maxwell, J. W. (1969). The relationship of birth order and socioeconomic status to the creativity of preschool children. *Child Development, 40*, 1241-1247.

Majoribanks, K. (1979). *Families and their learning environments.* London: Routledge & Kegan Paul.

Munroe, R. L., & Munroe, R. H. (1983). Birth order and intellectual performance in East Africa. *Journal of Cross-Cultural Psychology, 14*, 3-16.

Piper, J. (1974). *The teacher indicator of potential scale.* Redwood City, CA: Gifted Resource Center.

Renzulli, J. S. (1978). What makes giftedness? Reexamining a definition. *Phi Delta Kappan, 60*, 180-184.

Runco, M. A. (1984). Teachers' judgments of creativity and social validity of divergent thinking tests. *Perceptual and Motor Skills, 59*, 711-717. [Chapter 5]

Runco, M. A. (1985). Reliability and convergent validity of ideational flexibility as a function of academic achievement. *Perceptual and Motor Skills, 61*, 1075-1081. [Chapter 11]

Runco, M. A., & Albert, R. S. (1985). The reliability and validity of ideational originality in the divergent thinking of academically gifted and nongifted children. *Educational and Psychological Measurement, 45*, 483-501. [Chapter 10]

Runco, M. A., & Pezdek, K. (1984). The effect of radio and television on children's creativity. *Human Communications Research, 11*, 109-120. [Chapter 4]

Simonton, D. K. (1984). *Genius, creativity, and leadership.* Cambridge, MA: Harvard University Press.

Staffieri, R. J. (1970). Birth-order and creativity. *Journal of Clinical Psychology, 26*, 65-66.

Wallach, M. A., & Kogan, N., (1965). *Modes of thinking in young children.* New York: Holt, Rinehart, & Winston.

Wilks, L., & Thompson, P. (1979). Birth-order and creativity in young children. *Psychological Reports, 45*, 443-449.

Zajonc, R. S., & Markus, G. B. (1975). Birth order and intellectual development. *Psychological Review, 82*, 74-88.

## Chapter 3

# Independence and Creativity

### Abstract[*]

A 16-item questionnaire concerning independence and three divergent thinking tests were administered to three groups of preadolescent boys and their mothers as part of an on-going longitudinal investigation of exceptional giftedness. The subjects included one group of exceptionally gifted boys with IQs in excess of 150 ($n = 28$), a second group of exceptionally gifted boys selected for their math-science abilities (also well within the 99th percentile; $n = 26$), and a control group of gifted boys ($n = 37$, with a mean IQ of 133). The three groups were compared with one another in terms of (a) their own independence ratings; (b) their mothers' independence ratings; (c) correlations of boys' and mothers' independence ratings; and (d) correlations of independence ratings with IQ and scores from the divergent thinking tests. Results indicated significant differences among the three groups of mothers, and significant differences between the two exceptionally gifted groups and the control group. In addition, mothers' and subjects' independence scores were moderately correlated with IQ and divergent thinking test scores. These results are discussed and placed in the context of the longitudinal project of which they are a part.

[*]Adapted from: Albert, R. S., & Runco, M. A. (in press). Independence and cognitive ability in gifted and exceptionally gifted boys. *Journal of Youth and Adolescence, 18*.

Comparisons between high- and low-achieving persons of apparently equal talents in a variety of fields suggest that one of the major differences between the eminent and their lower ranked counterparts is the former's stronger, clearer sense of personal independence and more prolonged cognitive assertion, often in the face of personal loss and early adversity (Albert, 1980; Cox, 1926; Eiduson, 1962; Hammond, 1984; Oden, 1983; Rushton, Murray, & Paunonen, 1983; Simonton, 1987). In-depth research on productive and eminent individuals suggests that they are often highly self-sufficient and strongly self-motivated, somewhat introverted, clearly passionate in their interests, dominant in some of their interpersonal relationships, and both deeply serious and playful in their work. They invariably feel responsible and independent within their career and professional interests (MacKinnon, 1978; May, 1975; Roe, 1953). Although their personalities may differ, successful participants in a variety of fields usually exhibit these same performance characteristics (Simonton, 1987). Interestingly, self-esteem is not often mentioned by creators themselves or in the empirical research as an important personality disposition. This makes sense in light of the extensive biographical and autobiographical information about creative persons (especially non-scientists) who are highly distraught, depressed, even self-lacerating, but nonetheless are highly creative. On the other hand, there are creative and productive individuals who are apparently supremely self-confident (MacKinnon, 1978; May, 1975; Roe, 1953).

While high cognitive ability is among the salient characteristics of eminent individuals in a variety of fields (Barron, 1969; Cox, 1926; Helson, 1980; MacKinnon, 1965; Walberg, Rasher, & Hase, 1983), more than this is surely required. Eminent creativity requires a freedom of thought, feeling, and action sustained over time by an infrequent meshing of field-appropriate personality dispositions, abilities, and values. When one adds another necessity for high-level creativity—a sensitivity to significant problems coupled with a strong sense of responsibility—one sees how critical this "creative complex" is to the selection of and motivation to pursue difficult problems over long periods (Albert, 1975; Runco & Okuda, 1988). In the final analysis, these freedoms and meshings are essential to action, because performance is essential for the realization of the abilities and personality dispositions. To be able to act upon them, use them, and assert them, this is where independence and self-assertion enter the developmental equation.

In our model of family life, the families of gifted individuals simultaneously perform several interrelated actions from the child's early years through his or her adolescence (Albert, 1980; Albert & Runco, 1986, 1987). They encourage exploration and achievement (Seginer, 1983, 1986); they support the child's own growing effort to pursue his or her natural curiosity; and they make warm as opposed to clinging attachments. Moreover, such families protect the child from too abrupt and highly unpredictable changes. In order for the development of independence and curiosity to continue, such families encourage the child to manipulate and try to change some parts of his or her world for him- or herself. In this encouragement, the families need to clearly value and reward competence, and expect performance results.

The present investigation compares independence training in families of exceptionally gifted and conventionally gifted preadolescent boys. The primary hypothesis is that exceptionally gifted children differ from nominally gifted children as these children differ from those with average abilities and capacities (Albert, 1969; Albert & Runco, 1986). With the consistent differences between gifted and nongifted groups and between the Exceptionally High IQ and Math-Science groups that have already been found in a number of comparisons (Albert & Runco, 1986, 1987; Runco & Albert, 1986), it is reasonable to expect that the subjects and their mothers will differ in their judgments of independence. Based on the theories of independence and achievement outlined above, our expectation is that the exceptionally gifted subjects and mothers will give ratings indicative of higher independence than the nominally gifted subjects and their mothers. With the evidence that different domains of achievement have idiosyncratic developmental histories (Gardner, 1983), and our earlier findings that the High IQ subjects are more similar to their parents than the Math-Science subjects (Albert & Runco, 1986), we expect that the High IQ subjects will give ratings which are more strongly correlated with those of their mothers than those of the High Math-Science subjects and their mothers. Another prediction is that the independence ratings given by the mothers will be correlated with measures of their sons' creative potential. This prediction is based on earlier investigations of independence and general intelligence (Crutchfield, 1962; Lucito, 1964; Nakamura, 1958; Tuddenham, 1958), independence, achievement, and creativity (Allen & Levine, 1968; Aviram & Milgram, 1977; Bachman, 1986; Moustakas, 1967), and independence and originality (Barron, 1968).

## Method

### Subjects

One exceptionally gifted group was selected because their IQs at age 12 were in excess of 150 (average IQ = 159; $n = 26$). They were selected from the Mentally Gifted Minors programs of four school districts. The second sample was selected on the basis of math-science abilities well into the 99th national percentile (e.g., an average SAT math score of 655 at age 12; $n = 28$). These subjects were drawn from the Study of Mathematically Precocious Youth (Stanley, Keating, & Fox, 1974). The families of the samples are well in the upper-middle SES. The families of the High IQ subjects have an average of 2.8 children, and the families of the Math-Science subjects have an average of 2.5 children. The control group ($n = 37$; IQ mean of 133) of nominally gifted boys come from two seventh-grade classes of a large public intermediate school.

### Measures and Procedure

The subjects' age 12 creative potential was assessed with the Instances, Uses, and Similarities divergent thinking tests from the Wallach and Kogan (1965) battery. Each test contained three questions. A total divergent thinking score was calculated by adding the ideational fluency scores from the separate tests. Other scores from these tests (e.g., originality and flexibility) were not used because they are strongly correlated with fluency scores (Runco, 1986).

All subjects and their mothers were given the same 16-item Independence questionnaire (adapted from Winterbottom, 1958). This is a 16-item questionnaire asking about the most appropriate age for an individual to be involved in a variety of activities. The 16 questions are presented in Table 3-1. Each question has age 4 through age 16 as response options. This measure was chosen for its high reliability and the ease with which it can be administered to adolescents and adults. All measures administered to the exceptionally gifted subjects and their mothers were given in their homes, allowing as much time as needed to complete the tests. The control group received the divergent thinking tests and the Independence questionnaire in their classrooms, again with as much time as required. Their mothers completed the questionnaire at home.

## Results

The interitem ($\alpha$) reliability coefficients of the subjects' Independence questionnaire were as follows: control sample (.79), Math-Science sample (.85), Exceptionally High IQ sample (.74). Their mothers' were equally reliable: control mothers (.88), the mothers of Math-Science boys (.82), and the mothers of Exceptionally High IQ boys (.65). Table 3-1 presents the means and standard deviations of the ratings from the Independence questionnaire. A low score indicates a younger age and for a specific behavior, and therefore greater independence in the behavior.

Multivariate analyses of variance (MANOVA) were conducted to test the primary hypotheses of this investigation and compare the three groups in terms of subjects' and mothers' Independence judgments. Wilks' $\lambda$ was the criterion in these analyses, and the 16 items of the Independence questionnaire were the dependent variables. The first MANOVA established a significant difference among the ratings of independence given by the three samples of subjects in the multivariate test ($R_C = .55$, $F$ (32, 142) = 1.61, $p <$ .05) and the univariate tests for items 4 and 8. Contrasts indicated a significant difference between the ratings of the control subjects and the exceptionally gifted subjects in the multivariate test ($R_C = .54$, $F$ (16, 71) = 1.87, $p < .05$) and the univariate tests for items 4, 8, and 13. The difference between the two exceptionally gifted samples was not significant.

A second MANOVA indicated that there was a significant difference among the three groups of mothers' ratings, with two significant discriminant orthogonal functions ($R_C = .84$, $F$ (32, 98) = 4.56, $p < .001$, and $R_C = .67$, $F$ (15, 50) = 2.78, $p < .01$). This difference among the three groups was also apparent in the univariate tests of items 1, 3, 6, 7, 8, 9, 15, and 16. Contrasts indicated signficant differences between the ratings given by the control mothers and the mothers of the exceptionally gifted subjects in the multivariate test ($R_C = .70$, $F$ (16, 49) = 2.90, $p < .01$) and the univariate tests for items 3, 6, 7, 8, 9, 13, 15, and 16. Unlike the contrasts of the two samples of exceptionally gifted sons' ratings, there was a significant difference between the mothers of the Exceptionally High IQ subjects and the mothers of the Math-Science subjects in the multivariate test ($R_C = .80$, $F$ (16, 49) = 5.52, $p < .001$) and the univariate tests for items 1, 3, 7, 9, 15, and 16.

## Correlations

Product-moment correlations were used to determine whether or not mothers and sons gave similar independence ratings, and whether or not the ratings of both mothers and sons are related to the sons' cognitive ability. These analyses used a composite Independence score calculated for each subject and each mother from the average of the 16 questionnaire items. Table 3-2 presents the means and standard deviations of this composite for each of the groups.

Fluency scores from the divergent thinking tests are also presented in Table 3-2. Because divergent thinking tests may be sensitive to administration procedures, scores from these tests were transformed into z-scores (within each group), and these were used for the correlations. Both unadjusted coefficients ($r$) and coefficients which have been adjusted ($r'$) for attenuation due to the imperfect reliabilities of the tests are presented (Nunnally, 1978).

Results indicated that the Math-Science sons' and mothers' ratings were negatively related ($r = -.23$, $r' = -.28$), but the Exceptionally High IQ subjects' independence ratings were positively correlated with their mothers' independence ratings ($r = .13$, $r' = .19$). The difference between the adjusted coefficients approached statistical significance ($z = 1.54$, $p < .06$). The correlation between the sons and mothers of the control group was slight and negative ($r = -.08$, $r' = -.10$). While these coefficients are not large, keep in mind that they may be attenuated by the very restricted range of scores.

## Independence Ratings and Cognitive Ability

Because low scores on the questionnaire indicate younger ages for a particular activity, and represent earlier (or higher) independence, a negative correlation was predicted between independence ratings and cognitive ability scores. The exceptionally High IQ subjects' independence ratings were significantly and negatively related to IQ ($r = -.39$, $p < .05$, $r' = -.45$), but the scores for independence and IQ are unrelated in the control group. Although mothers' independence ratings were unrelated to their sons' IQ, they were significantly related to their sons' creative potential (divergent thinking test performance). For the entire sample of three groups of subjects, this coefficient was $r = -.29$ ($p < .05$, $r' = -.23$). Similar mother-son correlations were found in both of the exceptionally gifted samples: for the Exceptionally High IQ group ($r = -.29$, $r' = -.36$) and for the Math-Science group ($r = -.35$, $r' = -.37$).

Furthermore, subjects' own independence ratings were marginally related to their divergent thinking test scores in the Exceptionally High IQ group ($r = -.26$, $r' = -.30$). Again we stress that the coefficients are probably attenuated by the restricted range of scores.

Table 3-1

Mean Ratings for each Independence Questionnaire Item
and Each Group

| | Children | | | Mothers | | |
|---|---|---|---|---|---|---|
| | IQ | MS | Control | IQ | MS | Control |
| 1. Earn your own spending money | 10.8 | 11.3 | 9.9 | 11.0 | 7.9 | 11.0 |
| 2. Sleep overnight at a friend's | 5.9 | 5.9 | 5.7 | 6.4 | 5.8 | 5.9 |
| 3. Play where you want | 7.3 | 6.4 | 7.7 | 7.0 | 6.3 | 7.4 |
| 4. Make your own friends and visit their homes | 6.3 | 6.7 | 8.0 | 6.9 | 6.2 | 7.6 |
| 5. Stay alone at night until midnight | 11.3 | 10.3 | 11.3 | 12.1 | 11.2 | 12.7 |
| 6. Make decisions about clothes or money | 10.4 | 10.5 | 10.5 | 8.0 | 9.7 | 10.8 |
| 7. Act as a babysitter in another home | 12.8 | 13.0 | 12.8 | 14.1 | 9.4 | 13.8 |
| 8. Be able to go to bed on your own | 8.6 | 9.1 | 10.0 | 8.2 | 6.9 | 10.1 |
| 9. Go to the movies alone | 11.1 | 11.8 | 12.1 | 11.8 | 6.9 | 13.0 |
| 10. Go on an overnight trip (organized by school) | 10.4 | 10.3 | 10.3 | 10.2 | 10.4 | 11.4 |
| 11. Try new things without Mom or Dad for help | 10.2 | 10.2 | 10.4 | 8.7 | 9.8 | 9.6 |
| 12. Do well in school on your own | 9.7 | 9.6 | 10.1 | 7.6 | 9.0 | 9.3 |
| 13. Entertain self | 7.3 | 7.5 | 8.6 | 6.6 | 6.9 | 8.2 |
| 14. Do Well in competition | 7.1 | 6.9 | 7.9 | 7.0 | 5.8 | 7.7 |
| 15. Take part in parents' conversations/interests | 8.3 | 7.3 | 7.9 | 8.6 | 4.3 | 8.5 |
| 16. Try things without asking for help | 10.9 | 10.9 | 11.4 | 3.9 | 6.1 | 9.4 |

Note: IQ and MS (Math-Science) are the Exceptionally Gifted Groups.

Table 3-2

Means and Standard Errors for the Independence Composite
and the Divergent Thinking Test Scores

| | Group | | | | | |
|---|---|---|---|---|---|---|
| | High IQ ($n = 26$) | | Math-Science ($n = 28$) | | Control ($n = 37$) | |
| Mothers' Independence[a] | 8.6 | (1.3) | 6.3 | (2.2) | 9.7 | (1.6) |
| Subjects' Independence | 9.3 | (0.9) | 9.2 | (1.1) | 9.8 | (1.2) |
| Divergent Thinking Fluency[b] | 46.4 | (4.7) | 45.3 | (4.9) | 30.7 | (2.5) |

[a]The average of the 16 items presented in Table 3-1.
[b]The sum of three divergent thinking test scores.

## Discussion

The primary predictions of the present study concerning independence are supported by the results: The subjects and the mothers in the two exceptionally gifted samples gave significantly different independence ratings than the subjects and mothers in the control group. Moreover, the ratings of the Exceptional Math-Science group show earlier autonomy than both the Exceptionally High IQ group and the nominally gifted control group; and the independence ratings of the Exceptionally High IQ group reflect an earlier autonomy than the control group. These findings are consistent with the view that different levels and different domains of ability have different developmental histories (e.g., Albert, 1980; Albert & Runco, 1986; Gardner, 1983).

Although the magnitude of the correlation coefficients were only moderate (possibly reflecting a restricted range of subjects' scores), the relationships among independence, IQ, and divergent thinking test scores are also very consistent with earlier research. For example, Moustakas (1967) suggested that individuality and creativity are inextricably tied to one another. In his words, "to be creative means to experience life in one's own way" (p. 27). Barron (1969) pointed to a relationship between a lack of resistance to socialization as a loss in individuality. Aviram and Milgram (1977) gave empirical support for this relationship; and like the present investigation, they focused specifically on divergent thinking as an index of creative potential.

Keniston (1968) caught the complex nature of family dynamics and practices regarding independence training for gifted boys when he described the gifted, commited youth of the 1960s:

> Paradoxically, those who come from what to an outside observer would appear to be the best familites often underwent a severe struggle to emancipate themselves from these families. It may be that the very closeness, warmth, and encouragement toward independence in some of these families were what made adolescence both possible and necessary . . . . Put differently, many of these families seem to have given their children the strength and the need to challenge, reexamine, and partially reassimilate their parents' values, and eventually to achieve an unusual degree of individuality for themselves. (Keniston, 1968, pp. 102-103)

Although the present correlational results clearly suggest that cognitive ability and independence are related, they tell us little about causality. It is possible, for example, that children with high independence develop divergent thinking skills because of the opportunities they seek out in order to think and operate independently (see Scarr & McCartney, 1983). Or a child with outstanding cognitive ability, as a result of their parents' recognition and confidence, may be encouraged to use and explore their own abilities and initiative (Albert & Runco, 1986, 1987; Baumrind, 1971; Koenigs, Fiedler, & de Charms, 1977; Roe, 1953; Seginer, 1986). Families as facilitating environments (Winnicott, 1976) often value and encourage independence, especially those families in which giftedness is linked with valued achievement (Bloom, 1985; Keniston, 1968; Laband & Lentz, 1985). This encouragement (implicit and explicit) demonstrates to the child the parents' high priority for independence through achievement, and encourages efforts along these lines. Thus it is only a matter of time and everyday living that this parental emphasis comes through to the child as family values, themes, expectations, and "presses" (Marjoribanks, 1979), by way of parental modeling, rewarding, and overt respect for the child's own efforts (Baumrind, 1971).

## REFERENCES

Albert, R. S. (1969). The concept of genius and its implications for the study of creativity and giftedness. *American Psychololgist*, *24*, 743-753.

Albert, R. S. (1975). Toward a behavioral definition of genius. *American Psychologist*, *30*, 140-151.

Albert, R. S. (1980). Family position and the attainment of eminence: A study of special family positions and special family experiences. *Gifted Child Quarterly*, *24*, 87-95.

Albert, R. S., & Runco, M. A. (1986). The achievement of eminence: A model of exceptionally gifted boys and their families. In R. J. Sternberg & J. E. Davidson (Eds.), *Conceptions of giftedness* (pp. 332-357). New York: Cambridge University Press.

Albert, R. S., & Runco, M. A. (1987). The possible different personality dispositions of scientists and nonscientists. In D. N. Jackson & J. P. Rushton (Eds.), *Scientific excellence: Origins and assessment* (pp. 67-97). Beverly Hills, CA: Sage.

Allen, V. L., & Levine, J. M. (1968). Creativity and conformity. *Journal of Personality, 36,* 405-419.

Aviram, A., & Milgram, R. M. (1977). Dogmatisim, locus of control, and creativity in the Soviet Union, the United States, and Israel. *Psychological Reports, 40,* 27-34.

Bachman, E. B. (1986). The relations between type A behavior, clinically relevant behavior, and academic achievement. *Journal of Personality Assessment, 50,* 186-192.

Barron, F. (1968). *Creativity and personal freedom.* New York: Van Nostrand.

Barron, F. (1969). *Creative person, creative process.* New York: Holt, Rinehart, & Winston.

Baumrind, D. (1971). Current patterns of parental autonomy. *Developmental Psychology Monographs, 4* (1), 1-103.

Berglas, S. (1986). *The success syndrome: Hitting bottom when you reach the top.* New York: Plenum.

Bloom, B. S. (Ed.). (1985). *Developing talent in young people.* New York: Ballentine.

Cox, C. M. (1926). *Genetic studies of genius: The early mental traits of three hundred geniuses.* Stanford, CA: Stanford University Press.

Crutchfield, R. S. (1962). Conformity and creative thinking. In H. E. Gruber, G. Terrell, & M. Wertheimer (Eds.), *Contemporary approaches to creativity* (pp. 120-140). New York: Atherton.

Eiduson, B. T. (1962). *Scientists: Their psychological world.* New York: Basic Books

Gardner, H. (1983). *Frames of mind.* New York: Basic Books.

Hammond, A. L. (Ed.). (1984). *A passion to know: 20 profiles in science.* New York: Scribner's.

Heckhausen, H. (1983). Concern with one's competence: Developmental shifts in person-environment interaction. In D. Magnusson & V. L. Allen (Eds.), *Human development: An interactional perspective* (pp. 167-185). New York: Academic Press.

Helson, R. (1980). *Women and the mathematical mystique.* Baltimore: Johns Hopkins University Press.

Keniston, K. (1968). *Young radicals.* New York: Harcourt Brace Jovanovich.

Koenigs, S. S., Fiedler, M. L., & de Charms, R. (1977). Teachers' beliefs, classroom interaction and personal consation. *Journal of Applied Social Psychology, 7,* 95-114.

Laband, D. M., & Lentz, B. F. (1985). *The roots of success: Why children follow their parents' career footsteps.* New York: Praeger.

Lucito, L. F. (1964). Independence-conformity behavior as a function of intellect: Bright and dull children. *Exceptional Children, 31,* 5-13.

MacKinnon, D. W. (1965). Personality and the realization of creative potential. *American Psychologist, 20,* 273-281.

MacKinnon, D. W. (1978). *In search of human effectiveness.* Buffalo, NY: Creative Education Foundation.

Marjoribanks, K. (1979). *Families and their learning environments.* London: Routledge & Kegan Paul.

May, R. (1975). *The courage to create.* New York: Bantam.

Moustakas, C. (1967). Creativity and conformity in education. In R. L. Mooney & T. A. Razik (Eds.), *Explorations in creativity.* New York: Harper & Row.

Nakamura, C. Y. (1958). Conformity and problem solving. *Journal of Abnormal Social Psychology, 56,* 315-320.

Nunnally, J. C. (1978). *Psychometric theory* (2nd ed.). New York: McGraw-Hill.

Oden, M. (1983). A 40 year follow-up of giftedness: Fulfillment and unfulfillment. In R. S. Albert (Ed.), *Genius and eminence* (pp. 203-213). New York: Pergamon.

Poland, N. (1978, July-August). The most fascinating family in Britain. *Harvard Magazine,* pp. 29-32, 56-59.

Roe, A. (1953). *The making of a scientist.* New York: Dodd, Mead.

Runco, M. A. (1986). The discriminant validity of gifted children's divergent thinking test scores. *Gifted Child Quarterly, 30,* 78-82. [Chapter 16]

Runco, M. A., & Albert, R. S. (1986). Exceptional giftedness and intrafamilial divergent thinking. *Journal of Youth and Adolescence, 15,* 333-342. [Chapter 1]

Runco, M. A., & Okuda, S. M. (1988). Problem-discovery, divergent thinking, and the creative process. *Journal of Youth and Adolescence, 17,* 213-222. [Chapter 8]

Rushton, J. P., Murray, H. G., & Paunonen, S. V. (1983). Personality, research creativity, and teaching effectiveness in university professors. *Scientometrics, 5,* 93-116.

Scarr, S., & McCartney, K. (1983). How young people make their environments: A theory of genotype-environment effects. *Child Development, 54,* 424-435.

Seginer, R. (1983). Parents' educational expectations and children's academic achievement. *Merrill-Palmer Quarterly, 29,* 1-23.

Seginer, R. (1986). Mothers' behavior and sons' performance: An initial test of an academic achievement path model. *Merrill-Palmer Quarterly, 32,* 153-166.

Simonton, D. K. (1987). Developmental antecedents of achieved eminence. *Annals of Child Development* (Vol. 4, pp. 131-169). Greenwich, CT: JAI.

Stanley, J., Keating, D. P., & Fox, L. H. (Eds.). (1974). *Mathematical talents: Discovery, description, and development.* Baltimore: Johns Hopkins University Press.

Tuddenham, R. D. (1959). Correlates of yielding to a distorted group norm. *Journal of Personality, 27,* 272-284.

Walberg, H. S., Rasher, S. P., & Hase, K. (1983). IQ correlates with high eminence. In R. S. Albert (Ed.), *Genius and eminence* (pp. 52-56). New York: Pergamon.

Wallach, M. A., & Kogan, N. (1965). *Modes of thinking in young children.* New York: Holt, Rinehart, & Winston.

Winnicott, D. W. (1976). *The maturational processes and the facilitating environment.* London: Hogarth.

Winterbottom, M. R. (1958). The relation of need for achievement to learning experiences in independence and mastery. In J. W. Atkinson (Ed.), *Motives in fantasy, action, and society* (pp. 453-478). New York: Van Nostrand.

## Chapter 4

# Television, Radio,
# and Children's Creativity

### Abstract[*]

The literature on creativity posits that creative abilities are stable and relatively impervious to short-term interventions. Several studies have, however, reported differential effects of media on children's imaginative play and thinking. The results of these studies are difficult to interpret, owing to their reliance on nonstandardized measures of creativity. The present study examines the relative effects of television versus radio on children's creativity. Third and sixth graders were presented a story on television or radio and were then given an adapted version of the "Just Suppose" test of divergent thinking developed by Torrance (1974). Responses were scored in terms of ideational fluency, flexibility, and originality. The results indicated that the two media did not have a differential effect on children's creativity.

[*] Adapted from Runco, M. A., & Pezdek, K. (1984). The effect of television and radio on children's creativity. *Human Communication Research, 11,* 109-120.

A large number of researchers in the last 25 years have focused on the effects of television on children (see Murray, 1980, for a review of this literature). This is a particularly compelling issue given reports that children in this country watch an average of 27.6 hours of television a week (Lyle & Hoffman, 1972).

One approach to the study of television is to compare the effects of television with the effects of other media. As the amount of television viewing has increased in the past three decades, people on the average spend less time with verbal media such as reading and listening to the radio. The question addressed in the present study is that of the relative effects of television versus radio on children's cognitive processing. In particular, this study compares television and radio as stimuli for creative ideas in children.

Schramm, Lyle, and Parker (1961) in the United States, and Murray and Kippaz (1978) in Australia, reported that children in communities without access to television listened to the radio two to three times more than children with access to television. In terms of time spent reading, Furu (1971) in Japan, Himmelweit, Oppenheim, and Vince (1958) in England, and Werner (1975) in Norway, all reported a drop in the number of books read by children when television was introduced into communities. This relatively stable shift in allocation of time from strictly verbal media to television may have significant cognitive consequences for the viewer. The present study examines one potential cognitive consequence, that is, the differential effect of television and radio on children's creativity.

The interest in media as a stimulus for creativity in the present study follows from conflicting reports in the literature. On the one hand, the literature on creativity would predict that short-term interventions would have little or no effect on creativity. Here, creativity is defined as "the forming of associative elements into new combinations that either meet some specified requirements or are in some way useful" (Mednick, 1962, p. 221). Operationally, creativity can be defined as the production of divergent ideas (Guilford, 1968; Torrance, 1974; Wallach & Kogan, 1965). Creative individuals generate a high quality and quantity of ideas. For example, given an open-ended question, creative individuals will produce more ideas ("ideational fluency"), and more ideas that are statistically infrequent ("ideational originality"). Importantly, creativity defined in this manner has been demonstrated to be reliable and valid with kindergarten children (Ward, 1968), seven-year-old children (Rotter, Langland, & Berger, 1971), and college students (Wallach & Wing, 1969). Divergent thinking is independent of other forms of measures of intelligence, and generally correlates with other tests of creativity (Barron & Harrington, 1981). But, more relevant to the present study, creativity is considered to be a stable trait (e.g., Barron, 1955; Guilford, 1968). Therefore, reliable and valid measures of creativity should not be differentially affected by short-term exposure to television versus radio.

On the other hand, it has been suggested elsewhere that whereas listening to the radio actively stimulates creativity (Carnegie Commission, 1979; Morriset, 1976; Palmer, 1926), television does not influence "imaginativeness" (Singer, 1978; Singer & Singer, 1976a, 1976b; Tower, Singer, Singer & Biggs, 1979). Imaginativeness was operationally defined as "the extent to which a child transcended the constraints of reality in his or her play—for example, by using an object to represent another one, by adding vocalizations suggesting he or she was symbolizing a role or object, or introducing a story line" (Tower et al., 1979, p. 271).

Murray, Kwiatek, and Clarke (1982) examined the relationship between the average amount of television viewing in five- to eleven-year-old children and several measures of "fantasy and imagination." Imagination, measured in terms of (a) responses to the *Barron Inkblot Test*, and (b) responses to questions about involvement in fantasy, did not significantly relate to the amount of television viewing. However, in a second series of tasks, children were asked to make up stories. On this task, increased television viewing was related to the production of stories that were longer and included a greater diversity of characters. Conclusions from this study regarding the relationship between the amount of television viewing and "fantasy and imagination" are thus clearly restricted by our understanding of what these various indices measure.

Greenfield, Beagles-Roos, Farrar, and Gat (1981) had six- to eleven-year-old children complete a prematurely ended story that was presented on television or radio. The children were asked to "tell a story about what you think will happen next?" (p. 7). Responses were scored for imaginative elements, defined as "elements such as character, event or setting which had not appeared in the stimulus story" (p. 7). The results were that the radio presentation stimulated more novel ideas in the conclusions given by the children than did the television. The television story, in contrast, was associated with conclusions based more directly on elements of the presented story.

Meline (1976) compared the influence of audio-visual information with solely verbal information (audio-tape or text) on children's problem solving. Sixth- and seventh-grade children were asked to invent solutions to specific problems, and sample solutions for each problem were presented through audio-visual or solely verbal media. Each child was allowed one solution for each problem and six judges rated the solutions as either creative or not. The audio-visual sample solutions resulted in fewer creative solutions than did the solely verbal sample solutions.

The studies discussed above report interesting results concerning the effects of media on certain cognitive processes. The issue to be addressed in the present study, however, is that it is unclear exactly what cognitive processes were measured. Singer and Singer (1976a, 1976b) used a behavioral measure, and their focus was ostensibly on "the ability to use images" (cf. Singer, 1978, p. 153). Murray et al. (1982) measured "fantasy predisposition" and components of stories generated by children. Their results were not consistent on these two measures. Greenfield et al. (1981) scored "novel" ideas; although the cognitive process was never referred to as "creativity," the definition of scored responses was similar to Mednick's (1982) definition of creativity. In Meline's (1976) study, creative problem solving was defined as a process requiring, "on a first level, a departure from or freedom from and on a higher level, the transformation of given stimulus information" (p. 84).

These findings are inconsistent with the literature on creativity cited above that considers creative abilities to be generally stable, and not malleable. As such, creative abilities would not be expected to be differentially influenced by different stimulus media. In the one study that did utilize a standardized test of creativity to evaluate media effects, Stern (1973) reported no significant effects of television viewing on thinking. However, this study employed gifted children (fourth-, fifth-, and sixth-graders) and compared effects of exposure to cartoons versus situation comedies using only one form of media, television. The purpose of the present study is to clarify the effects of television versus radio on children's creativity by using a standardized test of creativity, known to be valid and reliable. Although the previous studies in this area are provocative, they are limited by the use of nonstandardized measures. This restriction is important because it is unclear what cognitive processes have been measured. The interpretation and generality of these findings are consequently limited.

The present study was designed to replicate the work of Greenfield et al. (1981) using standardized measures of creative potential. Children were presented a story either on television or radio. Immediately after the story, three separate standardized measures of divergent thinking were administered. Ideational fluency, flexibility, and originality in the responses of the two groups were compared. This study experimentally compares the effects of television versus radio on children's creativity, using a standardized test of creativity.

## Method

### Subjects

The subjects, 32 third-graders and 32 sixth-graders, were recruited from ethnically mixed, lower-middle class public schools in Montclair, California. Half of the children in each age group were males, and the other half females. The children were brought to the university campus by a parent. The parents completed a questionnaire on the television viewing habits of their children. Children in this sample watched an average of 23 hours of television each week. This average is consistent with national norms for children (Lyle & Hoffman, 1972).

### Materials and Design

Two different stories were used in the study to increase the generalizability of the results. The two stories used were *A Story, A Story,* an African folktale, and *Strega Nona,* the story of a magical old woman. Color animated videotapes of these two stories were obtained from Weston Woods Studios. New soundtracks were made for each story based on the original storybook text, using the same female narrator and style of narration for each. The same soundtrack was thus used in the television and radio conditions. *Strega Nona* was 7 min. 44 sec. long. *A Story, A Story* was 8 min. 29 sec. long. These were the same materials utilized by Greenfield et al. (1981).

The experiment utilized a 2 (grade) x 2 (media condition) x 2 (story) independent groups design. Half of the subjects in each grade were presented a story in the television form and the other half were presented only the audio version of a story in the "radio" condition. Subjects were randomly assigned to conditions to control for socioeconomic status, reading, television viewing, and radio listening differences.

## Procedure

Each child participated individually in a comfortable furnished room on the campus. The children were instructed that they would be presented a story either on television or on a tape recorder, "like listening to the radio." After the story, an adaptation of the "Just Suppose" test of Torrance (1974) was administered requiring subjects to generate ideas in response to a hypothetical situation that followed from the presented story. The instructions for the test were:

> Now you will be given a new situation, one that did not happen in the story. You are to suppose that it did happen and use your imagination to think of all of the exciting things that would happen if this situation had occurred. So pretend that the situation that I am going to tell you happened, and think of all the things that would have happened because of it. Make as many guesses as you can.

The children who were presented *Strega Nona* were then told:

> Just suppose Strega Nona did not come back when she did. What would have happened? What would Big Anthony have done? What would the townspeople have done? Remember, make as many guesses as you can.

The children who were presented *A Story, A Story* were then told:

> Just suppose the Fairy was too smart for Ananse and would not touch the gum baby. What would have happened? What would Ananse have done? What would the Sky God have done? Remember, make as many guesses as you can.

Each child was given five minutes to generate ideas. Responses were tape recorded and then transcribed for scoring. Each child was prompted once if he or she did not respond. The experimenter asked, "Can you think of anything at all?"

Two trained coders independently evaluated responses of each child. The scoring scheme developed by Torrance (1974) was used. Specifically, three scores were calculated for each child's responses. Fluency reflects the number of ideas given by the child. Flexibility reflects the number of distinct and different conceptual categories of ideas used by the child. Originality reflects the number of unique (i.e., statistically infrequent relative to the complete sample) ideas generated by the child. If a child responded, "Ananse would call the cops, and Ananse would go for help," they would be given two fluency points, one flexibility point, and the originality score would depend on the responses given by the other children. Inter-rater reliability, calculated with Pearson product-moment correlations, was .90 for fluency, .82 for flexibility, and .86 for originality.

## Results

A multivariate analysis of variance was performed on the mean fluency, flexibility, and originality data. Media condition, grade, and story were included in this analysis as between-subject factors. The range of scores for fluency was 1-12, flexibility 1-10, and originality 0-5. The means and standard errors of the three creativity indices are presented in Table 4-1.

The results of this analysis indicated that grade was the only factor that significantly influenced the creativity indices. This effect was evident in the multivariate test ($R_c$ = .37, $F$ (3,54) = 2.91, $p$ < .05) and in the univariate test for flexibility ($R$ = .28, $F$ (1,56) = 4.79, $p$ < .05). The effect size was nonsignificant for multivariate tests of story ($F$ (3,54) = .69) and media ($F$ (3,54) = .40), as were the univariate tests and the two- and three-way interactions.

An additional analysis was conducted to test whether performance on the divergent thinking test was significantly influenced by subjects' verbal ability. Verbal ability scores were obtained for each child from the school district psychologist. These scores were a standardized composite of the verbal subscales from the *Cooperative Primary Test* for third graders and from the *Comprehensive Test of Basic Skills* for the sixth graders. Three hierarchical multiple regression analyses were conducted using fluency, flexibility, and originality as criteria. Predictors added to the function, in order of inclusion, were the reading composite score, the square of this score, and the cube of this score. There were no significant first-order correlations (all $r$s < .20), nor quadratic (all $R^2_\Delta$ < .01) or cubic trends (all $R^2_\Delta$ < .003). Thus, the three creativity indices do not appear to be confounded by verbal ability.

Finally, in order to compare results on the three indices of creativity used in the present study with results reported by Torrance (1974), the interrelationships between the three creativity indices were evaluated with Pearson product-moment correlations. Fluency was significantly related to flexibility ($r$ = .85, $p$ < .001) and originality ($r$ = .37, $p$ < .01). These intercorrelations are similar to those reported by Torrance (1974), suggesting that these indices of creativity performed as they were designed to and in a manner consistent with previous research.

36

Table 4-1

Mean Fluency, Flexibility, and Originality Scores
as a Function of Grade and Media Condition

Third-Graders

| | | | | |
|---|---|---|---|---|
| Fluency | 3.38 | (.17) | 3.44 | (.44) |
| Flexibility | 2.06 | (.46) | 1.94 | (.21) |
| Originality | 1.06 | (.38) | 0.50 | (.24) |

Sixth-Graders

| | | | | |
|---|---|---|---|---|
| Fluency | 4.25 | (.74) | 4.44 | (.53) |
| Flexibility | 3.19 | (.60) | 2.94 | (.42) |
| Originality | 0.31 | (.15) | 0.75 | (.25) |

Note: Standard errors are in parentheses.

## Discussion

This study assessed the effects of television and radio on creativity as measured by a standardized test of divergent thinking. There were no differences between the two forms of media in terms of consequent ideational fluency, flexibility, or originality. Further, the three measures used performed as expected. That is, the three indices of divergent thinking were significantly intercorrelated, but not entirely oblique, and they were all unrelated to verbal ability.

These findings, both the nonsignificant media effects and the significant grade effect, are consistent with literature on creativity that holds that creative abilities are enduring traits (e.g., Barron, 1955; Guilford, 1968). These findings do not support the positions taken by the Carnegie Commission (1979) and Morriset (1976) that radio actively stimulates creativity. However, these positions were not data based. The results also contradict the finding of Greenfield et al. (1981). One explanation for this difference is that the experimental measures used in the two studies were different. In the Greenfield et al. study, children were asked to finish a prematurely ended story. This can be considered more of a convergent than divergent thinking task because it requires children to integrate presented information and infer how a story should logically end. The task is not, therefore, entirely open-ended, and not comparable to the divergent thinking task used in the present study. Because convergent thinking is not consistent with the definition of creativity, this could account for the difference in the results of Greenfield et al. (1981) and the present study.

Similarly, there were important procedural differences between the study of Meline (1976) and the present study. Simply put, Meline's task was also probably tapping a cognitive process that is unrelated to ideational fluency, originality, and flexibility. Meline asked subjects to give only one solution to each program, and subjects were explicitly instructed to give "the best . . . most original idea" (p. 84). Both of these procedures have been known to significantly influence ideation. The ideation of a subject when given instructions to be original is qualitatively and quantitatively different from the ideation of the same subject given less restrictive instructions (Harrington, 1975). With unrestricted instructions, ideation is more spontaneous, playful, and probably requires less effort than with restricted instructions (Wallach & Kogan, 1965). Along these same lines, the scoring procedures used by Meline (1976) focused on "departures" from, or "transformations" of given information. This is thus a measure of ideational distance, that is, remoteness. Although this is vaguely similar to Guilford and Guilford's (1980) "remoteness" index, distance is not a well-defined index of divergent thinking; and it is not related to ideational fluency, originality, or flexibility. These three divergent thinking indices are estimates of the number of unusualness of ideas and ideational categories regardless of their absolute distance from the given information. These three indices indicate that an original idea could be "close" to the given stimulus information. In fact, truly creative ideas are often viewed as both original and "close," that is, relevant to the task at hand (e.g., Bruner, 1962).

The crux of the issue is in the definition of "creativity." The present project does not presuppose that creativity is synonymous with divergent thinking. Divergent thinking tasks were used simply because they are the most commonly used estimate of creative potential and because they are psychometrically understood. In short, divergent thinking indices were employed because they are highly interpretable.

Overall, then, in making generalizations based on these data, one must be specific about the type of problem being presented by the media. Given the work of Greenfield et al. (1981) and Meline (1976), it may be that different forms of media differentially influence responses on convergent thinking tasks or tasks that require strategic ideation. However, the results of the present study suggest that ideational fluency, originality, and flexibility are not influenced differentially by the form of media with an open-ended divergent thinking task. Moreover, these indices of divergent thinking are distinct from other forms of measured intelligence, and predictive of real-world creative performance (Barron & Harrington, 1981; Wallach & Wing, 1969).

An alternative explanation of the results of the present study is that the experimental treatments, that is, the radio and television presentations, were not sufficiently robust to produce differences on any measure of cognitive processing. However, five additional dependent variables were included for other purposes (Pezdek & Lehrer, 1983). The given dependent variables assessed memory and comprehension in the radio and television conditions. Four of these five cognitive measures resulted in significant differences between the two media conditions. Therefore, the absence of media differences with the three creativity measures in the present study does not appear to be due to generally insufficient treatment effects.

Given that it is uncommon to present research that supports the null hypothesis, it is important to note that the conclusion that divergent thinking is not influenced differentially by television versus radio is not based entirely on this one investigation. Rather, this study is one application of the "trait" theory of creativity. For this reason, presenting support for the null hypothesis is justifiable in this study and follows from specific suggestions by Binder (1963).

The present study and the studies by Greenfield et al. (1981) and Meline (1976) do not test the possibility that creativity may be influenced significantly by more long-term media exposure. Indeed, this direction is interesting for future research. However, at present it can be concluded that creativity, measured by standardized tests of ideational fluency, flexibility, and originality, is not affected differentially by short-term exposure to television versus radio.

## REFERENCES

Barron, F. (1955). The disposition towards originality. *Journal of Abnormal Social Psychology, 51,* 478-485.

Barron, F., & Harrington, D. M. (1981). Creativity, intelligence and personality. *Annual Review of Psychology, 32,* 439-476.

Binder A. (1963). Further considerations on testing the null hypothesis and the strategy and tactics of investigating theoretical models. *Psychological Review, 70,* 107-115.

Bruner, J. S. (1962). The conditions of creativity. In J. S. Bruner (Ed.), *On knowing: Essays for the left hand* (pp.17-30). Cambridge, MA: Belknap.

Carnegie Commission on the Future of Public Broadcasting. (1979). *A public trust.* New York: Bantam.

Feldman, D. (1980). *Beyond universals in cognitive development.* Norwood, NJ: Ablex.

Furu, T. (1971). *The functions of television for children and adolescents.* Tokyo: Sophia University Press.

Greenfield, P., Geber, B., Beagles-Roos, J., Farrar, D., & Gat, I. (1981, April). *Television and radio experimentally compared: Effects of the medium on imagination and transmission of content.* Paper presented at the meeting of the Society for Research in Child Development, Boston.

Guilford, J. P. (1968). *Creativity, intelligence, and their educational implications.* San Diego, CA: Knapp.

Guilford, J. P., & Guilford, J. S. (1980). *Consequences manual of instructions and interpretations.* Orange, CA: Sheridan Psychological Services.

Harrington, D. M. (1975). Effects of explicit instructions to "be creative" on the psychological meaning of divergent thinking test scores. *Journal of Personality, 43,* 434-454.

Himmelweit, H. T., Oppenheim, A. N., & Vince, P. (1958). *Television and the child: An empirical study of the effects of television on the young.* London: Oxford University Press.

Lyle, J. I., & Hoffman, H. R. (1972). Children's use of television and other media. In E. A. Rubinstein, G. A. Comstock, & J. P. Murray (Eds.), *Television and social behavior (Vol. 4). Television in day-to-day life: Patterns of use.* Washington, DC: U.S. Government Printing Office.

Mednick, S. A. (1962). The associative basis of the creative process. *Psychological Review, 69,* 220-232.

Meline, C. W. (1976). Does the medium matter? *Journal of Communication, 26,* 81-89.

Morriset, L. N. (1976). Radio USA. In the *Annual Report* of the John and Mary Markle Foundation. New York.

Murray, J. P. (1980). *Television and youth.* Boys Town, NE: Boys Town Press.

Murray, J. P., & Kippaz, S. (1978). Children's social behavior in three towns with differing television experience. *Journal of Communication, 28,* 19-29.

Murray, J. P., Kwiatek, K., & Clarke, P. (1982, April). *Television and fantasy: Children's viewing and storytelling.* Paper presented at the meeting of the International Communication Association, Boston.

Palmer, R. (1926). *School broadcasting in Britain.* B.B.C. London: Jarrold and Sons Ltd.

Pezdek, K., & Lehrer, A. (1983, November). *The relationship between memory and comprehension of text versus television and radio.* Paper presented at the meeting of the Psychonomic Society, San Diego, CA.

Rotter, D. M., Langland, L., & Berger, D. (1971). The validity of tests of creative thinking in seven-year-old children. *Gifted Child Quarterly, 15,* 273-278.

Schramm, W., Lyle, J., & Parker, E.G. (1961). Children's learning from television. *Studies in Public Communication, 3,* 86-98.

Singer, D. G. (1978). Television and imaginative play. *Journal of Mental Imagery, 2,* 145-164.

Singer, D. G., & Singer, J. L. (1976a). Family television habits and the spontaneous play of preschool children. *American Journal of Orthopsychiatry, 46,* 496-502.

Singer, J. L., & Singer D. G. (1976b). Can TV stimulate imaginative play? *Journal of Communication, 26,* 74-80.

Stern, S. L. (1973). Television and creativity: The effects of viewing certain categories of commercial television broadcasting on divergent thinking abilities of intellectually gifted elementary students. *Dissertation Abstracts International, 34A,* 3716 (University Microfilms No. 73-31, 675).

Torrance, E. P. (1974). *Torrance tests of creative thinking.* Lexington, MA: Personnel Press.

Tower, R. B., Singer, D. G., Singer, J. L., & Biggs, A. (1979). Differential effects of television programming on preschoolers' cognition, imagination and social play. *American Journal of Orthopsychiatry, 49,* 265-281.

Wallach, M. A., & Kogan, N. (1965). *Modes of thinking in young children.* New York: Holt, Rinehart, & Winston.

Wallach, M. A., & Wing, C. W., Jr. (1969). *The talented student.* New York: Holt, Rinehart & Winston.

Ward, W.C. (1968). *Creativity in young children.* Child Development, *39,* 737-754.

Werner, A. (1975). The effects of television on children and adolescents: A case of sex and class socialization. *Journal of Communication, 25,* 450.

## Section II

# Educational Issues

The five chapters in this Section are primarily concerned with "What can we do about children's creative ideation?" and as such, they may be the most practical in the present volume. As you might expect, there are a number of strictly educational lessons in these chapters. Chapter 5, for instance, demonstrates that divergent thinking is associated with teachers' judgments about creativity, and Chapters 6 and 7 suggest that we encourage creative thinking by explicitly defining "originality" and "flexibility" for our students. The research in this Section also contributes to our understanding of the construct validity of divergent thinking tests. This is clearly seen in Chapters 6 through 9, with their separation of the ideational and metacognitive facets of divergent thinking.

Creativity is often operationalized as divergent thinking and assessed with tasks which require that an individual generate responses to an open-ended question (e.g., "Name all of the things you can think of that are triangular"). These tasks are typically scored for "ideational fluency," or the number of distinct responses, and "ideational originality," or the number of relatively unusual responses. Although there are many limitations inherent in these tests (Wallach, 1970, 1977), they have adequate reliability and validity with a wide range of criteria and populations (see Barron & Harrington, 1981; Hocevar, 1981).

The present project was designed to assess the social validity of divergent thinking tests. Social validity can be defined as the extent to which a traditional objective psychometric evaluation agrees with or predicts the subjective judgment of teachers, parents, supervisors, or "significant others" (Kazdin, 1977; Wolf, 1978). The rationale for social validation is that traditional psychometric assessments supply only one type of information, and that additional and meaningful information can also be obtained by asking those significant others who actually interact with—and make important decisions about—the individual to be tested. Parents, for example, might make decisions about their child's curriculum based on concerns or information that is different from the concerns or information used by a school counselor or teacher. Thus it is important to have parental input as well as that of the counselor or teacher. Put briefly, the primary virtue of social validation is that it uses criteria that are important in the real world.

Socially valid instruments have been constructed and used to complement the objective assessment of exceptional populations (Runco & Schreibman, 1983, 1987; Schreibman, Runco, Mills, & Koegel, 1982). Runco and Schreibman (1983), for instance, asked parents of autistic children to describe the important behavioral features of children on a videotape. Those features that were identified by several parents were incorporated into a questionnaire. A second group of parents then used this instrument to judge the behavior of autistic children. These parental judgments were in turn compared with the judgments made by trained behavior therapists. Schreibman et al. (1982) used a similar procedure with teachers, and here again, there were important similarities and differences between the subjective and objective evaluations. Runco and Schreibman concluded that their objective assessment procedures were socially valid in that there were significant correlations between the parents and teachers and the trained observers. And note that the work of Runco and Schreibman dealt with autistic children—a population that is notoriously difficult to assess. Similar accusations have been leveled against the assessment of creativity.

Subjective judgments have been utilized in the past as in the assessment of creativity (Getzels & Jackson, 1962; Holland, 1959; Karlins, Schuerhoff, & Kaplan, 1969; Lieberman, 1965; Mednick, 1963; Piers, Daniels, & Quackenbush, 1960; Richards, Cline, & Needham, 1964; Swenson, 1978; Yamamoto, 1963), but this previous research has had both a different purpose and a different methodology than the social validation paradigm. The previous research was concerned with developing a predictor of creativity for use in a wide variety of situations and which could be used independently of other measures. Social validation is used as a complement to traditional assessments and not intended as a replacement. It is, put simply, a criterion rather than a predictor. Moreover, previous research has relied on subjective judgments of teachers or experts, but has not used a socially valid instrument to obtain these judgments. Typically, previous research has relied on measures which are based on presumption, or at best theory, rather than on socially valid definitions of creativity. The only approximation to socially validating a measure of creativity is that of Swenson (1978). She questioned teachers about ostensibly creative classroom behaviors (e.g., "tries original ways to get out of work"), but she employed teachers of disadvantaged students, and her instrument was unrelated to divergent thinking ($r = .08$) and significantly related to intelligence ($r = .39$).

Divergent thinking tests have yet to receive a social validation that uses both a socially valid instrument (one that contains items that are meaningful to the significant others) and the subjective judgments of significant others. The present project utilized the social validation paradigm to (a) demonstrate its applicability to the assessment of creativity, and (b) evaluate the social validity of divergent thinking tests. The central question is, "Do these tests predict teachers' judgments of children's creativity?"

## Method

### Subjects

The children employed in this project ($N = 240$) were from a public intermediate school. Ninety-seven were "gifted" (having been nominated to the school district's Gifted and Talented program, and having IQs in excess of 130), 53 were "talented" (having also been nominated, but having IQs less than 130), and 90 were nongifted controls. the average age for the 51 fifth-grade children was 10-10, for the 59 sixth-grade children 11-9, for the 61 seventh-grade children 12-10, and for the 69 eighth-grade children 13-9. Forty-four percent were boys and 56% were girls. Three ethnicities were represented: Hispanic, Asian, and White—not of Hispanic origin.

Because the teachers of these children were to fill out evaluations of their students as a part of this investigation, it will be helpful to know the backgrounds of the six teachers. The teachers were all women; their ages ranged from 29 to 41 yrs, with a mean of 34-5; and their teaching experience ranged from 7 to 13 yrs., with a mean of 9-4. Four of the six had earned a MA degree, and the remaining two were in the process of obtaining MA degrees.

### The Questionnaire

The Teachers' Evaluation of Students' Creativity (TESC) was developed for this project. It contained 25 items, all of which are presented in Table 5-1. Twenty of these items were taken from the responses of 32 naive student teachers who were asked to (a) give synonyms of "creativity," (b) list behaviors that are observed in intermediate school children and that you consider to be "creative," and (c) list personality traits common to "creative" students. Because this task was given in written form, the teachers could respond simultaneously to all three requests, or respond to one at a time. Only those items suggested by three or more of the student teachers were included in the questionnaire. Four of the five remaining items were added to the questionnaire to avoid a possible response set. These four items (i.e., conforming, inflexible, insensitive, unoriginal) were simply antonyms of four of the items given by the student teachers. The last item on the questionnaire was the adjective "creative," which was also added by the experimenter.

The 25 items were randomly arranged on the Teacher Evaluation. An example of the wording for each question was "to what degree, or how often, is this child . . . ." Each item had seven possible responses: (1) rarely, (2) very little, (3) slightly, (4) moderately, (5) considerably, (6) very much, and (7) extremely. The instructions are given below. A total score was calculated by taking a mean of the 21 positively worded items.

### Divergent Thinking Tests

Five tests, each with three items, were used in this project. These were adapted from Wallach and Kogan (1965). Two of these (Pattern and Line Meanings) were figural tests, and three (Instances, Alternative Uses, and Similarities) were verbal.

### Procedure

The divergent thinking tests were administered to the children in their classroom. They were tested in groups by the experimenter. Testing sessions were 1 hr., and there were two sessions per day for one week. The administration procedures were adapted from Wallach and Kogan (1965).

The Teacher Evaluation was given to the teachers with the following instructions:

Please complete one questionnaire for each of your students that is participating in this project. Be sure to (a) distribute your responses across all seven possible answers; (b) take your time and carefully consider each item; and (c) remember that your ratings are completely confidential. If you have any questions, please ask.

### Results

The means and standard errors of the Teacher Evaluations, the divergent thinking tests, and the available IQs are presented in Table 5-2.

The reliability of the Teacher Evaluations was assessed with coefficient $\alpha$, a measure of internal consistency (Cronbach, 1970). The results indicated that the Teacher Evaluation was reliable: $\alpha$ was .96 overall, with a range of .91 to .97 for the six teachers.

The reliabilities of the divergent thinking tests were evaluated by calculating interitem and intertest Pearsonian correlations. These supported the reliability of the divergent thinking tests: The average interitem correlation was .64 for Fluency and .59 for Originality. Also, the average intertest correlation was .65 for Fluency and .36 for Originality.

Table 5-1

Items on the Teacher Evaluation

| | | |
|---|---|---|
| 1. Self-Directed | 9. Exploratory | 18. Challenging |
| 2. Curious | 10. Insensitive | 19. Uninhibited |
| 3. Conforming | 11. Unique | 20. Independent |
| 4. Original | 12. Innovative | 21. Sensitive |
| 5. Artistic | 13. Flexible | 22. Expressive |
| 6. Inflexible | 14. Unoriginal | 23. Inventive |
| 7. Intelligent | 15. Imaginative | 24. Good at Designing |
| 8. Interested in Many Things | 16. Always Questioning | 25. Creative |
| | 17. Nonconforming | |

Note: Items 3, 6, 10, and 14 were added by the experimenter to avoid a response set.

To evaluate possible gender and age effects on the TESC ratings, an analysis of variance was conducted using gender as the between-subjects factor and age as a covariate. The results of this analysis indicated that neither was significantly related to TESC ratings.

Table 5-2

Means and Standard Deviations (in parentheses)

| | Gifted | | Talented | | Control | |
|---|---|---|---|---|---|---|
| Teachers' Evaluation | 4.6 | (0.1) | 4.4 | (0.1) | 4.0 | (0.1) |
| Divergent Thinking Tests | | | | | | |
| Fluency | 42.2 | (2.2) | 37.4 | (2.6) | 36.3 | (1.8) |
| Originality | 36.2 | (3.5) | 29.5 | (4.0) | 26.7 | (2.1) |
| IQ | 140 | (0.8) | 119 | (0.9) | na | |

The social validity of the divergent thinking tests was evaluated by correlating the composite Fluency score (the total of the five tests) and the composite Originality score with the TESC ratings. Because the divergent thinking of gifted children is significantly different from that of talented and nongifted children (Runco & Albert, 1985), these Pearsonian correlations were calculated separately for the three groups of children. Also, all coefficients were adjusted for attenuation and range restriction (Bobko, 1983). This adjustment insures that the correlation coefficients are not biased by the imperfect reliability of the tests and differences between the standard errors of the three groups.

For the gifted children, scores on the Teachers' Evaluation of Students' Creativity were significantly correlated with scores on Fluency ($r = .30$, $p < .01$) and Originality ($r = .34$, $p < .001$). For the talented children, the Teacher Evaluations were significantly correlated with scores on Fluency ($r = .21$, $p < .05$) and Originality ($r = .28$, $p < .05$), and for the control group of children, the Teacher Evaluations were significantly correlated with scores on Fluency ($r = .28$, $p < .01$) and Originality ($r = .42$, $p < .001$).

Finally, in order to evaluate the discriminant validity of the Teacher Evaluations, correlations were computed between the Teacher Evaluation scores and the available IQs. These also were adjusted for attenuation and range restriction (Bobko, 1983). As expected, the resulting coefficient was negative and nonsignificant for the gifted ($r = -.12$) and talented children ($r = -.14$).

## Discussion

These results indicate that the Wallach and Kogan (1965) divergent thinking test battery does have social validity in terms of teacher judgments. That is, the divergent thinking test scores were significantly related to teachers' judgments about the creativity of their students. Although the amount of variance shared by the Teacher Evaluation and the divergent thinking tests was only moderate, this was to be expected. The Teacher Evaluation, like many observational techniques, probably was influenced by the personality traits and extracognitive characteristics of the children, as well as their cognitive skills (cf. Barron & Harrington, 1981). Furthermore, the correlations between the scores of the Teacher Evaluation and the divergent thinking tests were statistically significant. It may be concluded that divergent thinking test scores do in fact predict teachers' subjective judgments of creativity. Of course, this is not to say that divergent thinking tests or teacher judgments are accurate predictors of real-world creativity. The present study suggests only that a child's divergent thinking ability is a good predictor of teachers' judgments of creativity. Recall here that the social validation questionnaire is not a predictor; it is a criterion.

The TESC had very high interitem reliability, but given the nature of this measure, an evaluation of inter-rater reliability would also be informative.[1] Because a teacher's familiarity with his or her students is vital in making meaningful judgments (Gear, 1976; Holland, 1959), and there was only one qualified teacher for the students in the present research, this was not feasible. A "halo effect" is the most serious potential problem when using subjective judgments (Holland, 1959; Swenson, 1978; Wallach, 1970), and therefore it should be emphasized that the Teacher Evaluation was negatively related to IQ. This discriminant validity indicates that the

---

[1] Support for the interrater reliability and validity of the Teachers' Evaluation was later presented by Runco, M. A. (1987). Interrater agreement on a socially valid measure of students' creativity. *Psychological Reports, 61,* 1009-1010.

teachers were discriminating between creative children and other intellectually capable children.

The specific contents of the Teacher Evaluation are noteworthy. In particular, it is interesting that many of the items which were generated by student teachers (e.g., "flexible," "independent," "interested in many things") are very consistent with common theories of the creative personality (Albert, 1983). It appears that student teachers have a reliable prototype of "the creative individual" in much the same way as experts and laypersons have a reliable prototype of "intelligence" (Sternberg, Conway, Ketron, & Bernstein, 1981).

Finally, recall that this project was in part conducted to demonstrate that the social validation paradigm can be applied to the research on creativity. The agreement between the teachers and the scores on the divergent thinking tests is important, but the external validity of the Teachers' Evaluation of Students' *Creativity* should be examined further. For example, it would be interesting to replicate this study with art or science teachers. This is especially true because the general applicability of the social validation procedures to the psychometrics of creativity is now justified.

## REFERENCES

Albert, R. S. (Ed.). (1983). *Genius and eminence: The social psychology of creativity and exceptional achievement*. New York: Pergamon.

Barron, R., & Harrington, D. M. (1981). Creativity, intelligence, and personality. *Annual Review of Psychology, 32*, 439-476.

Bobko, P. (1983). An analysis of correlations corrected for attenuation and range restriction. *Journal of Applied Psychology, 68*, 584-589.

Cronbach, L. J. (1970). *Essentials of psychological testing* (3rd ed.). New York: Harper & Row.

Gear, G. H. (1976). Accuracy of teacher judgment in identifying intellectually gifted children: A review of the literature. *Gifted Child Quarterly, 20*, 478-489.

Getzels, J. W., & Jackson, P. W. (1962). *Creativity and intelligence: Explorations with gifted students*. New York: Wiley.

Hocevar, D. (1981). Measurement of creativity: Review and critique. *Journal of Personality Assessment, 45*, 450-464.

Holland, J. L. (1959). Some limitations of teacher ratings as predictors of creativity. *Journal of Educational Psychology, 50*, 219-223.

Karlins, M., Schuerhoff, C., & Kaplan, M. (1969). Some factors related to architectural creativity in graduating architecture students. *Journal of General Psychology, 81*, 203-215.

Kazdin, A. E. (1977). Assessing the clinical or applied importance of behavior change through social validation. *Behavior Modification, 1*, 427-451.

Lieberman, J. N. (1965). Playfulness and divergent thinking: An investigation of their relationship at the kindergarten level. *Journal of Genetic Psychology, 107*, 219-224.

Mednick, M. T. (1963). Research creativity in psychology graduate students. *Journal of Consulting Psychology, 27*, 265-266.

Piers, E. V., Daniels, J. M., & Quackenbush, J. F. (1964). The identification of creativity in adolescents. *Journal of Educational Psychology, 51,* 346-351.

Richards, J. M., Jr., Cline, V. B., & Needham, W. E. (1964). Creativity tests and teacher and self judgments of originality. *Journal of Experimental Education, 32,* 281-285.

Runco, M. A., & Albert, R. S. (1985). The reliability and validity of ideational originality in the divergent thinking of academically gifted and nongifted children. *Educational and Psychological Measurement, 45,* 483-501. [Chapter 10]

Runco, M. A., & Schreibman, L. (1983). Parental judgments of behavior therapy efficacy with autistic children: A social validation. *Journal of Autism and Developmental Disabilities, 13,* 237-248.

Runco, M. A., & Schreibman, L. (1987). Socially validating behavioral objectives in the treatment of autism. *Journal of Autism and Developmental Disorders, 17,* 141-147.

Schreibman, L., Runco, M. A., Mills, J. I., & Koegel, R. L. (1982). Teachers' judgments of improvements in autistic children in behavior therapy: A social validation. In R. L. Koegel, A. Rincover, & A. W. Egel (Eds.), *Educating and understanding autistic children* (pp. 78-87). Houston: College-Hill Press.

Sternberg, R. J., Conway, B. E., Ketron, J. L., & Bernstein, M. (1981). People's conceptions of intelligence. *Journal of Personality and Social Psychology, 41,* 37-55.

Swenson, E. V. (1978). Teacher-assessment of creative behavior in disadvantaged children. *Gifted Child Quarterly, 22,* 338-343.

Wallach, M. A. (1970). Creativity. In P. H. Musser (Ed.), *Carmichael's manual of child psychology* (Vol. 1, pp. 1211-1272). New York: Wiley.

Wallach, M. A. (1977). Tests tell us little about talent. In I. L. Janis (Ed.), *Current trends in psychology* (pp. 237-243). Los Altos, CA: William Kaufmann.

Wallach, M. A., & Kogan, N. (1965). *Modes of thinking in young children.* New York: Holt, Rinehart, & Winston.

Wolf, M. M. (1978). Social validity: The case for subjective measurement, or how applied behavior analysis is finding its heart. *Journal of Applied Behavior Analysis, 11,* 203-214.

Yamamoto, K. (1963). Relationships between creative thinking abilities of teachers and achievement of pupils. *Journal of Experimental Education, 32,* 3-25.

Chapter 6

# Enhancing the Originality of Ideas

### Abstract[*]

Explicit instructions to "be creative" are often used to estimate the role of task-perception in divergent thinking test performance. However, previous research on this topic has employed only nongifted individuals. The present investigation compared gifted ($n = 97$), talented ($n = 53$), and nongifted ($n = 90$) intermediate school children in terms of divergent thinking fluency, flexibility, and originality scores elicited by standard and explicit instructions. Results indicated that the scores of all groups were significantly different in the two instructional conditions. More importantly, there was a significant interaction between this instructional effect and children's level of ability. The explicit instructions enhanced the originality scores of the talented and nongifted children more than those of the gifted children; and the same instructions inhibited the fluency and flexibility scores of the gifted children more than those of the talented and nongifted children. These results have important implications for testing creativity and for our understanding of giftedness.

[*] Adapted from: Runco, M. A. (1986). Maximal performance on divergent thinking tests by gifted, talented, and nongifted children. *Psychology in the Schools*, 23, 308-315.

Divergent thinking tests are frequently used to estimate creative thinking potential. They involve open-ended questions to which a respondent may generate any number of ideational responses. Divergent thinking tests have sound theoretical support (Guilford, 1977; Wallach & Kogan, 1965), and divergent thinking ability is an important facet of giftedness (Albert & Runco, 1986; Renzulli, 1978). Of course, like most measures of intellectual ability, these tests are influenced by extracognitive factors. Harrington (1975), for example, proposed that "task-perception" is a crucial aspect of divergent thinking test performance. Moreover, he suggested that administering divergent thinking tests with explicit instructions to "be creative" would minimize individual differences resulting from task-perception. Presumably, any variability in performance after explicit instructions represents the purely cognitive component of divergent thinking test performance.

To test the role of task-perception, Harrington (1975) administered the Alternative Uses divergent thinking test with standard instructions to one group of college students, and the same test with explicit instructions to "be creative" to another group. Results indicated that the explicit instructions were very influential: Relative to subjects given standard instructions, the subjects given explicit instructions had high originality scores, giving many unusual responses, and low fluency scores, giving few common responses.

This explicit instructions technique is analogous to the maximal performance procedure used in personality assessment (Turner, 1978). The presupposition is that every examinee has a range of potential performance, and the most reliable index of behavior is at the maximum rather than a modal level. Modal performance might fluctuate in different contexts, and can improve or worsen depending upon the individual's perception of the exigencies of each particular setting. Maximal performance should be more stable because the individual's perception of the task is largely controlled, and behavior is at its peak.

Harrington (1975) demonstrated that maximal divergent thinking test performance can be elicited by administering explicit instructions to "be creative." Other investigations of maximal divergent thinking performance have reported sex differences (Evans & Forbach, 1983; Katz & Poag, 1979), an age-effect (Speller & Schumacher, 1975), and differences between various divergent thinking tests (Cummings, Hinton, & Gobdel, 1975). Unfortunately, no research has been conducted to compare gifted and nongifted children in terms of the effects of explicit instructions on divergent thinking. Gifted and nongifted individuals have different ideational tendencies (Guilford, 1977; Runco & Albert, 1985), and these may be at least partly the result of differences in task-perception. Therefore, giving explicit instructions might help us better understand the differences between gifted and nongifted children's divergent thinking. The primary purpose of the present investigation is to compare the divergent thinking of gifted and nongifted children in terms of the effects of explicit instructions.

A second reason to study the role of explicit instructions is essentially psychometric. More specifically, maximal performance scores have better predictive validity than those which are elicited by standard instructions (Datta, 1963; Harrington, 1975; Katz & Poag, 1979), but here again, gifted individuals have yet to be evaluated in this regard. Additionally, predictive validity is not the only index of a test's psychometric adequacy.

Divergent thinking test scores are, for instance, often correlated with scores from other intellectual measures, indicating a lack of discriminant validity (Boersma & O'Bryan, 1968; Runco & Albert, 1986), and ideational flexibility and originality have unique variance that is unreliable, indicating poor convergent validity (Hocevar, 1979; Runco, 1985; Runco & Albert, 1985). Perhaps explicit instructions will improve the discriminant and convergent validity of these tests, as they seem to improve predictive validity. The second purpose of this investigation is to evaluate the discriminant, convergent, and predictive validity of gifted and nongifted children's maximal performance divergent thinking test scores.

## Method

### Participants

A large sample of intermediate school children participated in this project ($N = 240$). According to school district criteria (teacher nominations and IQs), 97 of these children were "gifted," 53 were "talented," and 90 were nongifted. The range of IQ (Stanford-Binet or WISC-R, administered by a school district psychologist) was 98 to 165, and 130 was the cutoff between the gifted and talented groups. The gifted and talented groups had mean IQs of 141 and 119, respectively, and the standard deviations were 8 and 7. Boys and girls were approximately equally represented, as were the fifth through eighth grades.

### Measures and Procedure

This project was designed as a within-subject comparison of divergent thinking elicited by explicit instructions and divergent thinking elicited by standard instructions. Five tests were administered in the standard instructions condition. These were Instances, Pattern Meanings, Uses, Similarities, and Line Meanings (Wallach & Kogan, 1965), each with three items. Instructions and administration procedures from Wallach and Kogan (1965) were used. More specifically, the tests were described as games, with no particular correct or incorrect responses; there were no time limits, and the testing atmosphere was relaxed and permissive. The explicit instructions test had five items, with one item from each of the tests mentioned above. The testing atmosphere here was the same as the standard instructions condition, but instructions from Harrington (1975) were used. Put briefly, these instructions asked the children to "be creative" and "give only original responses." These instructions also informed the children that a creative idea was original and worthwhile, and defined an original idea as one that would be thought of by no one else. All instructions were given textually and orally.

The responses from the six divergent thinking tests were scored for ideational fluency, flexibility, and originality. Fluency reflects the number of distinct ideas; flexibility reflects the number of ideational categories in an individual's responses; and originality reflects the number of unusual or statistically infrequent ideas (relative to the pool of responses given by the entire sample of subjects). Each of the indices is described in detail by Runco

(1985) and Runco and Albert (1985). To allow comparisons between the two instructional conditions, scores were transformed into "item scores" (i.e., the sum of the standard instructions tests divided by 15, the number of items in those tests, and the sum of the explicit instructions tests divided by five, the number of items in that test).

A creative accomplishment self-report was also administered to the children to allow an evaluation of the predictive validity of the divergent thinking test scores. This measure reflects the quantity and quality of extracurricular activity in seven performance areas (i.e., writing, science, fine arts, crafts, public presentation, performing arts, and music) and is described in detail by Runco (1987). To allow an evaluation of the discriminant validity of the divergent thinking tests, *California Achievement Test* (CAT; McGraw-Hill, 1979) scores were obtained from school district records. The reading, language, and mathematics scores of the CAT were transformed into z-scores (within each grade level) and then added together to form a composite achievement test score.

The creativity tests were given to the children in their classrooms. The order of administration for the divergent thinking tests is presented in Table 6-1. (The explicit instructions test had to be administered last to avoid contamination of the standard instructions tests.) Testing required two hours each day for four days, with other tasks—including the creative accomplishment self-report—interspersed between the divergent thinking tests. Intermissions were given between tests, and the teachers were always present.

## Results

Table 6-1 presents the means and standard errors for each divergent thinking test, and presents them in the sequence in which they were administered. Note that there are no ascending or descending trends, and hence no indication of an order-effect (i.e., practice or fatigue).

To test for differences among the three groups of participants, a multivariate analysis of variance (MANOVA) was conducted. This included level of ability as a between-subjects factor, age (in months) as a covariate, and the six divergent thinking test scores (fluency, flexibility, and originality for verbal and figural tests) as dependent variables. Wilks' $\lambda$ was the criterion. The results indicated that age accounted for a significant amount of the variance in the divergent thinking test scores in the multivariate test ($R_c = .37$, $F (6,209) = 5.51$, $p < .001$) and the univariate tests for explicit instructions originality ($R = .14$, $F (1,214) = 4.39$, $p < .05$), and standard instructions fluency ($R = .33$, $F (1,214) = 26.12$, $p < .001$), flexibility ($R = .28$, $F (1,214) = 18.29$, $p < .001$) and originality ($R = .27$, $F (1,214) = 17.15$, $p < .001$). After this variance was controlled, the three groups were significantly different in the multivariate test ($F (12,418) = 2.03$, $p < .05$) and the univariate test for standard instructions flexibility ($F (1,214) = 3.83$, $p < .05$). Two contrasts were conducted to compare the scores of (a) the nongifted and talented children, and (b) the talented and gifted children. Results indicated that the talented and gifted children had significantly different scores in terms of the multivariate test ($F (6,209) = 2.31$, $p < .05$) and the univariate test for standard instructions flexibility ($F (1,214) = 5.34$, $p < .05$). The nongifted and talented groups were not significantly different. Table 6-1 presents the mean scores for each group and each test. To compare the divergent thinking test scores in the explicit instruction condition with those of the standard instruction condition, and to test the interaction between level of ability and instructional effect, a second MANOVA was conducted using level of ability as a between-subjects factor, age as a covariate, and "difference scores" (i.e., explicit instructions minus standard instructions) of fluency, flexibility, and originality as dependent variables. Difference scores have been used in similar pre- post-treatment comparisons (Runco & Schreibman, 1983) and were chosen instead of the regression approach in order to obtain a multivariate test of significance. Results indicated that after the variance attributable to age was controlled, there was a significant instructional effect in the multivariate test ($F$ (3,212) = 4.17, $p < .01$) and the univariate test for fluency ($F$ (1,214) = 6.92, $p < .01$). More importantly, there was an interaction between the instructional effect and level of ability in the multivariate test ($F$ (6,424) = 3.43, $p < .01$) and the univariate tests for fluency ($F$ (1,214) = 5.18, $p < .01$), flexibility ($F$ (1,214) = 9.69, $p < .001$), and originality ($F$ (1,214) = 3.11, $p < .05$). Table 6-2 presents the mean item scores for each group and both types of instructions. These data indicate that for all children, fluency and flexibility scores were higher in the standard instructions than the explicit instructions condition, and the originality scores were higher in the explicit instructions than the standard instructions condition. The interaction indicates that level of ability moderated the instructional effect. More precisely, explicit instructions enhanced the originality scores of the talented and nongifted children more than those of the gifted children, and inhibited the fluency and flexibility scores of the gifted children more than those of the talented and nongifted children.

Table 6-1

Means and Standard Errors (in parentheses) of Fluency, Flexibility, and Originality for the Tests with Standard Instructions

| | Gifted (n = 97) | | Talented (n = 53) | | Nongifted (n = 90) | |
|---|---|---|---|---|---|---|
| Fluency | | | | | | |
| Instances | 20.4 | (1.20) | 17.5 | (1.40) | 18.1 | (1.30) |
| Patterns | 3.9 | (0.31) | 3.5 | (0.33) | 3.6 | (0.19) |
| Uses | 7.5 | (0.50) | 7.3 | (1.15) | 5.7 | (0.32) |
| Similarities | 5.8 | (0.46) | 4.6 | (0.32) | 4.7 | (0.27) |
| Lines | 4.9 | (0.30) | 4.3 | (0.35) | 4.3 | (0.26) |
| Flexibility | | | | | | |
| Instances | 7.8 | (0.22) | 7.1 | (0.28) | 6.9 | (0.22) |
| Patterns | 3.1 | (0.20) | 2.9 | (0.23) | 2.9 | (0.13) |
| Uses | 4.6 | (0.20) | 4.3 | (0.27) | 3.7 | (0.14) |
| Similarities | 3.9 | (0.16) | 3.6 | (0.20) | 3.5 | (0.14) |
| Lines | 3.7 | (0.19) | 3.5 | (0.23) | 3.5 | (0.16) |
| Originality | | | | | | |
| Instances | 11.7 | (1.30) | 8.5 | (1.30) | 9.3 | (1.40) |
| Patterns | 5.7 | (0.70) | 5.2 | (0.62) | 4.9 | (0.36) |
| Uses | 8.2 | (1.02) | 7.9 | (2.40) | 4.8 | (0.46) |
| Similarities | 4.4 | (1.10) | 2.6 | (0.34) | 2.6 | (0.33) |
| Lines | 6.7 | (0.70) | 5.2 | (0.67) | 5.1 | (0.53) |

## Validity of the Divergent Thinking Test Scores

Pearson correlations were calculated in order to evaluate the discriminant, convergent, and predictive validity of the two sets of divergent thinking test scores. The correlation coefficients of the three groups of children were very similar, and therefore only the results for the entire sample will be presented.

In reference to discriminant validity, the fluency, flexibility, and originality scores from the explicit instructions conditions were negatively correlated with the CAT composite (average $r = -.11$), and all three standard instructions scores were positively and significantly correlated with the CAT composite (average $r = .45$, $p < .001$). In reference to convergent validity, the explicit instructions fluency scores were related to the flexibility and originality scores ($r = .78$ and .94, respectively), and the flexibility scores were related to the originality scores ($r = .67$). The standard instructions fluency scores were related to flexibility and originality scores ($r = .90$ and .80, respectively), as were the flexibility and originality scores ($r = .89$). In reference to predictive validity, neither the explicit instructions nor the standard instructions scores were related to quantity or quality scores of the creative activity questionnaire (average $r < .18$). All of these coefficients are probably attenuated due to the imperfect reliabilities of the tests (Nunnally, 1978).

Table 6-2

Means and Standard Errors (in parentheses) of the Standard and Explicit Instructions Divergent Thinking Test Scores

|  | Standard Instructions | | Explicit Instructions | |
|---|---|---|---|---|
| Fluency | | | | |
| Gifted | 8.5 | (0.46) | 5.5 | (0.38) |
| Talented | 7.6 | (0.56) | 6.7 | (0.87) |
| Nongifted | 7.2 | (0.36) | 6.1 | (0.44) |
| Flexibility | | | | |
| Gifted | 4.7 | (0.16) | 3.3 | (0.13) |
| Talented | 4.3 | (0.19) | 3.5 | (0.22) |
| Nongifted | 4.1 | (0.11) | 3.5 | (0.13) |
| Originality | | | | |
| Gifted | 7.1 | (0.69) | 9.0 | (0.75) |
| Talented | 5.9 | (0.89) | 10.9 | (1.96) |
| Nongifted | 5.3 | (0.44) | 9.6 | (0.81) |

Note: $n$ = 97 for the gifted group, 53 for the talented group, and 90 for the nongifted group.

## Discussion

These findings suggest that divergent thinking test scores elicited by explicit instructions are quite different from those elicited by standard instructions. More importantly, this instructional effect is moderated by the examinee's level of intellectual ability. The originality scores of the gifted children in the present investigation suggest that they spontaneously recognized what type of ideational strategy was appropriate for the open-ended tasks even when given only standard instructions. The talented and nongifted individuals, on the other hand, benefited from the explicit instructions and generated more original ideas in that instructional condition than they did in the standard instructions condition. In fact, in the explicit instructions condition, the originality scores of the talented and nongifted children were higher than those of the gifted children (see Table 6-2).

Thus, gifted children differ quite substantially from nongifted children in their perceptions of divergent thinking tasks, and we might induce that extracognitive ability is an important aspect of giftedness. Of course we should be very careful generalizing from the present findings to other gifted samples and other intellectual tasks. However, the conclusion that gifted and nongifted children differ in their extracognitive abilities is also supported by the work of Albert and Runco (1986), Renzulli (1978), and Davidson and Sternberg (1984). The work of Davidson and Sternberg is especially relevant here, for they demonstrated that nongifted children benefited more than gifted children from problem "precues."

Because divergent thinking tests are probably the most common measure of creativity, the findings of the present study have important psychometric implications that apply to examinees at all levels of ability. For example, the present findings reinforce the argument that divergent thinking tests reflect only creative potential, and other motivational and situational variables are involved in actual creative performance. These tests are reliable and valid; but in addition to divergent thinking, a truly creative act requires the recognition that a meaningful problem exists, an accurate perception of the task, and an interest in solving the problem in an original manner (Nicholls, 1972). Put briefly, the present findings indicate that individual differences in divergent thinking ability are explained most accurately in terms of cognitive ability and task-perception.

Another aspect of the present findings that is interesting from the psychometric perspective is that the divergent thinking test scores resulting from explicit instructions were negatively correlated with CAT scores, while those resulting from standard instructions were positively and significantly related to CAT scores. This is consistent with the view that the relationship between creativity and intelligence is influenced by the conditions under which the tests were administered (e.g., Wallach & Kogan, 1965), and it indicates that the scores elicited by the explicit instructions had discriminant validity while the standard instructions scores did not. The correlational analyses also indicated that neither instructional condition yielded favorable predictive validity coefficients. This was partly unexpected because of previous research on explicit instructions (Datta, 1963; Harrington, 1975; Katz & Poag, 1979). Still, this previous research correlated divergent thinking test scores with relevant personality traits rather than real-world performance, and the predictive validity of divergent thinking tests with real-world criteria has never been impressive (Hocevar, 1980).

The data in Table 6-1 indicate that the effects of explicit instructions are not the result of practice with divergent thinking tests. If practice influenced the children's scores, a more pronounced and linear increase in scores would be evident. One does see a trend in the verbal tests, but this is by no means clear-cut, and it is not apparent in the nonverbal tests. More importantly, this trend is the opposite of what one would expect from practice; it is more suggestive of a fatigue effect. Because the explicit instructions test was given last, fatigue would inhibit rather than enhance the influence of explicit instructions, and our findings would be on the conservative side. Of course, the possibility of any order-effect was minimized by giving the tests over several days rather than all on one day, and by interspersing other tests between the divergent thinking tests that were on the same day.

Not all types of instructions will reliably control task-perception and improve the discriminant validity of divergent thinking test scores (Koestner, Ryan, Bernieri, & Holt, 1984; Manske & Davis, 1968). As Koestner et al. (1984) point out, instructions should be informational rather than controlling. Future research could determine if explicit instructions can be used regularly—perhaps in a classroom—to inculcate an enduring capacity for originality.

Future research could also evaluate the effects of explicit instructions in other gifted populations. The definition of "giftedness" used in this project was that of the school district, and based only on IQs and nominations given by teachers. And yet, even with the narrow definition of giftedness, there was a robust effect of explicit instructions and the expected interaction between the instructional effect and level of ability. Giving explicit instructions does seem to control one extracognitive component of divergent thinking and help us better understand the differences between gifted and nongifted children.

## REFERENCES

Albert, R. S., & Runco, M. A. (1986). Achievement of eminence: A model of exceptionally gifted boys and their families. In R. J. Sternberg & J. E. Davidson (Eds.), *Conceptions of giftedness* (pp. 332-357). New York: Cambridge University Press.

Boersma, F. J., & O'Bryan, K. (1968). An investigation of the relationship between creativity and intelligence under two conditions of testing. *Journal of Personality, 36,* 341-348.

*California Achievement Test technical manual.* (1979). Monterey, CA: McGraw-Hill.

Cummings, L. L., Hinton, B. L., & Gobdel, B. C. (1975). Creative behavior as a function of task environment: Impact of objectives, procedures and controls. *Academy of Management Journal, 18,* 489-499.

Datta, L. (1963). Test instructions and identification of creative scientific talent. *Psychological Reports, 13,* 495-500.

Davidson, J. E., & Sternberg, R. J. (1984). The role of insight in intellectual giftedness. *Gifted Child Quarterly, 28,* 58-64.

Evans, R. G., & Forbach, G. B. (1983). Facilitation of performance on a divergent measure of creativity: A closer look at instructions to "be creative." *Applied Psychological Measurement, 7,* 181-187.

Guilford, J. P. (1977). *Way beyond the IQ.* Buffalo, NY: Creative Education Foundation.

Harrington, D. M. (1975). Effects of explicit instructions to be creative on the psychological meaning of divergent test scores. *Journal of Personality, 43,* 434-454.

Hocevar, D. (1979). Ideational fluency as a confounding factor in the measurement of originality. *Journal of Educational Psychology, 71,* 191-196.

Hocevar, D. (1980). Intelligence, divergent thinking, and creativity. *Intelligence, 4,* 25-40.

Katz, A. N., & Poag, J. R. (1979). Sex differences in instructions to "be creative" on divergent and nondivergent test scores. *Journal of Psychology, 47,* 518-530.

Koestner, R., Ryan, R. M., Bernieri, F., & Holt, K. (1984). Setting limits on children's behavior: The differential effect of controlling vs. informational styles on intrinsic motivation and creativity. *Journal of Personality, 52,* 233-248.

Manske, M. E., & Davis, G. A. (1968). Effects of simple instructional biases upon performance in the Unusual Uses test. *Journal of General Psychology, 79,* 25-33.

Nicholls, J. G. (1972). Creativity in the person who will never produce anything original and useful: The concept of creativity as a normally distributed trait. *American Psychologist, 27,* 717-727.

Nunnally, J. C. (1978). *Psychometric theory* (2nd ed.). New York: McGraw-Hill.

Renzulli, J. S. (1978). What makes giftedness? Reexamining a definition. *Phi Delta Kappan, 60,* 180-184.

Runco, M. A. (1985). The reliability and convergent validity of ideational flexibility as a function of academic achievement. *Perceptual and Motor Skills, 61,* 1075-1081. [Chapter 11]

Runco, M. A. (1987). The generality of creative performance in gifted and nongifted children. *Gifted Child Quarterly, 31, 121-125.* [Chapter 13]

Runco, M. A., & Albert, R. S. (1985). The reliability and validity of ideational originality in the divergent thinking of academically gifted and nongifted children. *Educational and Psychological Measurement, 45,* 483-501. [Chapter 10]

Runco, M. A., & Albert, R. S. (1986). The threshold theory regarding the creativity and intelligence.: An empirical test with gifted and nongifted children. *Creative Child and Adult Quarterly, 11,* 212-218. [Chapter 17]

Runco, M. A., & Schreibman, L. (1983). Parental judgments of behavior therapy efficacy with autistic children: A social validation. *Journal of Autism and Developmental Disorders, 13,* 237-248.

Speller, K. G., & Schumacher, G. M. (1975). Age and set in creative test performance. *Psychological Reports, 36,* 447-450.

Turner, R. G. (1978). Consistency, self-consciousness, and the predictive validity of typical and maximal personality measures. *Journal of Research in Personality, 12,* 117-132.

Wallach, M. A., & Kogan, N. (1965). *Modes of thinking in young children.* New York: Holt, Rinehart, & Winston.

## Chapter 7

# Enhancing the Flexibility of Ideas

### Abstract[*]

This investigation was conducted to examine the effects of instructions designed to enhance ideational originality and flexibility, and to test the prediction that flexibility is functionally related to originality. Twenty-nine adolescents received three divergent thinking tests with conventional (inexplicit) instructions, one test with explicit originality instructions, and one test with explicit flexibility instructions. Contrary to expectation, results indicated that originality scores were low when the adolescents were given the explicit flexibility instructions. This suggests that flexibility does not facilitate originality. However, the explicit originality instructions did elicit the highest originality scores, and the explicit flexibility instructions elicited the highest flexibility scores.

[*] Adapted from: Runco, M. A., & Okuda, S. M. 1990. The instructional enhancement of the flexibility and originality scores of divergent thinking tests. *Journal of Applied Cognitive Psychology, 4* (John Wiley and Sons, Ltd.).

Divergent thinking tests are often used to estimate the potential for creative thinking. Although divergent thinking tests are not perfect measures of creative thinking, they are reliable and predictive of some expressions of real-world creative performance (Milgram & Milgram, 1976; Runco, 1984, 1986a). Many techniques have been developed to enhance divergent thinking. For example, reinforcement (Milgram & Feingold, 1977), modeling (Belcher, 1975), and explicit instructions (Evans & Forbach, 1983; Harrington, 1975; Runco, 1986b) have each been used to enhance divergent thinking.

The explicit instruction approach is particularly promising. It parallels the "maximal performance" technique used in personality assessment wherein an examinee is directed to perform at their very best. The rationale for facilitating and assessing maximal performance is that every examinee has a range of possible performances, and the most reliable and replicable estimate of an individual's potential is probably their best—or maximal—performance.

Harrington (1975) ascertained that maximal performance on divergent thinking tests can be elicited by giving explicit instructions to "be creative." He compared the performance of a control group given only conventional and inexplicit instructions with that of an experimental group given instructions to "be creative." The experimental group was also instructed that a creative idea is both original and worthwhile. Results indicated that the experimental group generated significantly more original ideas than the control group. Runco (1986b) reported similar results from his administration of explicit instructions to gifted and nongifted children.

The previous research in this area has focused on explicit instructions to enhance originality. Originality is an integral constituent of creativity (Barron, 1968) and divergent thinking (Guilford, 1968). However, ideational flexibility is also very important. Flexibility can be operationalized as the number of categories or themes used when solving a problem. For example, if an examinee responses to the question, "Name all of the things you can think of that are strong," with "Superman, Batman, and Wonderwoman," only one ideational category is used. More flexible ideation would be seen in the responses, "Superman, gravity, and steel," for three ideational categories are used.

Flexibility scores can be used to verify the actual uniqueness of ostensibly original ideas (Runco, 1985). The reason for this is that originality is usually defined in terms of the number of subjects that give an idea; and if an examinee finds a unique category (e.g., superheroes), all responses in that category will be unique (i.e., given by only one subject) even though the examinee may give responses that are very similar. These ideas will each contribute to an individual's originality score even though they may each be links in one associative chain (Runco, 1986c). A low flexibility score is indicative of this type of spurious originality, and a high flexibility score indicates that ideas are unique relative to one another as well as unique within the sample of subjects. A truly creative individual would be expected to have high scores on both originality and flexibility. Flexibility scores are also important for the predictive validity of divergent thinking tests (Runco, 1986a).

Runco (1986b) reported that flexibility scores, like fluency scores, dropped when examinees were given explicit instructions. This was expected, for the instructions focused on the originality of the ideas (e.g., "give ideas that will be thought of by no one else"). The primary objective of the present investigation is to examine the effects of explicit instructions designed specifically to enhance ideational flexibility. The first prediction is that flexibility can be enhanced with special instructions. The second prediction is that enhancing flexibility will lead to an increase in originality. This prediction follows from Runco's (1986b) suggestion that there is a one-way functional relationship between flexibility and originality. Put briefly, the argument is that an individual using a variety of ideational categories (that is, having flexible ideation) should find a larger number of unique (and thus original) ideas than an individual using only one or a few categories. This prediction will be confirmed if instructions designed to enhance ideational flexibility elicit both high originality and high flexibility scores on the divergent thinking tasks.

Three sets of instructions were examined in the present investigation. The first instructions were conventional, inexplicit instructions. These were included to determine base rates for the three ideational scores. The second instructions were designed to maximize ideational originality, and they explicitly defined an original idea as unique. These instructions were included to replicate the findings of Harrington (1975) and Runco (1986b) and extend their work to adolescents. These instructions were also necessary to test the one-way functional relationship between originality and flexibility. The expectation was that they would confirm that enhancing originality does not increase flexibility scores. The third instructional set was unique to this investigation. It focused on ideational flexibility, and gave explicit guidelines to increase the flexibility of one's ideation.

## Method

### Subjects

The 29 adolescents involved in this investigation were participants in the Student Science Training Program at the Hilo campus of the University of Hawaii. This is a seven week program in calculus and physics. The participants (19 boys and 10 girls) were between the ages of 15 and 17 years. The mean PSAT Mathematics standard score was 65.1, with a standard deviation of 8.4, and the mean PSAT Verbal standard score was 53.7, with a standard deviation of 11.5. The data for the present study were collected as a distinct part of a project to identify effective selection criteria for participation in the summer program. For this reason, these subjects have been described in detail in an earlier report of problem discovery in adolescents (Runco & Okuda, 1988).

### Measures and Procedure

The divergent thinking tests used in this project were adapted from Wallach and Kogan (1965). They will be described in the order in which they were administered. Base rates for fluency, originality, and flexibility were established by administering an Instances test containing three items (e.g., "Name all of the things you can think of that are strong"), a Uses test containing three items (e.g., "Name all of the uses you can think of for a shoe"), and a Similarities test containing three items (e.g., "How are a potato and a carrot alike?"). One of these tests was administered each day for three days, and each was given with the conventional instructions. The instructions for the conventional instructions are identical to those used by Runco (1986b), and simply ask for as many responses as possible. On the fourth day a test was given with explicit instructions to "be creative." This test contained three items: one from each of the Instances, Uses, and Similarities tests. The instructions for the these items were adapted from Harrington (1985), and emphasize original and worthwhile ideas. Further, originality is defined in these instructions (as an idea that will be thought of by no one else). On the fifth and final day, a test was given with instructions written explicitly describing and encouraging ideational flexibility. This test also contained one item from each Instances, Uses, and Similarities. The instructions for enhancing flexibility were as follows.

> *Now we would like you to give as many different ideas as you can.* In other words, try to give a variety of ideas . . . like the earlier tasks, you should try to give as many ideas as possible; but now be flexible, approach each question from different angles, and focus on *variety.* For example, if you were asked to "Name square things," you could say, "notebook, textbook, cookbook, and schoolbook," but these ideas are all very similar. Instead, give a variety of ideas (e.g., "window, parking lot, television, and Lawrence Welk") . . . . It is very important for you to think of ideas that are unrelated to one another, and are in different categories. *Focus on variety.*

## Results

The reliability of the divergent thinking test scores was checked by calculating interitem (alpha) correlations. *Alpha* ($\alpha$) coefficients were as follows: Instances fluency (.69), originality (.62), and flexibility (.52); Uses fluency (.79), originality (.66), and flexibility (.62); and Similarities fluency (.76), originality (.57), and flexibility (.59).

Descriptive statistics for the fluency scores are presented in Table 7-1. Note that for each test fewer ideas were elicited by explicit instructions (the bottom two rows of Table 7-1) than conventional instructions. A *t*-test for dependent samples using the averages across tests indicated that the difference between the fluency scores elicited by the explicit originality instructions and the conventional instructions was significant ($t$ (28) = 3.80, $p$ < .001), as was the difference between the fluency scores of the explicit flexibility instructions and the conventional instructions ($t$ (28) = 3.79, $p$ < .001).

With these differences in fluency scores and the strong relationship among ideational indices (Runco, 1985), the originality and flexibility scores were transformed into ratio scores (i.e., originality divided by fluency, and flexibility divided by fluency); and these were used in subsequent analyses. Similar ratio scores have been used by Hocevar and Michael (1979), and Runco, Okuda, and Thurston (1987a).

Tables 7-2 and 7-3 present descriptive statistics for the flexibility and originality ratio scores. These data indicate that the originality scores elicited by the explicit originality instructions were higher than the originality scores of the other two sets of instructions. Similarly, the flexibility scores elicited by the explicit flexibility instructions were higher than the flexibility scores of the other two sets of instructions.

---

### Table 7-1

Means and Standard Deviations (in parentheses) of the Fluency Scores

| Instructions | Instances | | Uses | | Similar | | Average | |
|---|---|---|---|---|---|---|---|---|
| Conventional | 15.9 | (6.0) | 11.0 | (2.9) | 10.0 | (3.6) | 12.3 | (3.2) |
| Originality | 15.7 | (8.0) | 7.2 | (2.7) | 6.2 | (3.3) | 9.6 | (4.1) |
| Flexibility | 11.4 | (4.9) | 9.3 | (3.3) | 8.4 | (4.7) | 9.7 | (3.3) |

Note: Scores for the conventional instructions are averages of three test questions.

---

### Table 7-2

Means and Standard Deviations (in parentheses) of the Flexibility Ratio Scores

| Instructions | Instances | | Uses | | Similar | | Average | |
|---|---|---|---|---|---|---|---|---|
| Conventional | .55 | (.12) | .73 | (.10) | .61 | (.09) | .63 | (.07) |
| Originality | .55 | (.17) | .51 | (.17) | .68 | (.41) | .58 | (.17) |
| Flexibility | .64 | (.18) | .79 | (.13) | .83 | (.20) | .75 | (.09) |

Note: Scores for the conventional instructions are averages of three test questions.

Table 7-3

Means and Standard Deviations (in parentheses)
of the Originality Ratio Scores

|  | Instances | | Uses | | Similar | | Average | |
|---|---|---|---|---|---|---|---|---|
| Instructions | | | | | | | | |
| Conventional | .23 | (.09) | .25 | (.11) | .28 | (.11) | .25 | (.06) |
| Originality | .54 | (.22) | .45 | (.17) | .62 | (.59) | .54 | (.22) |
| Flexibility | .28 | (.16) | .33 | (.21) | .23 | (.21) | .28 | (.14) |

Note: Scores for the conventional instructions are
averages of three test questions.

The statistical significance of these differences was confirmed with $t$-tests for dependent samples (one-tailed probabilities). For example, using the averages presented in the last column of Table 7-2, the originality scores of the explicit originality condition were higher than the originality scores of the conventional ($t$ (28) = 6.93, $p$ < .001) and explicit flexibility instructional conditions ($t$ (28) = 6.25, $p$ < .001). Similarly, the flexibility scores of the explicit flexibility instructions were higher than those of the conventional ($t$ (28) = 7.09, $p$ < .001) and explicit originality instructions ($t$ (28) = 4.88, $p$ < .001).

## Discussion

The most important result of this investigation is that flexibility scores were enhanced with explicit instructions. A second significant finding is that originality scores dropped when the adolescents were given the explicit flexibility instructions. That originality scores were enhanced with explicit instructions confirms that explicit instructions are effective with adolescents as well as adults (Harrington, 1985) and school children (Runco, 1986b).

One explanation for these findings is that performance on divergent thinking tests requires both the ability to generate ideas and metacognitive and strategic skills. This explanation is consistent with previous work on the components of divergent thinking (Runco & Okuda, 1988; Runco, Okuda, & Thurston, 1987b). Runco et al. (1987b), for example, demonstrated that a useful strategy for responding to some open-ended tasks is to look for "environmental cues." A strategic component of divergent thinking is also implicit in Harrington's (1975) description of the role of "task perception" in creativity. In this view, the explicit instructions technique probably does not influence an examinees' ability to generate ideas, but rather manipulates the choice of specific ideational strategies.

That originality scores dropped when the examinees were given the explicit flexibility instructions refutes the prediction that originality is functionally tied to flexibility (Runco, 1986b). This drop was also unexpected because the examinees received explicit information about ideational flexibility after they received explicit information about originality. One might expect some transfer from the originality instructions to the test with the explicit flexibility instructions. However, there was no evidence of such a transfer. Apparently the effects of explicit instructions do not last long and may not transfer from one task to another (e.g., from the first explicit instructions test to the second). Because this is essentially the problem of generalization and maintenance of treatment, enduring instructional effects might be achieved by utilizing the technology of treatment generalization described by Walker and Buckley (1972). Put briefly, explicit instructions should probably be administered more than once, by several different examiners, and with a variety of tasks for more enduring effects. However, with the small sample of subjects in the present investigation, additional research on the effects of explicit instructions and the possibility of programming generalization and maintenance should be conducted.

## REFERENCES

Barron, F. (1968). *Creativity and personal freedom*. New York: Van Nostrand.

Belcher, T. L. (1975). Modeling original divergent responses: An integration. *Journal of Educational Psychology, 67*, 351-358.

Evans, R. G., & Forbach, G. B. (1983). Facilitation of performance on a divergent measure of creativity: A closer look at instructions to "be creative." *Applied Psychological Measurement, 7*, 181-187.

Guilford, J. P. (1968). *Intelligence, creativity, and their educational implications*. San Diego, CA: Knapp.

Harrington, D. M. (1975). Effects of explicit instructions to 'be creative' on the psychological meaning of divergent thinking test scores. *Journal of Personality, 43*, 434-454.

Hocevar, D., & Michael, W. (1979). The effects fo scoring formulas on the discriminant validity of tests of divergent thinking. *Educational and Psychological Measurement, 39*, 917-921.

Milgram, R. M., & Feingold, S. (1977). Concrete and verbal reinforement in creative thinking of disadvantaged children. *Perceptual and Motor Skills, 45*, 675-678.

Milgram, R. M., & Milgram, N. A. (1976). Creative thinking and creative performance in Israeli students. *Journal of Educational Psychology, 68*, 255-259.

Runco, M. A. (1984). Teachers' judgments of creativity and social validation of divergent thinking tests. *Perceptual and Motor Skills, 59*, 711-717. [Chapter 5]

Runco, M. A. (1985). Reliability and convergent validity of ideational flexibility as a function of academic achievement. *Perceptual and Motor Skills, 61*, 1075-1081. [Chapter 11]

Runco, M. A. (1986a). Divergent thinking and creative performance in gifted and nongifted children. *Educational and Psychological Measurement, 46*, 375-384. [Chapter 14]

Runco, M. A. (1986b). Maximal performance on divergent thinking tests by gifted, talented, and nongifted children. *Psychology in the Schools, 23*, 308-315. [Chapter 6]

Chapter 8

# Problem Finding and Creativity

## Abstract[*]

Previous empirical research suggests that problem discovery is an important step in the creative process. The present investigation was conducted to examine the role of problem discovery in the divergent thinking and creative performance of adolescents. Three divergent thinking tests were administered to a group of adolescents. Each test contained three presented problems and one discovered problem. The discovered problem allowed the adolescents to think of a problem and then provide solutions. Comparisons indicated that the adolescents generated significantly more responses to the discovered problems than the presented problems. Most important was that the unique variance of the discovered problems (controlling the variance shared with scores from the presented problems) was reliable and significantly related to five indices of creative performance. These results support the componential theory of divergent thinking and creativity, and are consistent with the developmental view of problem finding.

---

[*] Adapted from: Runco, M. A., & Okuda, S. M. (1988). Problem discovery, divergent thinking, and the creative process. *Journal of Youth and Adolescence, 17,* 211-220.

In recent years, many theorists have rejected the notion that creativity is a unitary trait, and have taken the position that creative performance is the result of an interaction of several abilities and skills. Runco (1986a), for example, suggested that both metacognitive strategy and cognitive ability per se are necessary "components" of the creative process. He demonstrated that gifted and nongifted children approach open-ended problems differently, with the former utilizing components that facilitate originality. Further empirical support for this view is given by Davidson and Sternberg (1984).

Although Runco (1986a) and Davidson and Sternberg (1984) have isolated several components, a comprehensive definition of creativity should incorporate the identification and definition of a problem or worthwhile task, and the generation, evaluation, application, and modification of solutions and ideas. Problem discovery is a particularly important component in the creative process because it occurs first, and because the quality of a problem may in part determine the quality of solutions. In Getzels' (1975) words, "a creative solution is the response to a creative problem" (p. 168). Additionally, although art, science, and other areas differ in some respects (e.g., prerequisite knowledge bases), the identification of a problem or task is probably crucial in all creative endeavors.

Csikszentmihalyi and Getzels (1970, 1971) were among the first to investigate creative problem finding. They presented 31 art students with a set of objects and asked the students to arrange the objects and compose a drawing. The students were observed while they worked, and their discovery-oriented behaviors were recorded. Discovery-oriented behavior was defined as the number of objects used before drawing; the amount of time spent exploring the objects before drawing; the uniqueness of the stimuli used; and changes in media or perspective. The drawings were rated for their originality, aesthetic value, and craftsmanship. Correlational analyses indicated that ratings of problem discovery behaviors were significantly related to the originality, aesthetic value, and craftsmanship of the completed drawings ($.42 < rs < .58$).

Moore (1985) took a similar approach with the verbal creativity of children. He allowed "middle school" children to choose an object, and then asked them to write an essay about it. Moore reported that students who wrote creative essays (judged by teachers) explored more objects than the students who wrote noncreative essays. These exploratory behaviors ostensibly were indicative of problem discovery. Moore (1985) also reported that the creative essays contained more changes in "object reality" and more words (an estimate of fluency) than the noncreative essays.

Wakefield (1985) examined the relationship of problem finding and divergent thinking by administering a series of visual (figural) divergent thinking tests to 23 fifth-grade children. The children were asked to describe all of the things that each figure could be, and they were scored for ideational fluency (i.e., the number of responses). One card in the series was completely blank, and the children were asked to first draw a figure (problem finding) and then provide ideas about it. Results indicated that the number of ideas given by the children to their own drawings was significantly correlated with the number of ideas given to the standard divergent thinking items ($r = .75$). Additionally, the scores from discovered problems had slightly better predictive validity than standard divergent thinking scores ($r = .46$ vs. $.33$). Similar findings were reported by Owen and Baum (1985).

Wakefield's (1985) investigation of problem finding and divergent thinking is particularly intriguing because divergent thinking is predictive of teachers' judgments of students' creativity (Runco, 1984) and children's writing, artistic, and crafts achievements (Runco, 1986b). Divergent thinking is also included in several definitions of giftedness (Albert & Runco, 1986; Renzulli, 1978). Still, problem-finding skills may in part depend upon mature cognitive structures (Arlin, 1975); and thus the results of Wakefield's (1985) study of fifth-graders may not generalize to other age groups. The primary objective of the present investigation is to examine the relationship between problem discovery and divergent thinking in adolescents.

The second objective of the present investigation is to isolate the problem discovery component of divergent thinking. Previous research has focused on the overlap of presented and discovered problems, and most analyses have been correlational. The present study is unique in its evaluation of differences between presented and discovered problems. The premise is that divergent thinking tasks that present problems require primarily ideational productivity, but divergent thinking tasks with discovered problems require both ideational productivity and the ability to define a workable task. There is an overlap between the two tasks, but the discovered tasks presumably involve a distinct problem-finding component. This can be determined by examining the unique variance of discovered problems. In this light, the present investigation is an empirical test of the componential view of the creative process.

The specific predictions tested in this investigation are concerned with the psychometric integrity and distinctiveness of the problem-finding component of adolescents' divergent thinking. The first prediction is that the unique variance of the scores elicited by a discovered divergent thinking task will be reliable and correlated with other indices of creative ability. This addresses the predictive validity of the scores (Anastasi, 1983). The second prediction is that scores on presented problems will be moderately but not highly correlated with scores on the discovered problems; and the last prediction is that the scores from the discovered problems will be unrelated or negatively correlated with scores from measures of academic ability. These final predictions are aimed at the discriminant validity of the problem discovery scores (Anastasi, 1983).

## Method

### Subjects

Twenty-nine students (19 males and 10 females) from a mathematics and science summer program participated in the study. This program involves seven weeks of intensive study in calculus and physics, and for many students, research experience under the supervision of an academic scientist. The program has a relatively selective admissions policy using four criteria: *Preliminary Scholastic Aptitude Test* (PSAT) mathematics scores, grade point average from mathematics and science courses, two letters of recommendation, and a personal essay. Most students were considered to be scientifically and mathematically talented, and many were considered to be gifted. The median mathematics PSAT percentile was 65 (with a range of 66 to 99), and the median verbal PSAT percentile was 52 (with a range of 31 to 99). The ages of the students ranged from 15 years 11 months to 17 years 7 months.

## Measures and Procedure

The Instances, Uses, and Similarities divergent thinking tests were used in this investigation. These are verbal tests. Each contained three standard "presented-problem" items and one "discovered-problem" item. The stimuli and instructions for the presented problems were adapted from Wallach and Kogan (1965). Each of these presents a task (e.g., "name all of the things you can think of that move on wheels") and examinees are asked to give as many ideas as possible. They are also informed that there are no incorrect answers, and that no grades are assigned.

The discovered problems were adapted from Wakefield (1985). Only instructions were presented on the discovered items. These instructions asked the examinees to define a task (i.e., find a problem), and then to provide solutions to it. For example, the following instructions were provided for the discovered problem of the Instances test:

> On the previous pages, you were asked to give "instances" of something (i.e., things that are square, strong, or move on wheels). Here we would like you to choose a category, and then list instances of it. Now you can choose something to make thinking of ideas easy! Be certain to choose a category that will allow you to give many responses. Keep in mind that the more ideas, the better!

Analogous instructions were provided for the discovered problems of Uses (". . . choose an object and then list uses for it . . .") and Similarities (". . . choose two objects that are alike, and then list your ideas of how the objects are similar . . ."). Each of the presented and discovered items was scored for the number of distinct ideas (ideational fluency). This scoring system is described in Runco and Albert (1986).

A Creative Activities Check List was administered and used as the criterion measure. This particular Check List was adapted from Hocevar (1980), and is similar in format to those used by Runco (1987) and Wallach and Wing (1969). It lists 55 creative activities in five different areas: mathematics (e.g., "How many times have you applied math in an original way to solve a practical problem?"); science (e.g., "How many times have you set up your own experimental laboratory or experimental conditions?"); art (e.g., "How many times have you painted an original picture?"); literature (e.g., "How many times have you had poem, short story, or the like published in a school publication?"); and crafts (e.g., "How many times have you designed and constructed a craft out of wood?"). All tests were administered in a classroom during the summer program. Testing required two hours each day for three days.

## Results

A multivariate analysis of variance with gender as a between subjects factor and age (in months) as a covariate indicated that there were no gender or age effects in the divergent thinking scores. All 29 cases were therefore used in subsequent analyses. Means and standard deviations for each item of the divergent thinking tests are presented in Table 8-1.

Table 8-1

Means and Standard Deviations
for the Divergent Thinking Test Scores

|  | Instances | | Uses | | Similarities | | Average | |
|---|---|---|---|---|---|---|---|---|
| Item 1 | 15.2 | (9.1) | 9.4 | (2.7) | 10.3 | (3.9) | 11.6 | (4.1) |
| Item 2 | 15.6 | (7.4) | 9.3 | (3.2) | 9.5 | (3.8) | 11.5 | (3.6) |
| Item 3 | 17.2 | (6.3) | 14.0 | (4.4) | 10.0 | (4.9) | 13.8 | (3.8) |
| Average | 15.9 | (6.0) | 10.9 | (2.9) | 9.9 | (3.4) | 11.5 | (3.1) |
| Item 4 | 25.3 | (13.6) | 17.9 | (9.9) | 13.9 | (6.4) | 19.1 | (7.3) |

Note: Items 1 through 3 represent the presented problems and Item 4 represents the discovered problem.

Order effects were examined by comparing the first and second items of each test, and comparing the second and third items of each test. Correlated $t$-tests revealed that the differences among the items of the Instances and Similarities tests were not significant. Scores on the third item of the Uses test were significantly higher than those on the second ($t$ (28) = 7.54, $p < .001$, $r = .65$).

### Differences Between Presented and Discovered Problems

Differences between presented and discovered problems were tested by comparing the average of the three presented items with the last item (the discovered problem) within each test (the bottom two rows of Table 8-1). Correlated $t$-tests were again used. Results indicated that the discovered item elicited significantly more ideas on the Instances test ($t$ (28) = 3.55, $p < .001$, $r = .13$), the Uses test ($t$ (28) = 3.90, $p < .001$, $r = .26$), and the Similarities test ($t$ (28) = 3.93, $p < .001$, $r = .52$). The mean correlation between the presented and discovered problems (using an $r$-to-$z$ transformation) was .32. A comparison of the average of the nine presented problems and the average of the three discovered problems also a revealed significant difference ($t$ (28) = 5.71, $p < .001$, $r = .28$).

### Unique Variance of the Discovered Problems

The unique variance of the discovered problems was examined in several ways. First, a canonical correlation was conducted to determine predictive validity. Canonical procedures calculate optimized composite scores, or "variates," for a set of predictors and a set of criteria. The canonical coefficient is the correlation between the two variates. The predictors were the mean scores (across tests) from the first, second, and third items of the three presented problems and the mean score of the three discovered problems. The criteria were the five area scores from the Activities Check List.

Results indicated that the predictor variate was significantly correlated with the criterion variate ($R_c$ = .78, $F$ (20, 67) = 2.22, $p$ < .01). More importantly, a hierarchical regression analysis indicated that the discovered problem scores were significantly correlated with the criterion variate (defined in the canonical analysis) after the variance shared with the presented problems was controlled ($R^2_\Delta$ = .09, $F$ (4, 24) = 5.41, $p$ < .05).

Two additional analyses were conducted to further examine the unique variance of the discovered problems. A regression analysis using the averages of the discovered and presented problems indicated that PSAT scores (a total of the verbal and mathematics scores after each was transformed into a $z$-score) accounted for only 2.5% of the unique variance of the discovered problems (for a description of this regression procedure, see Cohen & Cohen, 1975, chap. 6). Finally, a correlational analysis was conducted to evaluate the interitem reliability of the scores from the discovered problems. Results indicated that the scores from the three discovered problems were fairly reliable, with alpha coefficients of .53 before and .48 after controlling the scores from the presented problems.

## Discriminant Validity

Discriminant validity was evaluated by correlating the divergent thinking test scores and the Creative Activity Check List scores with PSAT scores. Results supported the discriminant validity of the creativity scores, for in general the divergent thinking test scores and the Creative Activity Check List scores were unrelated or negatively correlated with the PSAT scores. More specifically, the coefficients between the separate divergent thinking test scores and the PSAT scores ranged from .03 to .19. Similarly, only literature scores from the Check List were related to PSAT scores ($r$ = .39, $p$ < .05). Mathematics, science, art, and crafts scores were unrelated to PSAT scores (−.23 < $rs$ < .18).

## Discussion

These results confirm that problem discovery is associated with creative performance in adolescents. As predicted, the scores from the presented problems and the scores from the discovered problems were moderately correlated; but the discovered problems elicited significantly more ideas than the presented problems. Importantly, the relationship between discovered and presented problem scores was much smaller (mean $r$ = .32) than the coefficient reported by Wakefield (1985) in his work with fifth-grade children. This result is consistent with Arlin's (1975) position that problem finding is a developed skill, and only becomes distinct from problem-solving skill during adolescence.

The moderate association between presented and discovered problems is also consistent with the componential view of the creative process because both tasks involve the ability to generate ideas. The significant difference between the scores from the two types of problems was expected because the scores on the discovered problems reflect the problem-finding component of creativity in addition to ideational productivity. The most important findings for the componential theory of divergent thinking were those involving the unique variance of the discovered problems (controlling the variance shared with the presented problems). This presumably reflects problem-finding skill and is statistically independent of problem-solving skill (or ideational productivity). The unique variance of the scores from the discovered problems was reliable and predictive of creative activity. The distinctiveness of the problem discovery is also supported by the discriminant validity of the discovered problem scores. The analyses of discriminant validity relied on PSAT scores as criteria; but this type of composite criterion is often used (Runco & Albert, 1986b; Wakefield, 1985; Wallach & Wing, 1969). Hence, the distinctiveness and importance of the problem discovery component are supported by three types of psychometric evidence.

The difference between the two types of problems may have resulted from the discovered problems allowing examinees to select personally meaningful tasks. In this sense, the difference between the presented and the discovered problems may partly reflect an attitudinal component of divergent thinking. Csikszentmihalyi and Getzels (1970) demonstrated that artists' creativity is related to "an attitude for discovery," and the same may apply to adolescents. An alternative explanation is that the difference between the tests resulted from practice. The discovered problem of each test was administered after three presented problems. Note, however, that the scores on the second item in both Uses and Similarities was below those from the first item, and only the third item of Uses had a significant increase. Further, the average scores from Instances, Uses, and Similarities (Table 8-1) do not reflect a practice effect. Finally, the magnitude of the difference between the presented and discovered problems is difficult to account for in terms of practice alone.

Csikszentmihalyi and Getzels (1971) suggested that there is a continuum with "presented problem situations" on one extreme and "discovered problem situations" on the other. The two types of problems differ in the amount of initial information, the degree to which the method is initially apparent, and how much agreement there is concerning correct solutions. In these terms, the discovered problems in the present investigation were not entirely discovered because there were guidelines given in the instructions for each test. Bransford and Stein (1984) distinguished between the identification of a problem—simply recognizing that a problem exists— and the definition or operationalization of the problem. In these terms, the discovery tasks in the present investigation can be viewed as problems of definition rather than identification.

This distinction is a very important one, for real-world creativity probably requires both problem identification and problem definition. Additionally, this distinction and the continuum described by Csikszentmihalyi and Getzels (1971) might be useful in the educational setting. An educator could, for example, use various types of discovered and identification problems in the classroom to practice realistic problem-finding skills. Along the same lines, the results of the present investigation suggest that students' creativity and ideational fluency would be best exercised by assigning tasks that are extremely open-ended and allow students' own discovery.

Note that the individualized nature of the discovery problems required that only fluency scores were used in this investigation. Originality and flexibility are also important facets of divergent thinking (Runco, 1985, 1986c), but they are typically related to fluency (Runco, 1986d). Other components of divergent thinking and creativity should be examined in future research. Perhaps the critical and evaluative components of divergent thinking can be operationalized.

Also note that the criterion of creative performance used in this project only measures the quantity of creative activity. It tells us little about the quality of the examinees' accomplishments. Further, it was a self-report, and therefore potentially influenced by the examinees' memory and honesty. This particular measure has demonstrated its reliability many times in the past (for a review, see Runco, 1987), but future research should test the predictive validity of the problem-finding scores with other criteria of creative accomplishment.

The small sample of subjects in this project and the potentially restricted range of scores also suggest that additional research is needed. Given Arlin's (1975) argument that mature cognitive structures are necessary for problem finding, a comparison of the problem discovery of preoperational, concrete operational, and formal operational individuals would be extremely interesting. The present findings suggest that divergent thinking tests can be used to investigate problem finding, and they support the componential theory of problem discovery; but additional empirical research is needed to test the generality and applicability of this theory of the creative process.

## REFERENCES

Albert, R. S., & Runco, M. A. (1986). The achievement of eminence: A model of exceptionally gifted boys and their families. In R. J. Sternberg & J. E. Davidson (Eds.), *Conceptions of giftedness* (pp. 332-357). New York: Cambridge University Press.

Anastasi, A. (1983). *Psychological testing* (5th ed.). New York: Macmillan.

Arlin, P. K. (1975). Cognitive development in adulthood: A fifth stage? *Developmental Psychology, 11*, 602-606.

Bransford, J. D., & Stein, B. S. (1984). *The ideal problem solver*. New York: Freeman.

Cohen, J., & Cohen, P. (1975). *Applied regression/correlation analysis for the behavioral sciences*. Hillsdale, NJ: Erlbaum.

Csikszentmihalyi, M., & Getzels, J. W. (1970). Concern for discovery: An attitudinal component of creative production. *Journal of Personality, 38*, 91-105.

Csikszentmihalyi, M., & Getzels, J. W. (1971). Discovery-oriented behavior and the originality of creative products: A study with artists. *Journal of Personality and Social Psychology, 19*, 47-52.

Davidson, J. E., & Sternberg, R. J. (1984). The role of insight in intellectual giftedness. *Gifted Child Quarterly, 28*, 58-64.

Getzels, J. W. (1975). Problem-finding and the inventiveness of solutions. *Journal of Creative Behavior, 9*, 12-18.

Hocevar, D. (1980). Intelligence, divergent thinking, and creativity. *Intelligence, 4*, 25-40.

Moore, M. T. (1985). The relationship between the originality of essays and variables in the problem-discovery process: A study of creative and noncreative middle school students. *Research in the Teaching of English, 19*, 84-95.

Owen, S. V., & Baum, S. M. (1985). The validity of the measurement of originality. *Educational and Psychological Measurement, 45*, 939-944.

Renzulli, J. S. (1978). What makes giftedness? Reexamining a definition. *Phi Delta Kappan, 60*, 180-184.

Runco, M. A. (1984). Teachers' judgments of creativity and social validation of divergent thinking tests. *Perceptual and Motor Skills, 59*, 711-717. [Chapter 5]

Runco, M. A. (1985). Reliability and convergent validity of ideational flexibility as a function of academic achievement. *Perceptual and Motor Skills, 61*, 1075-1081. [Chapter 11]

Runco, M. A. (1986a). Maximal performance on divergent thinking tests by gifted, talented, and nongifted children. *Psychology in the Schools, 23*, 308-315. [Chapter 6]

Runco, M. A. (1986b). Divergent thinking and creative performance in gifted and nongifted children. *Educational and Psychological Measurement, 46*, 375-384. [Chapter 14]

Runco, M. A. (1986c). Flexibility and originality in children's divergent thinking. *Journal of Psychology, 120*, 345-352. [Chapter 18]

Runco, M. A. (1986d). The discriminant validity of gifted children's divergent thinking test scores. *Gifted Child Quarterly, 30*, 78-82. [Chapter 16]

Runco, M. A. (1987). The generality of creativity in gifted and nongifted children. *Gifted Child Quarterly, 31*, 121-125. [Chapter 13]

Runco, M. A., & Albert, R. S. (1986a). Exceptional giftedness and intrafamilial divergent thinking. *Journal of Youth and Adolescence, 15*, 333-342. [Chapter 1]

Runco, M. A., & Albert, R. S. (1986b). The threshold hypothesis regarding creativity and intelligence: An empirical test with gifted, talented, and nongifted children. *Creative Child and Adult Quarterly, 11*, 212-218. [Chapter 17]

Wakefield, J. F. (1985). Towards creativity: Problem finding in a divergent-thinking exercise. *Child Study Journal, 15*, 265-270.

Wallach, M. A., & Kogan N. (1965). *Modes of thinking in young children.* New York: Holt, Rinehart, & Winston.

Wallach, M. A., & Wing, C. W., Jr. (1969). *The talented student.* New York: Holt, Rinehart, & Winston.

Chapter 9

# Environmental Cues
# and Divergent Thinking

## Abstract[*]

Creative thinking seems to involve metacognitive—or strategic—skill in addition to purely cognitive ability. This investigation examined one strategy, namely, the use of environmental cues. Nine divergent thinking tasks were administered to 120 children in their classrooms. Teachers later evaluated their ideas, selecting ideas that may have been cued by the classroom environment. Surprisingly, only two of the nine had a significant proportion of ideas that were related to the immediate environment. One of these was from the Instances test, and the other was from Line Meanings. A MANOVA indicated that the proportion of original ideas increased significantly when the environmentally cued ideas were controlled. Further, scores which were adjusted for environmental cues had slightly higher predictive validity than unadjusted scores. Still, the difference between the predictive validity coefficients was unimpressive. Taken together, the results suggest that the testing environment has only a small influence on the divergent thinking of intermediate school children.

[*] Adapted from: Runco, M. A., Okuda, S. M., & Thurston, B. J. (1987, April). *Environmental cues in children's creative thinking.* Paper presented at the meeting of the Western Psychological Association in Long Beach, CA.

Divergent thinking tests are probably the most commonly used measure of children's creative thinking. They contain open-ended questions (e.g., "Name all of the things you can think of that are strong"), and an examinee is asked to generate a number of responses. Although these tests are theoretically related to creativity (Mednick, 1962; Wallach & Kogan, 1965) and have moderate empirical validity (Runco, 1986a, 1986b), one concern is that "environmental cues" may distort divergent thinking test results. For when asked to "Name all of the things you can think of that are rectangular," children may respond "door, window, book," and so on, giving primarily ideas that are suggested by the cues present in the immediate environment (Ward, 1969). Interestingly, Ward (1969) suggested that talented examinees do not use the immediate environment, but rely on their ideational skills.

The influence of environmental cues is important to understand because a fundamental assumption of divergent thinking tests is that they index cognitive ability and are impervious to the testing environment. There is also a related question of test reliability, for the examinee who uses ideational skill is more likely than the examinee who relies on environmental cues to find unique and original ideas.

A componential view of divergent thinking (Runco & Okuda, 1988) would suggest that using environmental cues is a legitimate strategy to use when faced with an open-ended task. Perhaps creative individuals are open to environmental cues as a starting point for their thinking. The cues may initiate a series of associations that will lead to a truly creative idea that is only very remotely related to the environment. Mednick's (1962) associative theory is pertinent here; but the point is that environmental cues may be used by creative examinees. The use of these cues may be an important metacognitive component of divergent thinking.

The present investigation is a within subject examination of the effects of environmental cues. Earlier research on this issue involved only preschool children, and examined only the frequency of environmentally imposed ideas. The objectives of the present investigation are to examine the frequency and validity of environmentally cued ideas in the divergent thinking of intermediate school children.

## Method

The subjects ($N = 120$) were between 11 and 13 years old, and the range of IQs was 98 to 165. All children received the Uses, Instances, and Line Meanings divergent thinking tests (Wallach & Kogan, 1965). Each test contained three questions (for a total of nine divergent thinking tasks), and each was administered in the examinees' classrooms (see Runco, Okuda, & Thurston, 1987).

After the data were collected, a lexicon containing every idea was compiled for each of the nine items. Three experienced teachers were then asked to rate each idea (on a zero-to-three scale) in terms of its relationship to the school environment. The instructions to the teachers are presented on the following page.

Three tests were administered and used as criteria for analyses of predictive validity. These were the How Do You Think test (Davis, 1975), the Teachers' Evaluation of Students' Creativity (Runco, 1984), and the Creative Activities Check List (Runco, 1986a) with quantity and quality of performance scores. IQs and *California Achievement Test* scores were obtained from students' records.

## Instructions to the Teachers

The following lists contain children's responses to open-ended questions (e.g., "name all fo the things that you can think of that are strong"). We are interested in determining which ideas are imposed or directly suggested by the school environment. Your task is to rate the degree to which each idea reflects the school environment. Use this rating scale: 3 means found in all classrooms; 2 means found in many classrooms; 1 means found in few classrooms; and 0 means never in a classroom. Include the students as part of the classroom. Please consider each, take your time, and do not evaluate the quality of the ideas (i.e., if they are "good" or "bad" ideas).

## Results

The teachers' ratings were reliable, with interrater agreement averaging 70%. Ideas which were given high ratings by the teachers were eliminated from the ideational pool. An examination of the frequency of environmentally cued ideas revealed that only two of the nine ideas had a notable proportion of environmentally related ideas. These were "square things" from the Instances test, with 29.7% of the ideas related to the environment, and one of the Line Meanings items, with 22.0%. The remaining seven of the divergent thinking items had very few responses that were suggested by the classroom environment, with a median of 12%.

Fluency and originality scores (Runco & Albert, 1985) were calculated for the two items that had notable proportions of environmentally cued ideas, with scores before (unadjusted) and after (adjusted) eliminating environmentally cued ideas. The means and standard deviations are given in Table 9-1.

### Before versus After Adjustment

A multivariate analysis of variance (MANOVA) was used to confirm that the adjusted and unadjusted scores were significantly different. The first analysis included difference scores (unadjusted minus adjusted) for the four divergent thinking indices (fluency and originality from each test). Sex and grade were included as between subject factors. Results indicated that there was a significant difference between the unadjusted and adjusted scores in the multivariate test ($R_c = .81$, $F (4, 100) = 46.38$, $p < .001$) and each of the univariate tests ($15.35 < Fs < 119.11$, all $p < .01$). The interaction between grade and the adjustment was significant ($R_c = .30$, $F (4, 100) = 2.52$, $p < .05$), with the eighth-graders having a larger difference between unadjusted and adjusted scores than the seventh-graders. The interaction with gender and the three-way interaction were not significant.

A second MANOVA was conducted using summation scores (unadjusted plus adjusted). The main effect for grade was significant ($R_c = .44$, $F (4, 100) = 5.83$, $p < .001$), with eighth-graders having higher scores than seventh-graders. Gender and the two-way interaction were not significant.

The differences between the adjusted and unadjusted scores were also confirmed with $t$-tests for dependent samples, with significant differences for Instances fluency ($t$ ( 112) = 10.05, $p < .001$), Instances originality ($t$ (112) = 10.74, $p < .001$), Line Meanings fluency ($t$ (119) = 4.11, $p < .001$), and Line Meanings originality ($t$ (119) = 4.33, $p < .001$).

Table 9-1

Means and Standard Deviations for Instances and Line Meanings

| | Instances | | | | Line Meanings | | | |
| | Before | | After | | Before | | After | |
| | M | SD | M | SD | M | SD | M | SD |
|---|---|---|---|---|---|---|---|---|
| Scores | | | | | | | | |
| Fluency | 16.2 | 16.1 | 8.5 | 9.9 | 3.8 | 2.7 | 2.7 | 2.2 |
| Originality | 2.7 | 4.7 | 2.0 | 3.4 | 1.3 | 1.9 | 1.1 | 1.6 |

## Originality Scores

One of the most important questions is whether or not the proportion of original ideas increases in the adjusted scores. To test this, an Originality-to-Fluency ratio was calculated for the unadjusted and adjusted scores of each test. These ratios were compared with $t$-tests (one-tailed) for dependent samples. Results indicated that the proportion of original ideas was significantly higher in the adjusted scores for Instances ($t$ (119) = 1.90, $p < .05$) and Line Meanings ($t$ (119) = 4.58, $p < .001$). The means and standard deviations for the ratios were as follows: Instances unadjusted (.264, .29) and adjusted (.293, .35); Line Meanings unadjusted (.199, .14) and adjusted (.153, .18).

## Validity

The validity of the adjusted and unadjusted scores was examined with correlational analyses. A canonical correlation indicated that the adjusted ratios were significantly related to the four criteria of creativity ($R_C = .37$, $p < .05$). The unadjusted ratios were unrelated to the same criteria ($R_C = .33$). Canonical analyses also indicated that both sets of ratios were unrelated to IQ and CAT scores. The matrix of product-moment correlations is presented in Table 9-2.

Note that all coefficient reported here may be attenuated due to the unreliability of the tests or the range of scores.

Table 9-2

Predictive and Discriminant Validity Coefficients

| | | | Criteria | | | |
|---|---|---|---|---|---|---|
| | HDYT | Teach. Eval. | Activ. Quan. | Activ. Qual. | IQ | CAT |
| Unadjusted | | | | | | |
| Fluency | | | | | | |
| Instances | 06 | 06 | 24 | −03 | 12 | 15 |
| Lines | 23 | 07 | 09 | −17 | 14 | 18 |
| Originality | | | | | | |
| Instances | 12 | 13 | 24 | 06 | 11 | 17 |
| Originality | 22 | 13 | 04 | 07 | 10 | 29 |
| Adjusted | | | | | | |
| Fluency | | | | | | |
| Instances | 03 | 06 | 18 | −09 | 17 | 23 |
| Lines | 20 | 06 | 07 | −11 | 15 | 19 |
| Originality | | | | | | |
| Instances | 11 | 19 | 24 | 05 | 12 | 26 |
| Originality | 19 | 13 | 03 | 05 | 16 | 27 |

Note: How Do You Think test (HDYT; Davis, 1975); Teachers' Evaluation of Students' Creativity (Runco, 1984); Creative Activity Quantity and Quality (Runco, 1986); IQ; and *California Achievement Test* composite.

## Discussion

These results suggest that the classroom environment does not significantly influence the divergent thinking test performance of seventh- and eighth-grade children. Only two of nine divergent thinking test items had a significant number of ideas that were related to the classroom. Further, when the environmentally cued ideas were controlled, the adjusted scores were only slightly more valid than the unadjusted scores. Only the increased proportion of original ideas is consistent with the view that divergent thinking is influenced by environmental cues.

The present results are incongruent with Ward's (1969) findings about environmental cues. However, in the present study, the ideas identified by the teachers were potentially but not definitely cued by the environment. Some of the ideas may have appeared to be environmentally cued even though they were not originally connected with the environment. These were eliminated with the present identification procedures, for we looked to ideas with high probabilities of being environmentally cued. But an idea could appear to be related to the environment and in reality be independent of the environment. For example, when asked to "List square things," a student could have responded with "Window" even without looking at the window.

Hence, the ideas chosen as related to the classroom may in fact have been given by the children without their using environmental cues, and we may have erroneously labeled some of the ideas.

A second potential problem is that the technique used in the present investigation may have missed ideas that were in fact related to the environment. In particular, a number of ideas may have been only indirectly cued by the environment. Surely, many of the ideas given resulted from the examinees scanning the environment, thinking about what they saw, and forming some associations. The end result would be an idea that is only remotely connected with the environmental cues, and would not be identified by the present scoring system.

A related difficulty is that interitem patterns should be taken into account. When responding to the question, "Name all of the things you can think of that are round," the second response (e.g., "Mars") may be dependent upon the first response (e.g., "Saturn"). Using interitem connections is another potential metacognitive strategy. Given the potential misidentification caused by interitem associations, and the importance of understanding metacognitive strategies for dealing with open-ended tasks, further research should be conducted along these lines. Other testing environments and divergent thinking tasks might also be worth examining. Perhaps the strategic use of environmental cues should be taught, at least as a way of finding an associative starting point. For now, it appears that environmental cues play only a small part in the divergent thinking process, and that divergent thinking tests are no more valid when environmentally cued ideas are taken into account.

## REFERENCES

Davis, G. A. (1975). In frumious pursuit of the creative person. *Journal of Creative Behavior, 9,* 75-87.

Mednick, S. A. (1962). The associative basis for the creative process. *Psychological Review, 69,* 220-232.

Runco, M.A. (1984). Teachers' judgments of creativity and social validation of divergent thinking tests. *Perceptual and Motor Skills, 59,* 711-717. [Chapter 5]

Runco, M. A. (1986a). Divergent thinking and creative performance in gifted and nongifted children. *Educational and Psychological Measurement, 46,* 375-384. [Chapter 14]

Runco, M. A. (1986b). Maximal performance on divergent thinking tests by gifted, talented, and nongifted children. *Psychology in the Schools, 23.* [Chapter 6]

Runco, M. A., & Albert, R. S. (1985). The reliability and validity of ideational originality in the divergent thinking of academically gifted and nongifted children. *Educational and Psychological Measurement, 45,* 483-501. [Chapter 10]

Runco, M. A., & Okuda, S. M. (1988). Problem-discovery, divergent thinking, and the creative process. *Journal of Youth and Adolescence, 17,* 211-220. [Chapter 8]

Runco, M. A., Okuda, S. M., & Thurston, B. J. (1987). The psychometric properties of four systems of scoring divergent thinking tests. *Journal of Psychoeducational Assessment, 2,* 149-156. [Chapter 12]

Wallach, M. A., & Kogan, N. (1965). *Modes of thinking in young children.* New York: Holt, Rinehart, & Winston.

Ward, W. C. (1969). Creativity and environmental cues in nursery school children. *Developmental Psychology, 1,* 543-547.

## Section III

# Dimensions of Divergent Thinking

The multidimensional nature of divergent thinking has been recognized since Guilford's early work. However, there is some controversy here, especially as of late. This may be the area of research which benefits the most from increasingly sensitive and powerful statistical procedures. The results of the four investigations described in this Section indicate that the various indices of divergent thinking are intercorrelated. Still, it would be premature to conclude that one index is sufficient to capture divergent thinking ability. Too often, fluency scores are used alone. Even with a high correlation among the indices—why fluency? Originality is more frequently emphasized in our theories of creativity. Also, as suggested in Chapter 14, the validity of divergent thinking tests is highest when several indices are taken into account. As suggested in Chapter 12, our best option may be to modify our scoring procedures, and to use several indices.

Divergent thinking (DT) is defined as the ability to produce a diversity of responses to an open-ended problem (Guilford, 1959). DT tests have been used for more than 20 years as one means to assess creative potential and have demonstrated adequate psychometric properties in various populations and age groups. These tests are typically game-like and open-ended, and responses are usually evaluated in terms of their quantity or "fluency" (the raw number of responses given) and their quality or "originality" (the uniqueness or statistical infrequency of the responses).

There are certain considerations that must be recognized when using divergent thinking tests, such as the age of the subjects (Burt, 1962; Torrance, 1974; Ward, 1968), the time constraints in test administration (Christensen, Guilford, & Wilson, 1957; Torrance & Ball, 1978; Vernon, 1971; Wallach & Kogan, 1965), the instructions given to the subjects (Elkind, Deblinger, & Alder, 1970; Harrington, 1975; Manske & Davis, 1968; Vernon, 1971), the particular type of test administered (Dewing, 1970; Richards, 1976; Torrance, 1968; Vernon, 1971), the number of subjects (Milgram & Milgram, 1976a), and the scoring techniques (Milgram & Milgram, 1976b; Vernon, 1971). As Barron and Harrington (1981) put it, "One can say that some DT tests, administered to some samples, under some conditions and scored according to some criteria, measure factors relevant to creativity criteria beyond those measured by indices of general intelligence" (p. 448). As we see it, the salient problem with DT tests is simply that they do not account for the multitude of influences that contribute to creative performance outside of the testing situation (Albert, 1975; McNemar, 1964; Nicholls, 1972; Wallach, 1970, 1971). Still, because they are probably the most frequently employed tests of creative ability, it is necessary to understand them as well as possible. The problem at hand is that of the reliability and convergent validity of one of the indices of DT, namely ideational originality.

Hocevar (1979a) demonstrated that DT originality is only spuriously reliable and valid. He reported that both fluency and originality had reliable interitem and intertest zero-order correlations in the DT of college students; but when the shared variance was partialed from originality, the reliability coefficients dropped to near zero. Hocevar (1979b) later utilized the same partial correlation procedures with the DT scores of elementary school children in which he evaluated the reliability of both originality and flexibility scores. The results indicated that both ideational indices were unreliable when fluency scores were controlled.

There are several reasons why these findings have limited generalizability. Hocevar demonstrated that fluency confounded originality and flexibility, but he relied on one type of test (verbal), one method of instruction, and one scoring procedure. Moreover, he employed only nongifted individuals as subjects. The empirical work of Dewing (1970), Howieson (1981), and Milgram and Milgram (1976a) indicates that Hocevar's (1979a, 1979b) findings may be limited to a nongifted population. Dewing (1970), for example, reported that the convergent validity coefficients of DT tests were significantly larger in creative children than in less creative children. More recently, Howieson (1981) demonstrated that the long-term predictive validity of DT scores, particularly originality, is significantly higher in creative than less creative individuals.

Another line of relevant research is that of Mednick (1962), Milgram and her associates (Milgram & Rabkin, 1980; Moran, Milgram, Sawyers, & Fu, 1983), and Ward (1969) on the associative hierarchies of gifted and nongifted individuals. Mednick (1962) predicted that the responses of an individual on an open-ended test would reflect an order-effect in which common ideas are generated first and unusual ideas later. That is, the associative strength of common ideas is ostensibly stronger than the associative strength of unusual ideas. Mednick also predicted that unoriginal individuals will generate only a few unusual ideas. However, individuals who produce quantitatively more original ideas supposedly generate only a moderate number of common ideas, and once these are expended, they will supply numerous unusual ideas. This prediction was for the most part supported by Milgram and Rabkin (1980), Moran et al. (1983), Phillips and Torrance (1977), Wallach and Kogan (1965), and Wallach and Wing (1969). Thus, original individuals seem to have a different pattern of concatenating ideas, and unusual ideas may not follow common ideas as they seem to in unoriginal individuals.

A third line of work supporting the prediction that ideational originality may be reliable only in gifted individuals includes Albert (1971, 1975, 1978, 1980a, 1980b) and the theoretical work of Jackson and Messick (1965), Nicholls (1972), and Wallach (1967, 1977). Albert, for instance, is extensively researching (a) the utility of standardized intellectual assessments in different gifted populations, and (b) the creative and other cognitive differences that exist between different levels of giftedness and in different areas of giftedness. Jackson and Messick (1965) suggested that creative individuals are more characterized by their ideation than noncreative individuals. They generate novel ideas that "transcend reality" and yet are appropriate to the task at hand. Wallach (1977) described the ideation of creative individuals as reflecting "tendencies to entertain the hypothetical," and to "pick up information from the periphery of one's attentional field" (p. 239).

The purpose of the present investigation is to utilize the partial correlation procedure in order to evaluate with several types of DT tests the reliability and convergent validity of originality in samples of gifted and nongifted children. The primary hypothesis is that gifted individuals will have psychometrically adequate ideational originality and nongifted individuals will not. The second hypothesis is that the psychometric properties of ideational originality are dependent upon the specific type of DT test employed (verbal or figural), and the third hypothesis is that the psychometric adequacy of ideational originality depends upon the specific method of test scoring. That is, it is hypothesized that the most stringent technique for scoring original ideas, using unique ideas (e.g., Wallach & Kogan, 1965; Wallach & Wing, 1969), will result in more psychometrically acceptable originality scores than will the less stringent technique of using unusual ideas (e.g., Hocevar, 1979a, 1979b; Milgram, Milgram, & Landau, 1974). This final comparison also facilitates the interpretation of the results in the light of previous research.

## Method

### Subjects

Intermediate school (fifth-, sixth-, seventh-, and eighth-grade) children were employed as subjects ($N$ = 240). All subjects were drawn from one large school because it had a large number of children in their Gifted and Talented (GT) program, all of whom were invited to participate in the present project. In addition, all of the nongifted children who shared a "home room" with the GT children were invited to participate. "Gifted" subjects ($n$ = 97) had been nominated to the GT program on the basis of their outstanding scores on the Teacher Indicator of Potential (TIP; Piper, 1974) and IQs above 130. "Talented" children ($n$ = 53) had also been nominated to the GT program on the basis of their TIP scores, but then their IQs were below 130. Nongifted children ($n$ = 90) were randomly chosen from the general school population.

Subjects' parents were sent a letter explaining the project, indicating the approval of the principal and the school district, and requesting (a) permission for the children to take a battery of creativity tests, and (b) demographic information. Eighty-nine percent of the parents granted permission, although a large number supplied only part of the demographic data. The average age for 51 fifth-graders was 10-10, 11-9 for the 59 sixth-graders, 12-10 for 61 seventh-graders, and 13-9 for the 69 eighth-graders. One hundred and six (44.2%) were boys and 134 (55.8%) were girls. Demographically three ethnicities were represented: Asian (48%), Hispanic (24%), and White—not of Hispanic origin (18%). The remaining 10% were of sundry ethnic backgrounds. Parents' educational level was evenly distributed, with a range of graduate training to elementary school. The total family income was also evenly distributed, although very few (2.9%) families reported earning less than $10,000 annually.

Six teachers filled out student evaluations. All six were female, with an age range of 29 to 41 and a mean of 34-5. Their teaching experience ranged from 7 to 13 years, with a mean of 9-4. Four had earned an MA degree, and two were in the process of obtaining an MA degree.

### Measures

Five DT tests from Wallach and Kogan (1965) were utilized. Each had three items. Three tests were verbal: (a) Instances (e.g., "Name all of the things you can think of that are square"); (b) Uses (e.g., "List all the uses you can think of for a shoe"); and (c) Similarities (e.g., "How are a potato and a carrot alike?"). The two figural tests were (d) Pattern Meanings and (e) Line Meanings. All five tests are described or depicted in Wallach and Kogan (1965).

A Creative Activities Check List (CACL) was also used. This measure is similar in content and format to that of Hocevar (1978), Milgram and Milgram (1976b), and Wallach and Wing (1969). The present version was adapted from Hocevar (1978) so that all of the CACL activities are appropriate for the present age group. It contains 65 activities in seven scales, or "domains" (i.e., Art, Writing, Science, Performing Arts, Crafts, Music, and Public Presentation). Each domain has at least six items. An example of the wording is, "How many times have you written a short story?" Possible responses were (1) Never, (2) Once or twice, (3) Three to five times, or (4) Six or more times. A total CACL score was obtained by calculating a score for each scale (an average, based on the number of items in that scale), and adding together these scores. Thus the seven domains were equally represented in the total score.

Our third measure was the Teachers' Evaluation of Students' Creativity (TESC; Runco, 1984). This contains 25 randomly arranged behavioral descriptors. Each has seven possible Likert-type responses. An example of the wording is "to what degree, or how often, is this child original?" with the responses ranging from (1) "rarely" to (7) "extremely." A total score was calculated by taking an average of the items. This type of questionnaire has demonstrated adequate reliability and predictive validity with teachers in previous research (Runco, 1984; Runco & Schreibman, 1983).

*California Achievement Test* (CAT) reading, language, and mathematics scores (Form C; McGraw-Hill, 1979) for all children, and the IQs of the GT children, were obtained from school district records.

## Procedure

Each creativity test was administered to the children in their classrooms. The presentation format and procedures were adapted from Wallach and Kogan (1965). The children were specifically encouraged to work alone, and to avoid discussing the tests on their breaks. Teachers were always present in the classrooms. After all tests were administered, the children were carefully debriefed.

Two criteria were used to form four experimental groups, as in Wallach and Wing (1969). These were the total unusual-originality score from the five DT tests, and a composite achievement score. The latter was constructed from the CAT with the same procedure applied to the Scholastic Aptitude Test by Wallach and Wing (1969). That is, the standardized mathematics, reading, and language scores were transformed into $z$-scores and added together. Next, the sample of children was divided at the median to form a high-CAT group and a low-CAT group. Subjects' unusual-originality scores were dealt with in a similar way within these two groups in order to select children for the high achievement-high originality ("High-High"), high achievement-low originality ("High-Low"), low achievement-high originality ("Low-High"), and low achievement-low originality ("Low-Low") groups. Because testing spanned five consecutive school days, 15 children had incomplete data due to absences. Careful inspection of the data indicated that these were not systematic absences, but given the multivariate statistical procedures involved here, the groups included only children with complete data ($N = 225$).

## Scoring Divergent Thinking

The DT tests were scored for three indices. Fluency, the first index, was defined as the number of distinct ideas (Milgram et al., 1974). The two originality indices were scored as follows. A lexicon of all subjects' responses was compiled for each item in order to score originality in terms of response "uniqueness" (Wallach & Kogan, 1965; Wallach & Wing, 1969) and "unusualness" (Hocevar, 1978; Milgram et al., 1974). "Unique" responses oc-

93

curred when a response was given by only one individual, and "unusual" responses were scored as the weighted sum of statistically infrequent responses: three points if the response was unique, two points if less than 2.5% of the sample gave it, and one point if less than 5.0% of the sample did so. A total score for each test was calculated by finding the mean of the item scores. A grand total for each child was calculated by adding together the scores from all five DT tests.

## Results

### Reliability of the Measures

The internal consistency of fluency, the CACL, and the TESC was evaluated with the coefficient alpha, an estimate of the average interitem correlation (Cronbach, 1970). Each of the criterion measures was adequately reliable: $\alpha$ was .94 for the CACL, .74 for Instances fluency, .89 for Uses fluency, .64 for Similarities fluency, .88 for Pattern Meanings fluency, .87 for Line Meanings fluency, and .96 for the TESC. Although there are no fixed rules for comparing and interpreting interitem and intertest coefficients (see Nunnally, 1978, chap. 7), these coefficients are similar in magnitude to the correlation coefficients reported in previous research. The CACL scales and the fluency totals from the five DT tests were evaluated further by calculating one average intertest correlation. Both sets of measures were significantly correlated (average $r = .51$ and .41, respectively, both $p < .001$).

The reliability of unusual-originality and unique-originality was evaluated as in Hocevar's (1979a, 1979b) research with average interitem correlations before (zero-order correlation) and after (partial correlation) fluency was controlled. Partialing involved removing the common variance of fluency on a particular test from the originality interitem correlations within that test. The mean (across tests) zero-order coefficients for the unusual-originality scores of the four groups were: Low-Low (.16), Low-High (.47), High-Low (.22), and High-High (.61). The mean partial coefficients for these groups were $-.08$, $-.01$, $-.09$, and $-.10$.

The mean zero-order coefficients for the unique-originality scores of the four groups were: Low-Low (.07), Low-High (.38), High-Low (.11), and High-High (.58). The partial coefficients for these groups were .20, .22, .04, and .10.

The zero-order coefficients suggest that the two high DT groups had much more reliable originality scores than the two low DT groups. This was true for both unusual-originality (.53 versus .19) and unique-originality (.48 versus .09). Also, the figural tests appeared to be more reliable than the verbal tests. Importantly, only four of the tests had adequate average interitem correlations after fluency was controlled. These were Instances and Pattern Meanings for the Low-High group and Instances and Uses for the High-High group. Both of these were with unusual-originality scoring, and both were in the high-originality groups.

Because these coefficients reflect the range of scores for a variable, and because the range of DT scores was different in the four experimental groups, these correlations were adjusted to take into account each group's variability (Cohen & Cohen, 1975, p. 65). These adjusted coefficients were very similar to the unadjusted coefficients and therefore these findings cannot be attributed to differences in the range of scores.

## Convergent and Discriminant Validity

The convergent validity of unusual-originality and unique-originality was evaluated in terms of intertest correlations between the five DT tests before and after fluency was controlled. In this case the total fluency score from the entire battery of DT tests was partialed. Because these correlations were potentially attenuated (Nunnally, 1978), only those tests that had adequate interitem correlations were included in this evaluation. The first intertest evaluation therefore included only the two high DT groups. These are summarized in Table 10-1.

Table 10-1

Average Zero-Order and Partial Intertest Correlations
for Unusual- and Unique-Originality

### Unusual Originality

| | Adjusted $r$ | | Unadjusted $r$ | |
| | Zero-Order | Partial | Zero-Order | Partial |
|---|---|---|---|---|
| Group | | | | |
| High-High | .34 | −.18 | .21 | −.06 |
| Low-High | .27 | −.26 | .13 | −.12 |

### Unique Originality

| | Adjusted $r$ | | Unadjusted $r$ | |
| | Zero-Order | Partial | Zero-Order | Partial |
|---|---|---|---|---|
| Group | | | | |
| High-High | .52 | .09 | .25 | .04 |
| Low-High | .02 | −.16 | .01 | −.16 |

Note: The High-High group is the High Achievement, High Originality group; the Low-High group is the Low Achievement, High Originality group; and so on.

Nunnally's (1978, p. 220) adjustment for test attenuation was applied to these correlations, and the average adjusted correlations are included in Table 10-1. Also, Cohen and Cohen's (1975) adjustment for range restriction was applied, but the pattern of results was comparable to that of the unadjusted coefficients. That is, there was a clear difference between the average correlations in the two high DT groups. Furthermore, none of the coefficients are statistically adequate after partialing fluency, even when adjusted to account for attenuation.

To test the second hypothesis, another intertest evaluation was conducted using only the figural tests. This analysis included all four experimental groups, but excluded the unique-originality coefficients for the low DT groups because of their inadequate interitem correlations. The correlations between the Pattern and Line Meaning tests are presented in Table 10-2. Note that these coefficients do reflect adequate convergent validity after fluency was partialed. In fact, these correlations were high enough to preclude the adjustment for attenuation. The adjusted correlations would exceed 1.0 for the high-originality groups, meaning that the correlations were as high as possible given the reliability of the two tests. The adjusted coefficients for the low-originality groups would also reflect adequately reliability ($r = .56$ and $.78$, respectively). Still, note that these correlations reflect differences between the groups, with the high DT groups again having the most reliable scores, particularly in unique-originality.

The convergent validity of the DT indices was then evaluated by correlating them with the CACL and the TESC. These correlations indicated that these measures had adequate convergent validity. More specifically, the correlations of fluency, unusual-originality, and unique-originality with the CAL were all significant ($r = .23, .31,$ and $.31$, respectively, all $p < .001$) as were there correlations with the TESC ($r = .24, .45,$ and $.50$, respectively, all $p < .001$).

A final evaluation of the convergent validity of the DT indices was conducted by intercorrelating them with one another. This analysis indicated that fluency was significantly correlated with unusual-originality ($r = .90, p < .001$) and unique-originality ($r = .79, p < .001$), as were unusual-originality and unique-originality ($r = .97, p < .001$). (Again, adjustments for attenuation were possible but uninterpretable, all exceeding 1.0.)

The discriminant validity of the DT indices was evaluated by correlating them with the CAT composite. However, given the widely respected "threshold hypothesis" of intelligence which posits that creativity and intelligence are independent only at upper levels of intelligence (e.g., Barron, 1969; MacKinnon, 1962; Oden, 1968; Runco & Albert, 1986; Terman, 1954; Yamamoto, 1965), this correlation was conducted within each of the experimental groups. These correlations indicated that the DT indices and the CAT were highly related in the High-High group (average $r = .85$) but unrelated in the Low-Low group (average $r = -.19$). Thus, contrary to the threshold hypothesis, DT has discriminant validity at the lower levels of intelligence (when achievement was used to estimate intelligence).

Table 10-2

Average Zero-Order and Partial Correlations
for the Figural Tests

| Group | Unusual-Originality | | Unique-Originality | |
|---|---|---|---|---|
| | Zero-Order | Partial | Zero-Order | Partial |
| High-High | .68 | .62 | .77 | .70 |
| Low-High | .45 | .35 | .23 | .18 |
| High-Low | .31 | .21 | | |
| Low-Low | .16 | .11 | | |

Note: The High-High group is the High Achievement, High Originality group; the Low-High group is the Low Achievement, High Originality group; and so on. The Unique-Originality coefficients for the High-Low and Low-Low groups were too low to be included in two of the Unique-Originality analyses.

A final evaluation, conducted in order to make these findings more interpretable, involved the available IQs. It must be emphasized that we had IQs for only a subsample of students (i.e., those children nominated for the GT program). Therefore, the results of this analysis must be judged cautiously. It was a $t$-test comparison of the two high-CAT groups with the two low-CAT groups. As expected, the high-achievement groups had significantly higher IQs than the low-achievement groups ($t$ (146) = 3.61, $p <$ .001).

## Discussion

The results of this investigation support the basic premise that the psychometric adequacy of ideational originality is determined to a large degree by the cognitive ability of the subjects involved. The primary hypothesis, that the psychometric adequacy of ideational originality is a function of the level of achievement and ideational productivity, was clearly supported. The second hypothesis was also clearly supported in that there were significant differences between the figural DT tests and the verbal DT tests. However, the third hypothesis was not supported in that the more stringent unique-originality scoring method did not result in more psychometrically adequate originality scores than the unusual-originality scoring method. The less stringent unusual-originality scoring was often more adequate, especially in the interitem correlations.

## Group Differences

The reliability and validity coefficients indicated definite differences between the four experimental groups, and it appears that the psychometric quality of ideational originality is greatly influenced by both level of achievement and ideational productivity. The High-High group had the largest interitem and intertest correlations, followed by the Low-High group, the High-Low group, and finally the Low-Low group. The fact that the two high DT groups were more reliably original than either low DT groups was to be expected based on the associative theory of creativity (Mednick, 1962) and results of research on associative hierarchies (e.g., Milgram & Rabkin, 1980; Moran et al., 1983). And again, it is important to note that these differences were not influenced by the differences in range of scores on the dependent measures (Cohen & Cohen, 1975; Yamamoto, 1965).

Group differences were readily apparent in both the interitem and intertest correlations, both before and after ideational fluency were partialed. These differences are consistent with Nicholls' (1972) view of the non-normal distribution of DT. He suggested that individuals who produce original ideas may indeed have some reliable ability that less original individuals more or less lack. The group differences are also consistent with the theoretical work of Mednick (1962), Jackson and Messick (1965), and Wallach (1967). They each offer intriguing explanations of creative individuals' ideation. The present work reinforces their theories by demonstrating that the psychometric properties of ideational originality are different for individuals measuring at different levels of achievement and ideational productivity. In brief, the DT of original and unoriginal individuals differs both quantitatively and qualitatively.

It may seem obvious that individuals who produce a greater number of original ideas will also produce them more reliably than less original individuals. But keep in mind that reliability is an estimate of response stability, and statistically speaking, an individual who produces few original ideas can do so just as consistently as an individual producing a large number of original ideas. In fact, if an individual produces an extremely large number of ideas on a particular task or a particular item on a test, it might be simply because they concentrated on that particular task, and thus had very little time, interest, or energy for later tasks. Their ideational originality would not necessarily be reliable; it might be quite unreliable. Our point here is that reliability is a psychometric quality that is derived from but not equivalent to the absolute quantity of responses.

The finding that the High-High group was more reliably original than the Low-High group and that the High-Low group was more reliably original than the Low-Low group was partly unexpected because, in a sense, this is inconsistent with the widely held threshold hypothesis (e.g., Barron, 1969; MacKinnon, 1962; Oden, 1968; Runco & Albert, 1986; Terman, 1954; Yamamoto, 1965). One explanation for this inconsistency is that the relationship of achievement and originality is a result of the particular measures used in the present study. Perhaps the present measures were unlike those used in the research that supports the threshold hypothesis. However, using achievement as an estimate of "intelligence" is a somewhat common practice, at least with adolescents and adults (e.g., Madaus, 1967; Schubert, 1973; Wallach & Wing, 1969). In fact, Stanley (1977) strongly suggested that achievement tests are more accurate and meaningful than IQ tests. Chauncey and Hilton (1965) also have argued that achievement tests are accurate and reliable, and their focus was on the exceptionally gifted populations.

This leads us to believe that the inconsistency between the threshold hypothesis and the results of the present investigation reflects a problem with the threshold hypothesis itself. And as far as we know, this hypothesis has only been examined twice in the past 15 years (cf. Barron & Harrington, 1981). Our research suggests that the validity of this hypothesis relies heavily on one's definition of convergent thinking, or "intelligence" (Runco & Albert, 1986). Of central relevance here is that the DT tests in the present investigation did have discriminant validity, but only at certain levels of achievement.

## Figural-Verbal Differences

Of the two types of tests, only the figural tests (Pattern Meanings and Line Meanings) were psychometrically adequate after ideational fluency was partialed. Also, as Table 10-2 indicates, there are sizeable differences between the four groups' figural tests coefficients. Even after ideational fluency was controlled, the High-High group had the highest reliability coefficients, followed by the Low-High group, the High-Low group, and finally the Low-Low group. And here again, these findings were apparent even when the range of scores was taken into account.

Our findings that the figural tests were more reliable and valid than the verbal tests suggest that an individual has the greatest chance of generating consistently more original responses when the situation or stimuli are unfamiliar. The figural DT tests are abstract drawings, none of which represent any one referent, while the verbal stimuli all have some familiar meaning. As Mednick (1962) stated:

> The greater the number of instances in which an individual has solved problems with given materials in a certain manner, the less is the likelihood of his attaining a creative solution using these materials. (p. 223)

In this view, the difference between the two types of tests is a matter of their being differentially accessible to divergent thinking strategies. The verbal tests can be "solved" by generating associations to the words or to the referents of the words, while the figural tasks, on the other hand, are unfamiliar and must be "solved" by trial-and-error, effortful, on-the-spot associations. In Mednick's (1962) terms, verbal tests allow associations to be made based on "similarity," including rhyme and homonymity, whereas the figural tests can be solved through "serendipity" or accidental associations. Presumably serendipity would facilitate originality by minimizing the probability of the same idea being given by more than one individual. In this sense, the figural tests can be defined as "nonentrenched" tasks while the verbal tests are more "entrenched" (Sternberg, 1982). Still, the above differences between the figural and verbal tests are probably a result of both ideational processes and motivational differences. The figural tests, due to their unfamiliarity, may be more challenging tasks and perhaps more "game-like" than the verbal tests. The result of this is that the figural tests might stimulate effortful ideational strategies, while the verbal stimulate rote ideation. Hence, the figural tests elicit more reliably original responses than the verbal tests.

The general conclusion is that there are significant differences between gifted and nongifted children, and between verbal and figural DT tests. Keep in mind, however, that DT tests are sensitive to the conditions under which they are administered (e.g., the level of permissiveness, or game-like versus test-like atmosphere, the instructions given to the subject, the homogeneity of tests employed, and the procedures for scoring unusual ideas), and that the results from the DT in one condition or population are not necessarily indicative of DT test results in another condition or population. More importantly, because giftedness can be defined in various ways (e.g., behaviorally or psychometrically), it should be emphasized that the present investigation relied on academic achievement as the main criterion of "giftedness." There is evidence that these findings might change if group formation was based on IQ or another measure. Further research should address this possibility.

## REFERENCES

Albert, R. S. (1971). Cognitive development and parental loss among the gifted, the exceptionally gifted, and the creative. *Psychological Reports, 29,* 19-26.

Albert, R. S. (1975). Toward a behavioral definition of genius. *American Psychologist, 30,* 140-151.

Albert, R. S. (1978). Observations and suggestions regarding giftedness, familial influence and the achievement of eminence. *Gifted Child Quarterly, 22,* 201-211.

Albert R. S. (1980a). Genius. In R.H. Woody (Ed.), *The encyclopedia of clinical assessment* (Vol. 2, pp. 729-743). San Francisco: Jossey-Bass.

Albert, R.S. (1980b). Family position and the attainment of eminence: A study of special family positions and special family experiences. *Gifted Child Quarterly, 24,* 87-95.

Barron, F. (1969). *Creative person, creative process.* New York: Holt, Rinehart, & Winston.

Barron, F., & Harrington, D.M. (1981). Creativity, intelligence, and personality. *Annual Review of Psychology, 32,* 439-476.

Burt, C. L. (1962). Critical note: The psychology of creative ability. *British Journal of Educational Psychology, 32,* 292-298.

*California achievement test technical manual.* (1979). Monterey, CA: McGraw-Hill.

Chauncey, H., & Hilton, T. L. (1965). Are aptitude tests valid for the highly able? *Science, 148,* 1297-1304.

Christensen, P. R., Guilford, J. P., & Wilson, R. C. (1957). Relations of creative responses to working time and instructions. *Journal of Experimental Psychology, 53,* 82-88.

Cohen, J., & Cohen, P. (1975). *Applied multiple regression/correlational analysis for the behavior sciences.* Hillsdale, NJ: Erlbaum.

Cronbach, L. J. (1970). *Essentials of psychological testing* (3rd ed.). New York: Harper & Row.

Dewing, K. (1970). The reliability and validity of selected tests of creative thinking in a sample of seventh-grade West Australian children. *British Journal of Educational Psychology, 40,* 35-42.

Elkind, D., Deblinger, J., & Adler, D. (1970). Motivation and creativity: The context effect. *American Educational Research Journal, 7,* 351-357.

Guilford, J. P. (1959). Three faces of the intellect. American Psychologist, *14,* 469-479.

Harrington, D. M. (1975). Effects of explicit instructions to be creative on the psychological meaning of divergent thinking test scores. *Journal of Personality, 43,* 434-454.

Hocevar, D. (1978). Studies in the evaluation of tests of divergent thinking. *Dissertation Abstracts International, 35,* 4658A-4686A. (University Microfilms No. 78-69)

Hocevar, D. (1979a). Ideational fluency as a confounding factor in the measurement of originality. *Journal of Educational Psychology, 71,* 191-196.

Hocevar, D. (1979b). The unidimensional nature of creative thinking in fifth grade children. *Child Study Journal, 9,* 273-278.

Howieson, N. (1981). A longitudinal study of creativity: 1965-1975. *Journal of Creative Behavior, 15,* 117-134.

Jackson, P. W., & Messick, S. (1965). The person, the product, and the response: Conceptual problems in the assessment of creativity. *Journal of Personality, 33,* 309-329.

MacKinnon, D. W. (1962). The nature and nurture of creative talent. *American Psychologist, 17,* 484-495.

Madaus, G. F. (1967). Divergent thinking and intelligence: Another look at a controversial question. *Journal of Educational Measurement, 4,* 227-235.

Manske, M. E., & Davis, G. A. (1968). Effects of simple instructional biases upon performance in the Unusual Uses test. *Journal of General Psychology, 79,* 25-33.

McNemar, Q. (1964). Lost: Our intelligence? Why? *American Psychologist, 19,* 871-882.

Mednick, S. A. (1962). The associative basis for the creative process. *Psychological Review, 69,* 220-232.

Milgram, R. M., & Milgram, N. A. (1976a). Group versus individual administration in the measurement of creative thinking in gifted and nongifted children. *Child Development, 47,* 563-565.

Milgram, R. M., & Milgram, N. A. (1976b). Creative thinking and creative performance in Isreali students. *Journal of Educational Psychology, 68,* 255-259.

Milgram, R. M., Milgram N., & Landau, E. (1974). *Identification of gifted children in Israel: A theoretical and empirical investigation* (Technical Research Report). Ramat-Aviv, Israel: Tel-Aviv University.

Milgram, R. M., & Rabkin, L. (1980). Developmental test of Mednick's associative hierarchies of original thinking. *Development Psychology, 16,* 157-158.

Moran, J. D., Milgram, R. M., Sawyers, J. K., & Fu, V. R. (1983). Original thinking in preschool children. *Child Development, 54,* 921-926.

Nicholls, J. G. (1972). Creativity in the person who will never produce anything original and useful: The concept of creativity as a normally distributed trait. *American Psychologist, 27,* 717-727.

Nunnally, J. C. (1978). *Psychometric theory* (2nd ed.). New York: McGraw-Hill.

Oden, M. (1968). The fulfillment of a promise: 40 year follow-up. *Genetic Psychology Monographs, 77,* 3-93.

Phillips, V. K., & Torrance, E. P. (1977). Levels of originality at earlier and later stages of creativity test tasks. *Journal of Creative Behavior, 11,* 147. (Abstract)

Piper, J. (1974). *The teacher indicator of potential scale.* Redwood City, CA: Gifted Resource Center.

Richards, R. L. (1976). A comparison of selected Guiford and Wallach-Kogan creative thinking tests in conjunction with measures of intelligence. *Journal of Creative Behavior, 10,* 151-164.

Runco, M. A. (1984). Teachers' judgments of creativity and social validation of divergent thinking tests. *Perceptual and Motor Skills, 59,* 711-717. [Chapter 5]

Runco, M. A., & Albert, R. S. (1986). The threshold theory regarding creativity and intelligence: An empirical test with gifted and nongifted children. *Creative Child and Adult Quarterly, 11,* 212-218. [Chapter 17]

Runco, M. A., & Schreibman, L. (1983). Parental judgments of behavior efficacy with autistic children: A social validation. *Journal of Autism and Developmental Disorders, 13,* 237-248.

Schubert, D. S. P. (1973). Intelligence as necessary but not sufficient for creativity. *Journal of Genetic Psychology, 122,* 45-47.

Stanley, J. C. (1977). The predictive value of the SAT for brilliant seventh- and eighth-graders. *College Board Review, 106,* 2-8.

Sternberg, R. J. (1982). Nonentrenchment in the assessment of intellectual giftedness. *Gifted Child Quarterly, 26,* 63-67.

Terman, L. M. (1954). The discovery and encouragement of exceptional talent. *American Psychologist, 9,* 221-230.

Torrance, E. P. (1968). Examples and rationales of test tasks for assessing creative abilities. *Journal of Creative Behavior, 2,* 165-178.

Torrance, E. P. (1974). *Torrance tests of creative thinking.* Lexington, MA: Personnel Press.

Torrance, E. P., & Ball, O. (1978). Effects of increasing the time limit of the Just Suppose test. *Journal of Creative Behavior, 12,* 281. (Abstract)

Vernon, P. E. (1971). Effects of administration and scoring on divergent thinking. *British Journal of Educational Psychology, 41,* 245-247.

Wallach, M. A. (1967). Creativity and the expression of possibilities. In J. Kagan (Ed.), *Creativity and learning* (pp. 36-57). Boston: Houghton-Mifflin.

Wallach, M. A. (1970). Creativity. In P. H. Mussen (Ed.), *Carmichael's manual of child psychology* (Vol. 1, pp. 1211-1272). New York: Wiley.

Wallach, M. A. (1971). *The intelligence-creativity distinction.* Morristown, NY: General Learning Press.

Wallach, M. A. (1977). Tests tell us little about talent. In I. L. Janice (Ed.), *Current trends in psychology* (pp. 237-243). Los Altos, CA: William Kaufmann.

Wallach, M. A., & Kogan, N. (1965). *Modes of thinking in young children.* New York: Holt, Rinehart, & Winston.

Wallach, M. A., & Wing, C. W., Jr. (1969). *The talented student.* New York: Holt, Rinehart, & Winston.

Ward, W. C. (1968). Creativity in young children. *Child Development, 39,* 737-754.

Ward, W. C. (1969). Rate and uniqueness in children's creative responding. *Child Development, 40,* 869-878.

Yamamoto, K. (1965). Effects of restriction of range and test unreliability on correlation between measures of intelligence and creative thinking. *British Journal of Educational Psychology, 35,* 300-305.

## Chapter 11

# Ideational Flexibility

### Abstract[*]

Recent evidence suggests that ideational flexibility shares a significant amount of its variance with ideational fluency, and more importantly, that the unique variance of flexibility is unreliable and invalid in terms of interitem and intertest correlations. However, these findings have been demonstrated only with nongifted individuals. The present study used partial-correlation procedures to evaluate the unique variance of flexibility in the divergent thinking of 230 gifted and nongifted children. Four groups (quartiles of a composite achievement test score) were compared in terms of the reliability and convergent validity of their flexibility scores. Results confirmed that there were significant differences between the four groups, and that the unique variance of flexibility was only reliable and valid in the children in the high-achievement quartile.

[*] Adapted from: Runco, M. A. (1985). The reliability and convergent validity of ideational flexibility as a function of level of academic achievement. *Perceptual and Motor Skills, 61,* 1075-1081.

Divergent thinking tests have been used for many years as measures of creative potential. These tests involve open-ended questions to which an individual can supply any number of responses. Typically, the number of responses is taken as an index of "ideational fluency," and is used independently of the other ideational indices. However, "ideational flexibility," the number of response categories, is also very important because it increases the universe of possible ideational classes, and thereby increases the probability of finding a divergent or truly "creative" idea. Guilford (1968) suggests that flexibility is antithetical to ideational rigidity and "functional fixedness." He distinguishes between "spontaneous flexibility," where a respondent inadvertently changes ideational categories, and "adaptive flexibility," where a respondent is required to change ideational strategies. The former can ostensibly be seen in the Unusual Uses test (e.g., "Name all of the uses you can think of for a brick")and the latter in the Plot Titles test (e.g., "Suggest as many titles as you can for this short story .. .").

Torrance (1974) suggested that fluency, flexibility, and originality should all be considered when interpreting an individual's divergent thinking potential, for otherwise divergent thinking ability can be overestimated or underestimated. For instance, an examinee could very possibly discover an ideational category that is discovered by no one else. And because "ideational originality" is defined as the number of unusual ideas, every response in that category will be viewed as original even though they are all thematically similar. This clearly should not be the case because only the first idea in that category is original in the true sense of the word. Taking the flexibility index into account will guard against this type of biased originality score by distinguishing between divergent thinking which is both original and flexible and divergent thinking which is only original or flexible.

Runco (1986) argued that ideational flexibility is important for the predictive validity of divergent thinking tests. With a large sample of intermediate school children, five divergent thinking tests, and canonical statistical procedures, he demonstrated that ideational fluency, flexibility, and originality were singly unrelated to real-world creative performance, but their interaction was strongly related to creative performance. In short, only the interaction of fluency, flexibility, and originality had predictive validity.

Thus, ideational flexibility is important both theoretically and practically. And yet fluency is often used alone when administering divergent thinking tests. This practice is ostensibly justified by reports of a significant overlap between the ideational indices. Hocevar (1979a), for example, used partial-correlational analyses to evaluate the ideational flexibility of fifth-grade children, and he found that fluency and flexibility shared a large portion of their variance. More importantly, he reported the unique variance of flexibility was unreliable: Interitem and intertest coefficients were negative or near zero after fluency scores were partialed.

Note that this partial-correlational research employed only nongifted individuals. This limits the generalizability of the findings because the qualitative and quantitative differences between the divergent thinking of gifted and nongifted individuals are recognized in theory (Albert & Runco 1986; Mednick, 1962; Wallach, 1967, 1970) and supported by empirical research (Dewing, 1970; Mednick, Mednick, & Jung, 1964; Runco &

106

Albert, 1985, 1986). Hence, to fully understand the reliability and validity of ideational flexibility, a comparision of gifted and nongifted samples is needed. This is the objective of the present investigation.

## Method

### Subjects

Intermediate school children participated in this project ($N = 230$). The average age was 12-5, with a range of 9-9 to 14-4. Fifty-six percent of the sample was female and 44% was male. This sample included 97 "gifted" children, 53 "talented" children, and 90 nongifted children. The mean IQ for the gifted children was 140.5, with a standard deviation of 8.4 and a range of 130-165. The mean IQ for the talented group was 119.7, with a standard deviation of 6.7 and a range of 98-128. The nongifted children shared a "home room" with the gifted and talented children, but had not been nominated to the Gifted and Talented program of their school district and consequently were never given an IQ test. For the present investigation, subject groups were formed on the basis of *California Achievement Test* (CAT) scores rather than IQs. This strategy was used because CAT data were available for every child, including the nongifted children, and have been used in the past for similar group comparisons. A CAT composite was formed by standardizing (within grade levels) the mathematics, language, and reading CAT scores and calculating an average of the three. This composite achievement score was then used to form four groups of subjects, or quartiles.

### Measures and Procedure

Three verbal divergent thinking tests (Instances, Uses, and Similarities) and two figural tests (Pattern Meanings and Line Meanings) from Wallach and Kogan (1965) were administered to the children in their classrooms, with the teachers present. The instructions and administration format were adapted from Wallach and Kogan (1965). Each test contained three items. An example of a question from the Instances test is, "Name all of the things you can think of that are round"; an example from the Uses test is, "List all of the uses you can think of for a newspaper"; an example of Similarities is, "How are a potato and a carrot alike"; and the figural tests are depicted in Wallach and Kogan (1965). All tests were scored for ideational fluency and flexibility. The number of flexibility categories ranged from 12 to 24 for the five tests.

### Results

The first analysis was an evaluation of the reliability of the fluency and flexibility indices across all tests and groups. Both indices were reliable with a Cronbach's *alpha* of .88 for fluency and .87 for flexibility. Given the subjectivity involved in scoring flexibility, the reliability of this index was also checked by comparing the judgments of two trained judges. These judges independently categorized the responses of 40 randomly selected subjects for each test item. This evaluation indicated that the scoring system was highly reliable with judges agreeing on 89.2% of the categorizations for the verbal tests and 90.9% of the categorizations for the figural.

The primary hypothesis of this investigation was tested by evaluating the reliability and convergent validity of flexibility within each of the four groups of children. To insure that the results could be interpreted in the light of earlier research on flexibility in nongifted children (Hocevar, 1979a), partial-correlation procedures were used. For interitem correlations, this involved correlating the three items within each test before and after partialing the total fluency score from that particular test. To preclude problems involved with the skewed distribution of $r$, and to allow direct comparions between subject groups, each individual coefficient was transformed into $z'$, then the average of $z'$ was calculated for each test, and then the average $z'$ was transformed back into $r$ (see Guilford, 1956; Dunlop, Jones, & Bittner, 1983). These reliability coefficients are presented in Table 11-1. Tests of significance (Cohen & Cohen, 1975, chap. 2) indicated that before partialing, group differences were significant only in the Instances test $(X^2(3) = 8.34, p < .05)$. After partialing, however, the four groups of children were significantly different in terms of the reliability coefficients of Uses $(X^2(3) = 10.31, p < .05)$, Similarities $(X^2(3) = 10.15, p < .05)$, and Line Meanings $(X^2(3) = 11.38, p < .01)$. More importantly, the coefficients in Table 11-1 suggest that only the coefficients of Uses, Similarities, and Line Meanings in the high achievement group had acceptable reliability coefficients after controlling fluency. (See Nunnally [1978] for guidelines to interpret reliability coefficients.) $F$-max tests (Kirk, 1968) indicated that differences between the groups and between the tests were not due to heteroscedasticity.

Given these test reliabilities, only Uses, Similarities, and Line Meanings were used in the analysis of convergent validity. Convergent validity was evaluated as in the research of Hocevar (1979a, 1979b) and Runco and Albert (1985). Here, partialing involved intercorrelating the flexibility scores of the three tests (within each group) before and after controlling the total fluency scores (i.e., the sum of these three tests). The resulting zero-order ($r$) and partial ($r'$) coefficients were as follows: Quartile Four ($r = .56, r' = .32$), Quartile Three ($r = .47, r' = .14$), Quartile Two ($r = .46, r' = -.07$), and Quartile One ($r = .44, r' = -.12$). The difference between the zero-order coefficients of the four groups was not statistically significant, but the partial coefficients were significantly different ($X^2(3) = 7.39, p < .05$). Most important is that only Quartile Four—the high achievement group—had acceptable convergent validity coefficients after partialing. (See Nunnally [1978] for guidelines to interpret validity coefficients.)

Because the intertest coefficients were potentially attenuated by the reliabilities of the tests, and potentially biased because of differences in the variances of the different groups, the coefficients were adjusted using a method of Guilford and Fruchter (1973). These adjusted coefficients were slightly different from the unadjusted coefficients, but the differences between the groups and between the zero-order and partial coefficients were still quite obvious.

Table 11-1

Average Interitem Correlation Coefficients[a] for Flexibility
Before ($r$) and After ($r'$) Controlling Fluency

| Measure | Quartile[b] One | | Quartile Two | | Quartile Three | | Quartile Four | |
|---|---|---|---|---|---|---|---|---|
| | $r$ | $r'$ | $r$ | $r'$ | $r$ | $r'$ | $r$ | $r'$ |
| Instances | 52 | 04 | 52 | 08 | 38 | 08 | 50 | –07 |
| Uses | 39 | 15 | 50 | –07 | 48 | –12 | 73 | 41 |
| Similarities | 59 | 01 | 53 | –12 | 54 | –20 | 52 | 36 |
| Patterns | 55 | 02 | 76 | 20 | 71 | –23 | 77 | –06 |
| Lines | 50 | –05 | 51 | –17 | 64 | –26 | 71 | 32 |
| Means | 51 | 05 | 57 | –02 | 56 | –15 | 66 | 20 |

[a]Means were calculated by (a) transforming $r$ to $z'$, (b) averaging $z'$, and (c) transforming $z'$ to $r$.

[b]*California Achievement Test* (1979) quartiles, with four as the high achievement group.

## Discussion

The primary hypothesis of this project was supported in that there were significant differences between the reliability and convergent validity coefficients of flexibility in the four groups of children. As predicted, the high achievement group (Quartile Four) had the most reliable and valid flexibility scores. In fact, after controlling fluency, they were the only group to have adequate reliability and convergent validity coefficients. These findings are very consistent with the earlier work suggesting that gifted samples have idiosyncratic ideational predilections (Mednick, 1962; Runco 1986; Runco & Albert, 1985; Wallach, 1967, 1970). A point to emphasize is that the group differences did not simply result from heteroscedasticity.

This investigation presupposed that ideational flexibility is presently defined and measured in a realistic fashion. Other definitions of divergent thinking indices are available (Hocevar & Michael, 1979; Harrington, Block, & Block, 1983). Also, although there is some evidence that various divergent thinking test batteries are comparable (Richards, 1976), generalizations from the present findings to all divergent thinking tasks must be made judiciously. This point is demonstrated in the present study by the differences between the five tests (Table 11-1).

One implication of these results is that divergent thinking tests should not be scored in the same manner for all levels of ability. Perhaps the fluency index is sufficient for nongifted individuals, while flexibility and fluency should both be used for gifted individuals. On a more theoretical level, these findings suggest that ideational flexibility may not be normally distributed in the general population, a hypothesis that is consistent with McNemar's (1964) argument about the non-normal distribution of creativity. In psychometric terms, flexibility was only reliable and valid in high achievement children, and therefore flexibility may be the component of creativity that is not normally distributed. Recall here that ideational flexibility is a crucial facet of creative performance (Guilford, 1968; Runco, 1986; Torrance, 1974).

One might question using an achievement test to delineate subject groups. However, justification for this procedure is given by Chauncey and Hilton (1965), Runco and Albert (1986), and Stanley (1977). Furthermore, many of the participants in this project were "gifted" in the conventional sense (the IQ). If a replication is conducted, it could employ multiple criteria for giftedness, and perhaps an alternative scoring scheme for ideational flexibility.

## REFERENCES

Albert, R. S., & Runco, M. A. (1986). Achievement of eminence: A model of exceptionally gifted boys and their families. In R. J. Sternberg & J. E. Davidson (Eds.), *Conceptions of giftedness* (pp. 332-357). New York: Cambridge University Press.

Chauncey, H., & Hilton, T. L. (1965). Are aptitude tests valid for the highly able? *Science, 148,* 1297-1304.

Cohen, J., & Cohen, P. (1956). *Applied multiple regression/correlation analysis for the behavioral sciences.* Hillsdale, NJ: Erlbaum.

Dewing, K. (1970). The reliability and validity of selected tests of creative thinking in a sample of seventh-grade West Australian children. *British Journal of Educational Psychology, 40,* 35-42.

Dunlop, W. P., Jones, M. B., & Bittner, A. C. (1983). Average correlations vs. correlated averages. *Bulletin of the Psychonomic Society, 21,* 213-216.

Guilford, J. P. (1956). *Fundamental statistics in psychology and education.* New York: McGraw-Hill.

Guilford, J. P. (1968). *Intelligence, creativity, and their educational implications.* San Diego, CA: Knapp.

Guilford, J. P., & Fruchter, B. (1973). *Fundamental statistics in psychology and education* (5th ed.). New York: McGraw-Hill.

Harrington, D. M., Block, J., & Block, J. H. (1983). Predicting creativity in preadolescence from divergent thinking in early childhood. *Journal of Personality and Social Psychology, 45,* 609-623.

Hocevar, D. (1979a). The unidimensional nature of creative thinking in fifth grade children. *Child Study Journal, 9,* 273-278.

Hocevar, D. (1979b). Ideational fluency as a confounding factor in the measurement of originality. *Journal of Educational Psychology, 71,* 191-196.

Hocevar, D., & Michael, W.B. (1979). The effects of scoring formulas on the discriminant validity of tests of divergent thinking. *Educational and Psychological Measurement, 39,* 917-921.

Kirk, R. E. (1968). *Experimental design: Procedures for the behavioral sciences.* Belmont, CA: Wadsworth.

McNemar, Q. (1964). Lost: Our intelligence? Why? *American Psychologist, 19,* 871-882.

Mednick, M. T., Mednick, S. A., & Jung, C. I. (1964). Continual association as a function of level of creativity and type of verbal stimulus. *Journal of Abnormal and Social Psychology, 69,* 511-515.

Mednick, S. A. (1962). The associative basis for the creative process. *Psychological Review, 69,* 220-232.

Nunnally. J. C. (1978). *Psychometric theory* (2nd ed.). New York: McGraw-Hill.

Richards, R. L. (1976). A comparison of selected Guilford and Wallach-Kogan creative thinking tests in conjunction with measures of intelligence. *Journal of Creative Behavior, 10,* 151-164.

Runco, M. A. (1986). Divergent thinking and creative performance in gifted and nongifted children. *Educational and Psychological Measurement, 46,* 375-384. [Chapter 14]

Runco, M. A., & Albert, R. S. (1985). The reliability and validity of ideational originality in the divergent thinking of academically gifted and nongifted children. *Educational and Psychological Measurement, 45,* 483-501. [Chapter 10]

Runco, M. A., & Albert, R. S. (1986). The threshold theory regarding creativity and intelligence: An empirical test with gifted and nongifted children. *Creative Child and Adult Quarterly, 11,* 212-220. [Chapter 17]

Stanley, J. C. (1977). The predictive value of the SAT for brilliant seventh- and eighth-graders. *College Board Review, 106,* 2-8.

Torrance, E. P. (1974). *Torrance tests of creative thinking.* Lexington, MA: Personnel Press.

Wallach, M. A. (1967). Creativity and the expression of possibilities. In J. Kagan (Ed.), *Creativity and learning* (pp. 36-57). Boston: Houghton-Mifflin.

Wallach, M. A. (1970). Creativity. In P. H. Mussen (Ed.), *Carmichael's manual of child psychology* (Vol. 1, pp. 1211-1272). New York: Wiley.

Wallach, M. A., & Kogan, N. (1965). *Modes of thinking in young children.* New York: Holt, Rinehart, & Winston.

## Chapter 12

# Four Indices of Divergent Thinking

### Abstract[*]

The traditional system for scoring divergent thinking tests has been criticized for its lack of predictive and discriminant validity. The present investigation was conducted to evaluate alternative scoring systems. Two divergent thinking tests (Uses and Line Meanings) were administered to 120 seventh- and eighth-grade children; and the psychometric properties (i.e., reliability, and predictive and discriminant validity) of four scoring systems were evaluated and compared. Correlational analyses indicated (a) that the Uses test had notably higher validity coefficients than Line Meanings; (b) that the summation score (the sum of fluency, originality, and flexibility), the uncommon score (the number of ideas given by less than 5% of the sample), and the weighted-fluency score had the highest validity coefficients; (c) that ratio scores (e.g., flexibility divided by fluency) were generally unreliable and invalid; and (d) that all divergent thinking test scores were unrelated to IQ but were related to achievement test scores. These findings have practical and theoretical implications for the testing of divergent thinking and creativity.

[*] Adapted from: Runco, M. A., Okuda, S. M., & Thurston, B. J. (1987). The psychometric properties of four systems for scoring divergent thinking tests. *Journal of Psychoeducational Assessment, 5*, 149-156.

Divergent thinking tests are probably the most commonly used measure of the potential for creative thinking. These tests contain open-ended questions (e.g., "Name all of the things you can think of that are rectangular," "How are an apple and an orange alike?") and an examinee may generate numerous responses. Typically, divergent thinking tests are scored in terms of the number of responses (fluency), the number of unique or unusual responses (originality), and the number of categories in the responses (flexibility). However, this scoring system has been criticized because of its marginal predictive (Kogan & Pankove, 1974; Runco, 1986a) and discriminant validity (Hocevar, 1979; Runco, 1985, 1986b; Runco & Albert, 1985).

Fortunately there are alternative scoring systems. One possibility is to use a summation index (Yamamoto, 1964a, 1964b). This is calculated simply by adding together fluency, originality, and flexibility scores. The disadvantage of the summation score is that it may rely too heavily on ideational productivity. An individual who generates many ideas will have a high fluency score, and in all probability, high originality and flexibility scores. The components of the summation score are therefore at least partly redundant. Still, this score is consistent with existing theories of the ideational processes in that it represents three facets of divergent thinking (Guilford, 1968; Runco, 1986b, 1986c; Torrance, 1974), and it should therefore be evaluated and compared to other scoring alternatives.

Moran, Milgram, Sawyers, and Fu (1983) recommend using two indices: one for the number of common ideas, and one for the number of uncommon ideas. (Moran et al. [1983] use the labels "popular" and "original" for the two indices; however, to avoid confusion among the various indices in the present investigation, the labels "common" and "uncommon" were used.)

A score for the common index is calculated as the number of ideas that are given by more than 5% of the sample, and a score for the uncommon index is calculated as the number of ideas that is given by less than 5% of the sample. This system has an advantage over the traditional and summation scoring systems, for the common and uncommon indices do not overlap. In the traditional scoring system, for example, one idea can contribute to fluency, originality, and flexibility scores. The common and uncommon scores are derived from entirely different responses.

A third scoring system uses ratio scores. Hocevar and Michael (1979) and Runco (1986c), for example, calculated ratio scores by dividing originality and flexibility scores by fluency scores. Ratio scores can be criticized because the absolute number of ideas is essentially lost when a ratio is calculated. An examinee with two ideas, one of which is unique, will have the same ratio score as an examinee with 20 ideas, 10 of which are unique. The advantages of the ratio scores include their circumventing the problem of overlapping scores, and their representing several facets of divergent thinking, as suggested by Guilford (1968), Runco (1986b, 1986c), and Torrance (1974). Hence, ratio scores offer reasonable alternatives for scoring divergent thinking tests.

A fourth scoring alternative was operationalized especially for this investigation. This weighted-fluency score is calculated by assigning weights to each idea, and adding together the weights. Weights are determined by the relative frequency of the ideas (i.e., the number of examinees that give the same idea). Unlike earlier research using general categories (one for all ideas given by less than 5% of the sample, another for ideas given by between 6% and 10%, and so on), the new procedure calculates relative frequency in a precise manner. For example, if an idea is given by eight examinees in a sample of 120 subjects, the score for this idea would be .067 (8 divided by 120). To keep high scores in line with high divergent thinking ability, this quotient is subtracted from 1.00; and the difference (.933) is the weight for that idea. In a sample of 120 examinees, a unique idea would receive a weight of .992 and an idea given by 24 examinees will receive a weight of .800. A weighted-fluency sum can be calculated by adding together all of the weights.

Given the the popularity of divergent thinking tests, and the dubious reliability and validity of the traditional scoring system (Hocevar, 1979; Runco, 1985; Runco & Albert, 1985), an evaluation of alternative scoring systems should be conducted. Hocevar and Michael (1979) started in this direction; however, they only compared traditional and ratio scoring systems, and they only considered discriminant validity. In the present investigation, two divergent thinking tests were administered to a heterogeneous sample of gifted and nongifted children; and the psychometric properties (i.e., reliability, and predictive and discriminant validity) of four scoring systems were evaluated and compared. The specific objectives include determining (a) if any of the indices should not be used because of poor psychometric qualities; (b) if there is one or more empirically attractive indices; and (c) if the various indices are intercorrelated. This last point is especially important, for it will indicate the degree to which the findings from studies using different indices are comparable.

## Method

### Subjects

Participants in this project were 60 sixth- and 60 seventh-grade children from a public intermediate school. The range of ages was 11 to 13 years, and the range of IQs (WISC-R or Stanford-Binet) was 98 to 165. Boys and girls were approximately equally represented.

### Measures and Procedure

Two divergent thinking tests from Wallach and Kogan (1965) were administered to the children in groups, in the classrooms, with the teachers present. Uses is a verbal test, and Line Meanings is a nonverbal (or visual) test. Each test had three questions. Predictive validity was evaluated with five criteria: scores from the quantity and quality scales of the Creative Activities Check List (Runco, in press); the Teachers' Evaluation of Students' Creativity (TESC; Runco, 1984), the How Do You Think test (HDYT; Davis, 1975), and the art-writing scale of the Biographical Inventory of Creativity (BIC; Schaefer & Anastasi, 1968). Testing required two hours each day for three consecutive days. The IQ and a composite of *California Achievement Tests* (CAT) were obtained from school records and used as criteria for discriminant validity. The CAT composite was simply a sum of the language, reading, and mathematics scores after each was transformed into a z-score (within grade levels).

## Results

The reliability of the indices was evaluated with α, a measure of in-teritem consistency. The α coefficients for the Uses and Line Meanings tests, respectively, were as follows: summation (.78 and .85); uncommon (.77 and .85); common (.61 and .53); originality-ratio (.61 and .57); flexibility-ratio (.38 and .48); and weighted-fluency (.61 and −.09). Because the two flexibil-ity-ratio scores and weighted-fluency from Line Meanings were unreliable, they were excluded from subsequent analyses.

Table 12-1 presents predictive validity coefficients. Coefficients that have been adjusted for the unreliability of the predictor are also presented (Nunnally, 1978). These adjusted coefficients may be viewed as hypothetical coefficients that use perfectly reliable predictors.

To facilitate the interpretation of the validity coefficients, the aver-age validity coefficient (across the five criteria, using an r-to-z procedure) for each index is presented in Table 12-2. Correlations between each index and a factor score are also presented in Table 12-2. This factor score was calculated with a principal components analysis of the five criteria. One factor (with an eigenvalue of 2.27) was extracted, and it accounted for 45.5% of the variance in the scores. The factor loadings were .821 for the Activity quantity score, .719 for the Activity quality score, .419 for the TESC, .719 for the HDYT test, and .625 for the BIC.

Table 12-2 also presents unadjusted and adjusted discriminant validity coefficients for the divergent thinking indices using the IQ and CAT scores as criteria. These indicate that each of the divergent thinking indices has adequate discriminant validity coefficients in terms of the IQ. However, most of the indices are moderately correlated with CAT scores. IQ and the CAT are nearly unrelated ($r = .16$).

Table 12-3 presents the intercorrelations of the divergent thinking in-dices. Coefficients from the Uses test are presented below the diagonal of the matrix, and coefficients from Line Meanings are presented above the diagonal. Entries on the diagonal are intertest (Uses with Line Meanings) coefficients. Only unadjusted coefficients are presented in Table 12-3, but they too would be attenuated by the reliabilities of the tests. Moreover, all of the coefficients in Tables 12-1, 12-2, and 12-3 may have been influenced by the range of scores (Nunnally, 1978; Runco & Albert, 1986), and this may contribute to differences among the indices. However, descriptive data are presented in Table 12-4, and these suggest that the scores for this sample are relatively unrestricted. Also, recall that the IQ had a range of 98 to 165.

Table 12-1

Unadjusted (r) and Adjusted[a] (r') Predictive Validity Coefficients for the Divergent Thinking Indices

| | Activity Quantity | | Activity Quality | | TESC[b] | | HDYT[c] | | BIC[d] | |
|---|---|---|---|---|---|---|---|---|---|---|
| | r | r' | r | r' | r | r' | r | r' | r | r' |
| **Summation** | | | | | | | | | | |
| Uses | 39 | 44 | 19 | 22 | 23 | 26 | 45 | 51 | 11 | 12 |
| Lines | 15 | 16 | 04 | 04 | 01 | 01 | 21 | 23 | 08 | 09 |
| **Common** | | | | | | | | | | |
| Uses | 11 | 14 | 04 | 05 | 08 | 10 | 25 | 32 | 10 | 13 |
| Lines | 18 | 25 | 01 | 01 | −26 | −36 | 14 | 19 | 09 | 12 |
| **Uncommon** | | | | | | | | | | |
| Uses | 34 | 39 | 17 | 19 | 25 | 28 | 42 | 48 | 09 | 10 |
| Lines | 10 | 11 | 02 | 02 | 09 | 10 | 21 | 22 | 10 | 11 |
| **Originality-Ratio** | | | | | | | | | | |
| Uses | 08 | 10 | 16 | 20 | 24 | 31 | 18 | 23 | −05 | −06 |
| Lines | 03 | 04 | 03 | 04 | 16 | 21 | 15 | 20 | 11 | 15 |
| **Weighted-Fluency** | | | | | | | | | | |
| Uses | 34 | 44 | 17 | 22 | 25 | 32 | 43 | 55 | 11 | 14 |

[a]Adjusted to take the reliability ($\alpha$) of the predictor into account (Nunnally, 1978).

[b]Teachers' Evaluation of Students' Creativity (Runco, 1984)

[c]How Do You Think test (Davis, 1975)

[d]Biographical Inventory of Creativity (Schaefer & Anastasi, 1968)

Table 12-2

Mean Unadjusted (r) and Adjusted[a] (r') Validity Coefficients
and Correlations with Factor Scores

| | Mean | | Factor Scores | | IQ | | CAT | |
|---|---|---|---|---|---|---|---|---|
| | r | r' | r | r' | r | r' | r | r' |
| **Summation** | | | | | | | | |
| Uses | 24 | 27 | 42 | 48 | 07 | 08 | 29 | 33 |
| Lines | 10 | 11 | 11 | 12 | 10 | 11 | 23 | 25 |
| **Common** | | | | | | | | |
| Uses | 12 | 15 | 07 | 09 | −05 | −06 | 26 | 33 |
| Lines | 03 | 04 | 01 | 01 | 19 | 26 | −05 | −07 |
| **Uncommon** | | | | | | | | |
| Uses | 25 | 28 | 36 | 41 | 06 | 07 | 29 | 33 |
| Lines | 11 | 12 | 09 | 10 | 07 | 08 | 25 | 27 |
| **Originality-Ratio** | | | | | | | | |
| Uses | 13 | 17 | 19 | 24 | 13 | 17 | 12 | 15 |
| Lines | 10 | 13 | 15 | 20 | 10 | 13 | 23 | 30 |
| **Weighted-Fluency** | | | | | | | | |
| Uses | 26 | 33 | 36 | 46 | 05 | 06 | 31 | 40 |

[a] Adjusted to take the reliability of the index ($\alpha$) into account (Nunnally, 1978). The mean and factor scores reflect the five criteria from Table 12-1. An r-to-z was used in averaging.

Table 12-3

Intercorrelations of the Indices

|  | 1 | 2 | 3 | 4 | 5 |
|---|---|---|---|---|---|
| 1. Summation | 33 | 39 | 96 | 59 | 82 |
| 2. Common | 47 | 31 | 29 | −14 | 53 |
| 3. Uncommon | 98 | 43 | 37 | 65 | 84 |
| 4. Originality-Ratio | 68 | 17 | 70 | 34 | 46 |
| 5. Weighted-Fluency | 97 | 59 | 97 | 67 | 35 |

Note: Coefficients from the Uses test are below the diagonal and Line Meanings are above. Coefficients on the diagonal are intertest correlations (Uses with Line Meanings).

Table 12-4

Means and Standard Deviations
for the DT Indices and the Criteria

|  | Mean | SD |
|---|---|---|
| Summation |  |  |
| Uses | 73.0 | 86.3 |
| Lines | 55.5 | 46.4 |
| Common |  |  |
| Uses | 11.4 | 4.9 |
| Lines | 6.1 | 3.0 |
| Uncommon |  |  |
| Uses | 11.3 | 16.0 |
| Lines | 7.7 | 7.3 |
| Originality-Ratio |  |  |
| Uses | 3.4 | 2.1 |
| Lines | 5.2 | 2.9 |
| Weighted-Fluency |  |  |
| Uses | 19.1 | 17.6 |
| Criteria |  |  |
| Activity Quantity | 2.0 | 0.4 |
| Activity Quality | 3.5 | 1.5 |
| TESC[a] | 4.4 | 1.1 |
| HDYT[b] | 290.5 | 36.4 |
| BIC[c] | 4.3 | 12.9 |

[a]Teachers' Evaluation of Students' Creativity (Runco, 1984)

[b]How Do You Think test (Davis, 1975)

[c]Biographical Inventory of Creativity (Schaefer & Anastasi, 1968)

## Discussion

These results suggest that the flexibility-ratio scores from both tests and the weighted-fluency score from Line Meanings are unreliable, and should probably not be used as indices of divergent thinking. The coefficients in Tables 12-1 and 12-2 suggest that the summation, uncommon, and weighted-fluency indices are the most valid indices of the four scoring systems. These coefficients are not exceedingly large, but they are similar to the validity coefficients reported in other psychometric investigations of divergent thinking (see Runco, 1986a).

The coefficients in Tables 12-1 and 12-2 also suggest that the Uses test had much higher validity coefficients than the Line Meanings test. Indeed, most of the validity coefficients from Line Meanings were too low to be useful. One explanation for the difference between the verbal and nonverbal test scores is that the criterion measures were verbal. However, divergent thinking tests are typically unrelated to verbal ability (Runco & Pezdek, 1984). Moreover, the verbal-nonverbal difference is consistent with the work of Guilford (1968), Roid (1984), Runco (1986b), and Runco and Albert (1985).

The coefficients in Table 12-3 indicate that the summation, uncommon, and weighted-fluency scores were strongly related to one another. This suggests that findings from investigations using one of these indices can probably predict results from investigations using one of the other indices. Put simply, the three indices are essentially interchangeable.

Theoretical and practical considerations are involved in choosing an index, in addition to psychometric evidence. The summation index, for example, is congruent with the theories of Guilford (1968), Runco (1986b, 1986c), and Torrance (1974). They argue that divergent thinking is a multifaceted ability, and that several indices should be taken into account to fully capture the range of ideational processes. On the other hand, simply adding together the fluency, originality, and flexibility scores may not be the best method of integrating the scores. Anastasi (1982) discussed a cutoff method of dealing with multiple test scores, and Runco (1986a) demonstrated that interactions between fluency, originality, and flexibility can be tested with multiple regression techniques. Another approach is to use nonoverlapping scores. Unfortunately, the flexibility-ratio scores were unreliable, and the originality-ratio scores were invalid.

An additional consideration is that of the relativity of the uncommon and originality scores. By definition, these indices depend upon the number of subjects in the experimental sample; and an uncommon idea in one group may not be uncommon in another group. For this reason, Jackson and Messick (1967) suggest that indices that depend upon response frequency be used only as a first step in identifying creative ideas. An evaluation of the appropriateness or elegance of the uncommon ideas may then be made to better identify truly creative ideas. The problem with this two-step process is that evaluations of appropriateness and elegance are typically determined subjectively; and this introduces the issue of interrater reliability.

The discriminant validity coefficients in the present investigation suggest that the relationship between divergent thinking and academic achievement holds up with verbal and nonverbal tests, and with a variety of divergent thinking indices. Getzels and Jackson (1962), Runco and Albert (1986), and Wakefield (1985) also reported that divergent thinking test scores are related to achievement test scores and are unrelated to IQs. This is interesting because it reinforces the notion that students with outstanding divergent thinking ability can excel in academic achievement without having notable IQs. In Wakefield's (1985) terms, it is an example of academic "overachievement."

With the criterion problem plaguing the research on creativity (Nicholls, 1983), an important secondary finding in this investigation is that the HDYT test is a very useful and psychometrically sound criterion. Because the HDYT test focuses on the attitudinal component of creativity (Davis,

1975), future research could examine the predictive validity of the interaction of HDYT and divergent thinking test scores. Runco (1986a) demonstrated how product terms can be included in multiple regression equations to test the predictive validity of interactions. Future research should also be conducted to examine the external validity of these results. For example, although the sample of subjects was fairly heterogeneous in terms of the IQ, it would be interesting to compare divergent thinking test indices in other age groups.

Finally, future research should be conducted to evaluate and compare other available systems for scoring divergent thinking tests. For instance, Runco (1986c) scored divergent thinking tests for the number of thematic changes; Christensen, Guilford, and Wilson (1959) and Hocevar (1979) used subjective judgments of originality; Feldman, Marrinan, and Hartfeldt (1972) used "transformational power"; and Ball and Torrance (1980) described a "streamlined" scoring system (using fluency, flexibility, originality, abstractness, and resistance to premature closure). These indices could be compared to the indices tested here; but for now it appears that summation, uncommon, and weighted-fluency scores from the verbal divergent thinking test are the indices of choice.

## REFERENCES

Anastasi, A. (1982). *Psychological testing* (5th ed.). New York: Macmillan.

Ball, O. E., & Torrance, E. P. (1980). Effectiveness of new materials developed for training the streamlined scoring of the TTCT, figural A and B forms. *Journal of Creative Behavior, 14,* 199-203.

Christensen, P. R., Guilford, J. P., & Wilson, R. C. (1959). Relation of creative responses to working time and instructions. *Journal of Experimental Psychology, 53,* 82-88.

Davis, G. A. (1975). In frumious pursuit of the creative person. *Journal of Creative Behavior, 9,* 75-87.

Feldman, D. H., Marrinan, B. M., & Hartfeldt, S. D. (1972). Transformational power as a possible index of creativity. *Psychological Reports, 30,* 335-338.

Getzels, J. W., & Jackson, P. W. (1962). *Creativity and intelligence: Explorations with gifted students.* New York: Wiley.

Guilford, J. P. (1968). *Intelligence, creativity, and their educational implications.* San Diego, CA: Knapp.

Hocevar, D. (1979). Fluency as a confounding factor in the measurement of originality. *Journal of Educational Psychology, 71,* 191-196.

Hocevar, D., & Michael, W. (1979). The effects of scoring formulas on the discriminant validity of tests of divergent thinking. *Educational and Psychological Measurement, 39,* 917-921.

Jackson, P. W., & Messick, S. (1967). The person, the product, and the response: Conceptual problems in the assessment of creativity. In J. Kagan (Ed.), *Creativity and learning* (pp. 1-19). Boston, MA: Beacon Press.

Kogan, N., & Pankove, E. (1974). Long-term predictive validity of divergent thinking tests: Some negative evidence. *Journal of Educational Psychology, 66,* 802-810.

Moran, J. D., Milgram, R. M., Sawyers, J. K., & Fu, V. R. (1983). Original thinking in preschool children. *Child Development, 54,* 921-926.

Nicholls, J. G. (1983). Creativity in the person who will never do anything original or useful. In R. S. Albert (Ed.), *Genius and creativity: The social psychology of eminence and exceptional achievement* (pp. 265-279). Elmsford, NY: Pergamon.

Nunnally, J. C. (1978). *Psychometric theory* (2nd ed.). New York: McGraw-Hill.

Roid, G. H. (1984). Construct validity of the figural, symbolic, and semantic dimensions of the structure-of-intellect learning abilities test. *Educational and Psychological Measurement, 44,* 692-702.

Runco, M. A. (1984). Teachers' judgments of creativity and social validation of divergent thinking tests. *Perceptual and Motor Skills, 59,* 711-717. [Chapter 5]

Runco, M. A. (1985). Reliability and convergent validity of ideational flexibility as a function of academic achievement. *Perceptual and Motor Skills, 61,* 1075-1091. [Chapter 11]

Runco, M. A. (1986a). Divergent thinking and creative performance in gifted and nongifted children. *Educational and Psychological Measurement, 46,* 375-384. [Chapter 14]

Runco, M. A. (1986b). The discriminant validity of gifted children's divergent thinking test scores. *Gifted Child Quarterly, 30,* 78-82. [Chapter 16]

Runco, M. A. (1986c). Flexibility and originality in children's divergent thinking. *Journal of Psychology, 120,* 345-352. [Chapter 18]

Runco, M. A. (1987). The generality of creative performance in gifted and nongifted children. *Gifted Child Quarterly, 31,* 121-125. [Chapter 13]

Runco, M. A., & Albert, R. S. (1985). The reliability and validity of ideational originality in the divergent thinking of academically gifted and nongifted children. *Educational and Psychological Measurement, 45,* 483-501. [Chapter 10]

Runco, M. A., & Albert, R. S. (1986). The threshold hypothesis regarding creativity and intelligence: An empirical investigation with gifted and nongifted children. *Creative Child and Adult Quarterly, 11,* 212-220. [Chapter 17].

Runco, M. A., & Pezdek, K. (1984). The effect of television and radio on children's creativity. *Human Communications Research, 11,* 109-120. [Chapter 4]

Schaefer, C. E., & Anastasi, A. (1968). A biographical inventory for identifying creativity in adolescent boys. *Journal of Applied Psychology, 52,* 42-48.

Torrance, E. P. (1974). *Torrance tests of creative thinking.* Lexington, MA: Personnel Press.

Wakefield, J. F. (1985). Towards creativity: Problem-finding in a divergent-thinking exercise. *Child Study Journal, 15,* 265-270.

Wallach, M. A., & Kogan, N. (1965). *Modes of thinking in young children.* New York: Holt, Rinehart, & Winston.

Yamamoto, K. (1964a). Threshold of intelligence in academic achievement of highly creative students. *The Journal of Experimental Education, 32,* 401-405.

Yamamoto, K. (1964b). Role of creative thinking and intelligence in high school achievement. *Psychological Reports, 14,* 783-789.

Chapter 13

# High and Low Divergent Thinkers

### Abstract[*]

To evaluate the generality of creativity, gifted and nongifted children ($N =$ 228) were given a creative performance questionnaire. Questionnaires were scored for quality and quantity in seven performance domains: writing, music, crafts, art, science, performing arts, and public presentation. The generality of performance was tested by checking the intercorrelations of the seven domains. Results indicated that the quality and quantity of creative performance were largely unrelated, and differences between gifted and nongifted children were slight. Additionally, for both gifted and nongifted children, quantity performance scores of the seven domains were significantly correlated (median $r = .46$), and quality performance scores were only weakly correlated (median $r = .16$). These findings indicate that there is some generality of creativity when performance is indexed by the number of activities, but there is specificity to the quality of creativity when such performance is defined as unusual, self-motivated, and useful.

[*] Adapted from: Runco, M. A. (1987). The generality of creative performance in gifted and nongifted children. *Gifted Child Quarterly, 31,* 121-125.

The creativity of individuals within particular fields of endeavor has often been investigated. This research implicitly or explicitly presupposes that creativity is specialized within a given area. Examples of this research are Amos (1978), Gardner (1982), and Getzels and Csikszentmihalyi (1976) with artists; Barron (1968) with artists and writers; Bachtold and Werner (1970) with psychologists; Helson (1980) with mathematicians; MacKinnon (1962) with architects; Simonton (1984) with political leaders; and Chambers (1964), Eiduson (1962), and Kuhn (1963) with scientists. Others have discussed the specialization of talent in children and adolescents (e.g., Albert & Runco, 1986; Holland & Astin, 1962; Milgram & Milgram, 1976; Stanley, Keating, & Fox, 1974; Schaefer & Anastasi, 1968; Walberg, 1969; Wallach & Wing, 1969). Reviews of this research are given by Albert (1983) and Barron and Harrington (1981).

Given this corpus of research on the specialization of creativity, it is surprising that Hocevar (1976) reported a "generalized disposition to distribute one's creative efforts across areas" (p. 807). This conclusion was based on his study in which he administered a creative performance checklist to 239 college students. This checklist required the students to indicate how many times they had performed certain creative activities, and hence this was strictly an index of the quantity of creative performance. Areas of activity included fine arts, crafts, performing arts, math-science, literature, and music. Hocevar (1976) reported that the areas were moderately intercorrelated, with coefficients ranging from .17 to .76.

One explanation for Hocevar's (1976) finding a generality of creative performance is that he employed only nongifted individuals. The aforementioned research on the specialization of creativity focused on gifted or exceptionally gifted individuals, and they may have more focus or concentration in their creative efforts than nongifted individuals. With this in mind, the first hypothesis of the present project is that the generality of creative performance is a function of the level of intellectual ability.

A second possible explanation for Hocevar's (1976) findings is that his creative performance instrument was unreliable or invalid. However, this type of instrument has been used extensively in the past, and has more than adequate psychometric properties (Holland, 1961; Holland & Astin, 1962; Howieson, 1981; Kogan & Pankove, 1972, 1974; Rotter, Langland, & Berger, 1971; Wallach & Wing, 1969). Still, Hocevar (1976) relied solely on the quantity of creative performance, specifically the number and frequency of creative activities; and the quality of these activities is also important (Milgram & Milgram, 1976; Runco, 1986; Skager, Schultz, & Klein, 1965). In fact, the quality of creative performance is theoretically more important than its quantity (Anderson 1960; Simonton, 1984; Taylor, 1984). Hence, the second hypothesis of the present study is that creative performance quality will differ from creative performance quantity in terms of its generality.

## Method

### Subjects

There were 228 children involved in this project. Ninety-seven were "gifted," having been nominated to the Gifted and Talented program of their school and having IQs in excess of 130; 53 were "talented," having been nominated to the Gifted and Talented program but having IQs below 130; and 78 were nongifted. The four intermediate school grades (5th, 6th, 7th, and 8th) were fairly equally represented, as were the two sexes.

### Measures

Creative performance was measured with a 65-item questionnaire. This self-report was adapted from Hocevar (1978) in that all of the activities that were appropriate for intermediate school children were used. Seven performance domains were represented: writing (e.g., wrote a short story), music (e.g., composed music), crafts (e.g., designed a craft out of wood), art (e.g., painted a picture), science (e.g., conducted an original experiment), performing arts (e.g., choreographed a dance), and public presentation (won an award for a speech). Each area had at least six items. An example of the wording is, "How many times have you . . . painted a picture?" The possible responses were (a) Never, (b) Once or twice, (c) Three to five times, and (d) Six or more times. Scores for performance quantity were calculated by finding the average rating of the items in each domain.

To evaluate the quality of creative performance, a procedure similar to that of Milgram and Milgram (1976) was used in that the children were also requested to give detailed information about their most creative activity in each of the seven performance domains. They were asked to describe the activity, explain why they performed that particular activity, and explain to what end it was used. Quality of creative performance was evaluated with a ten-point system developed especially for this project. High quality ratings indicated that the activity was unusual, highly self-motivated, and applied in a noteworthy fashion (e.g., winning an art show, recording music). Low scores were indicative of relatively common activities which lacked self-motivation and serious application (e.g., paint-by-numbers).

The Instances, Similarities, Uses, Pattern Meanings, and Line Meanings divergent thinking (DT) tests from Wallach and Kogan (1965) were also used in this study. Each test had three items. A total DT score was calculated simply by adding together the five fluency scores.

### Procedure

The tests were administered to the children in their classrooms, with the teacher present. The instructions were given orally and textually by the experimenter. Instructions for the creative performance questionnaire were adapted from Hocevar (1978), and the instructions for the open-ended (quality) part of this questionnaire were adapted from Milgram and Milgram

(1976). Instructions and administration format for the DT tests were adapted from Wallach and Kogan (1965). These particular data are a part of a large research project and therefore testing required two hours a day for four consecutive days.

## Defining Subject Groups

Because one hypothesis of this investigation involves differences between gifted and nongifted individuals, the procedure and rationale for group definition should be explicitly described. This is particularly true because the issue here is that of creativity, but the participants of this project had been previously labeled "gifted," "talented," or "nongifted" based on teacher nominations and IQs.

First, the data from all gifted, talented, and nongifted children were pooled. Two groups were then formed. One was a high DT group ($n$ = 114) and was composed of those individuals who were above the median total DT score. A low DT group ($n$ = 114) was composed of those individuals at or below the median total DT score. The rationale for this procedure is that IQ would be untenable as the criterion for group formation because of its nonlinear relationship with creativity (e.g., Runco & Albert, 1986). DT was an appropriate criterion because it is thought to be one component of giftedness (Albert & Runco, 1986; Renzulli, 1978) and the primary difference between creative and noncreative individuals (Tyler, 1974). Furthermore, DT is related to certain forms of real-world creative performance (Runco, 1984, 1986), and has been used for group contrasts in earlier research (Dewing, 1970; Runco & Albert, 1985; Ward, 1969). Finally, recall that many of the subjects in this project were "gifted" in the conventional sense (including IQ). Clearly, DT is not synonymous with giftedness, but was appropriate for the formation of groups.

## Results

The reliability of the quantity score from the creative performance was evaluated with coefficient $\alpha$, an index of the average interitem correlation (Cronbach, 1970). The $\alpha$ coefficients for the performance areas were as follows: writing (.69), music (.82), crafts (.85), art (.74), science (.78), performing arts (.79), and public presentation (.74). Given the subjectivity involved in scoring the quality of creative performance, its reliability was evaluated in terms of interrater agreement. Two raters independently judged a randomly selected sample (one-third) of the performance questionnaires. Results indicated that these raters gave identical judgments on 77% of the categorical assignments.

The correlation between quantity and quality of creative performance was calculated within the two groups. For the high DT group, the Pearson correlation coefficients of quantity with quality were as follows: writing ($r$ = .16, $p$ <.05), music ($r$ = .26, $p$ <.01), crafts ($r$ = .16, $p$ <.05), art ($r$ = .31, $p$ <.001), science ($r$ = .40, $p$ <.001), performing arts ($r$ = .36, $p$ <.001), and public presentation ($r$ = .12). For the low DT group, quantity-quality correlation coefficients were as follows: writing ($r$ = .31, $p$ <.001), music ($r$ = .45, $p$ <.001), crafts ($r = .18$, $p$ <.05), art ($r = .23$, $p$ <.01), science ($r = .37$, $p$ <.001), performing arts ($r = .34$, $p$ <.001), and public presentation ($r = -.08$).

In order to address the hypothesis concerning the generality of creativity in gifted versus nongifted individuals, correlations were calculated between the quantity scores of the various performance domains, and then between the quality scores of the performing domains. The quantity intercorrelations are presented in Table 13-1 and the quality intercorrelations are presented in Table 13-2. Note that in both tables, the low DT group is above the diagonal and the high DT group is below.

---

Table 13-1

Correlations Among the Quantity Scores

|  | 1 | 2 | 3 | 4 | 5 | 6 | 7 |
|---|---|---|---|---|---|---|---|
| 1. Writing | — | 34*** | 60*** | 48*** | 33*** | 56*** | 52*** |
| 2. Music | 34*** | — | 31*** | 29*** | 23** | 42*** | 14 |
| 3. Crafts | 66*** | 45*** | — | 70*** | 34*** | 58*** | 23** |
| 4. Art | 41*** | 30*** | 55*** | — | 46*** | 46*** | 49*** |
| 5. Science | 50*** | 38*** | 58*** | 48*** | — | 27** | 46*** |
| 6. Prf. Arts | 56*** | 51*** | 46*** | 63*** | 51*** | 59*** | — |
| 7. Pblc. Pres. | 58*** | 41*** | 63*** | 45*** | 60*** | 48*** | — |

Note: Decimals have been omitted, with **$p$ < .01, and ***$p$ < .001. The low DT group is above the diagonal, and the high DT group is below.

---

These coefficients indicate that there is only a small difference between the low DT group and the high DT group in terms of either quantity intercorrelations or quality intercorrelations. There is, however, a large difference between the coefficients of the quantity scores and the intercorrelations of the quality scores: The median coefficient for the quantity scores is .46 (with a range of .14 to .70) for the low DT group and .49 (with a range of .30 to .66) for the high DT group. The median intercorrelations for the quality scores is .16 (with a range of −.01 to .35) for the low DT group and .20 (with a range of .03 to .42) for the high DT group.

Table 13-2

Correlations Among the Quality Scores

|  | 1 | 2 | 3 | 4 | 5 | 6 | 7 |
|---|---|---|---|---|---|---|---|
| 1. Writing | — | 12 | 19* | 18* | 11 | 19* | 24** |
| 2. Music | 12 | — | 15 | 09 | 22* | 16 | 01 |
| 3. Crafts | 03 | 19* | — | 21* | 24** | 33*** | 11** |
| 4. Art | 05 | 29*** | 27** | — | 08 | 28** | 21* |
| 5. Science | 25** | 42*** | 11 | 19* | — | 14 | 35*** |
| 6. Prf. Arts | 25** | 32*** | 07 | 21* | 18* | — | 13 |
| 7. Pblc. Pres. | 17* | 40*** | 20* | 35*** | 33*** | 18* | — |

Note. Decimals have been omitted, with $*p < .05$, $**p < .01$, and $***p < .001$. The low DT group is above the diagonal, and the high DT group is below.

## Discussion

These findings indicate that both the low and the high divergent thinking groups demonstrated moderate generality in the quantity of creative performance and both groups demonstrated moderate specificity in the quality of their creative performance. These findings also suggest that gifted and nongifted children do not differ significantly from one another in the generality of their creative performance. The only notable difference between the high divergent thinking group and the low divergent thinking group was the pattern of interarea quality correlations. For example, in the high divergent thinking group, music was significantly related to all other performance areas, as was public presentation. For the low divergent thinking group, only writing and crafts scores were related to several other performance areas.

The quantity-quality correlations within the performance areas and the overall difference between Tables 13-1 and 13-2 indicate that the quantity of one's creative performance is at best slightly related to the quality of creative performance.

Additional support for this is given by Runco (1986) in an evaluation of the predictive validity of divergent thinking tests. The practical implications of the quality-quantity distinction are very important. Most obvious is that a large body of research utilizes self-report measures of creative performance, and usually this research relies on either quantity or quality scoring (e.g., Bull & Davis, 1980; Holland, 1961; Holland & Astin,

1962; Howieson, 1981; Kogan & Pankove, 1972, 1974; Rotter et al., 1971; Skager et al., 1965; Taft & Gilchrist, 1970; Wallach & Wing, 1969). Put briefly, quantity and quality of creative performance should both be considered, perhaps with a ratio score (quality divided by quantity).

The quantity-quality distinction is also important on a more theoretical level because it suggests that a large quantity of creative performance is not sufficient—and perhaps not necessary—for high quality creative performance. In a sense, this contradicts the "constant probability model" wherein every activity has an equal chance of being "creative," and thus the more one produces, the higher the probability of achievement (Simonton, 1984). Also of theoretical importance is that quality performance scores reflected domain-specificity, as expected by the work on the specialization of creative performance (e.g., Albert & Runco, 1986; Barron, 1968; Eiduson, 1962; Helson, 1980; MacKinnon, 1962; Simonton, 1984; Stanley et al., 1974; Walberg, 1969). And keep in mind that it is the quality rather than quantity of one's work that is likely to earn a reputation for a creator (Anderson, 1960; Simonton, 1984; Taylor, 1984).

Two aspects of the present project should be taken into account before generalizations are made. First, the participants of this study were children and adolescents, and this in itself limits the quantity and perhaps the quality of performance. Time is surely required to perform some high quality activity; and hence a youth, regardless of ability, might not yet have the opportunity to perform a large quantity and quality of creative activities. The second consideration is that the correlation coefficients reported here are probably smaller than would be the case in a sample with a wider range of scores, or if the tests used were perfectly reliable (Nunnally, 1978). Adjustments for range restriction and attenuation could be applied; however, the findings of the present study were unambiguous. There is an empirical distinction between the quantity and the quality of creativity with the former reflecting a generality of performance and the latter reflecting a specificity of performance.

## REFERENCES

Albert, R. S. (1983). *Genius and eminence: The social psychology of creativity and exceptional achievement.* New York: Pergamon Press.

Albert, R. S., & Runco, M. A. (1986). Achievement and eminence: A model of exceptionally gifted boys and their families. In R. J. Sternberg & J. E. Davidson (Eds.), *Conceptions of giftedness* (pp. 332-357). New York: Cambridge University Press.

Amos, S.P. (1978). Personality differences between established and less-established male and female creative artists. *Journal of Personality Assessment, 42,* 374-377.

Anderson, J. E. (1960). The nature of abilities. In E. P. Torrance (Ed.), *Talent and education* (pp. 9-31). Minneapolis: University of Minnesota Press.

Bachtold, L. M., & Werner, E. E. (1970). Personality profiles of gifted women: Psychologists. *American Psychologist, 25,* 234-243.

Barron, F. (1968). *Creativity and personal freedom.* New York: Van Nostrand.

Barron, F., & Harrington, D. M. (1981). Creativity, intelligence, and personality. *Annual Review of Psychology, 32,* 439-476.

Bull, K. S., & Davis, G. A. (1980). Evaluating creative potential using the statement of past creative activities. *Journal of Creative Behavior, 14,* 249-257.

Chambers, J. A. (1964). Relating personality and biographical factors to scientific creativity. *Psychological Monographs, 78,* 1-20.

Cronbach, L. (1970). *Essentials of psychological testing* (3rd ed.). New York: Harper & Row.

Dewing, K. (1970). The reliability and validity of selected tests of creative thinking in a sample of seventh-grade West Australian children. *British Journal of Educational Psychology, 40,* 35-42.

Eiduson, B. T. (1962). *Scientists: Their psychological world.* New York: Basic Books.

Gardner, H. (1982). *Art, mind, and brain: A cognitive approach to creativity.* New York: Basic Books

Getzels, J. W., & Csikszentmihalyi, M. (1976). *The creative vision: A longitudinal study of problem-finding in art.* New York: Wiley.

Helson, R. (1980). *Women and the mathematical mystique.* Baltimore, MD: Johns Hopkins University Press.

Hocevar, D. (1976). Dimensions of creativity. *Psychological Reports, 39,* 869-870.

Hocevar, D. (1978). Studies in the evaluation of tests of divergent thinking. (Doctoral dissertation, Cornell University, 1977). *Dissertation Abstracts International, 38,* 4685A-4686A. (University Microfilms No. 78-69).

Holland, J. L. (1961). Creative and academic performance among talented adolescents. *Journal of Educational Psychology, 52,* 136-147.

Holland, J. L., & Astin, A. W. (1962). The prediction of the academic, artistic, scientific and social achievement of undergraduates of superior scholastic aptitude. *Journal of Educational Psychology, 53,* 132-143.

Howieson, N. (1981). A longitudinal study of creativity: 1965-1975. *Journal of Creative Behavior, 15,* 117-134.

Kogan, N., & Pankove, E. (1972). Creative ability over a five-year span. *Child Development, 43,* 427-442.

Kogan, N., & Pankove, E. (1974). Long-term predictive validity of divergent-thinking tests: Some negative evidence. *Journal of Educational Psychology, 66,* 802-810.

Kuhn, T. S. (1963). The essential tension: Tradition and motivation in scientific research. In C. W. Taylor & F. Barron (Eds.), *Scientific creativity: Its recognition and development* (pp. 341-354). New York: Wiley.

MacKinnon, D. W. (1962). The nature and nurture of creative talent. *American Psychologist, 17,* 484-495.

Milgram, R. M., & Milgram, N. A. (1976). Creative thinking and creative performance of Israeli students. *Journal of Educational Psychology, 68,* 255-259.

Nunnally, J. C. (1978). *Psychometric theory* (2nd ed.) New York: McGraw-Hill.

Renzulli, J. S. (1978). What makes giftedness? Reexamining a definition. *Phi Delta Kappan, 60,* 180-184.

Rotter, D. M., Langland, L., & Berger, D. (1971). The validity of tests of creative thinking in seven-year-old children. *Gifted Child Quarterly, 16,* 273-278.

Runco, M. A. (1984). Teachers' judgments of creativity and social validation of divergent thinking tests. *Perceptual and Motor Skills, 59*, 711-711. [Chapter 5]

Runco, M. A. (1986). Divergent thinking and creative performance in gifted and nongifted children. *Educational and Psychological Measurement, 46*, 375-384. [Chapter 14]

Runco, M. A., & Albert, R. S. (1985). The reliability and validity of ideational originality in the divergent thinking of academically gifted and nongifted children. *Educational and Psychological Measurement, 45*, 483-501. [Chapter 10]

Runco, M. A., & Albert, R. S. (1986). The threshold hypothesis regarding creativity and intelligence: An empirical test with gifted and nongifted children. *Creative Child and Adult Quarterly, 11*, 212-220. [Chapter 17]

Schaefer, C. E., & Anastasi, A. (1968). A biographical inventory for identifying creativity in adolescent boys. *Journal of Applied Psychology, 52*, 42-48.

Simonton, D. K. (1984). *Genius, creativity, and leadership.* Cambridge, MA: Harvard University Press.

Skager, R. W., Schultz, C. B., & Klein, S. P. (1965). Quality and quantity of accomplishment as measures of creativity. *Journal of Educational Psychology, 56*, 31-39.

Stanley, J., Keating, D. P., & Fox, L. H. (Eds.). (1974). *Mathematical talent: Discovery, description, and development.* Baltimore: Johns Hopkins University Press.

Taft, R., & Gilchrist, M. B. (1970). Creative attitudes and creative productivity: A comparison of two aspects of creativity among students. *Journal of Educational Psychology, 61*, 136-143.

Taylor, C. W. (1984). Developing Creative excellence in students: The neglected history-making ingredient which would keep our nation from being at risk. *Gifted Child Quarterly, 28*, 106-109.

Tyler, L. E. (1974). *Individual differences: Abilities and motivational directions.* Englewood Cliffs, NJ: Prentice-Hall.

Walberg, H. J. (1969). A portrait of the artist and scientist as young men. *Exceptional Children, 36*, 5-12.

Wallach, M. A., & Kogan, N. (1965). *Modes of thinking in young children.* New York: Holt, Rinehart, & Winston.

Wallach, M. A., & Wing, E. W., Jr. (1969). *The talented student.* New York: Holt, Rinehart, & Winston.

Ward, W. C. (1969). Creativity and environmental cues in nursery school children. *Developmental Psychology, 1*, 543-542.

## Section IV

# Issues of Validity

All of the research presented in this volume presupposes that divergent thinking tests are valid. Section IV focuses on research examining the validity of divergent thinking tests. Several types of validity are investigated: Chapters 14 and 15 focus on "predictive validity"; Chapter 16 and 17 focus on discriminant validity"; and all of the chapters contribute to our understanding of the "construct validity" of divergent thinking tests. One point to emphasize is that validity is not dichotomous, but is instead a matter of degree. In fact, there are no set criteria of "adequate" validity. The appropriate level of validity depends upon the type of test, and the objectives of testing. The chapters in Section IV suggest that divergent thinking test are moderately valid, but one must use several indices of ideational skill and take into account a child's level of ability.

## Chapter 14

# Predicting Creative Performance from Divergent Thinking

### Abstract[*]

Because intellectual measures often have idiosyncratic psychometric properties in exceptional populations, the relationship between divergent thinking test scores and creative performance was evaluated and compared in gifted and nongifted children ($N$ = 212). The criterion of creative performance was a self-report which estimates the quantity and quality of extracurricular activity in seven domains. Results of canonical and bivariate analyses indicated that divergent thinking and creative performance scores were moderately related in the gifted sample, but unrelated in the nongifted sample. Additionally, the quantity of extracurricular performance was more predictable than its quality. Finally, there were particular areas of performance (e.g., writing and art) that were more strongly related to divergent thinking than other areas (e.g., music and science). These results are discussed in the context of the criterion-related validity of divergent thinking tests.

---

[*] Adapted from: Runco, M. A. (1986). Divergent thinking and creative performance in gifted and nongifted children. *Educational and Psychological Measurement, 46*, 375-384.

Divergent thinking can be operationalized as the ability to generate numerous and diverse ideas. It is assessed with tests that contain open-ended questions, and responses from these tests are usually scored for ideational "fluency," "originality," and "flexibility." Divergent thinking is influenced by motivational and situational factors, and is of course not completely synonymous with creative ability. Still, divergent thinking tests are psychometrically reliable, and widely employed as estimates of creative potential.

Probably the most important concern about divergent thinking tests is that of their relationship with real-world creative performance. This is the issue of "concurrent validity" when the predictor and the criterion are contemporaneous, and "predictive validity" when the predictor is temporally removed from the criterion. Wallach and Wing (1969), for example, compared divergent thinking and achievement tests in terms of their accuracy in predicting the accomplishment of high school students. They reported that divergent thinking was related to accomplishment in the areas of leadership, art, writing, and science, but unrelated to accomplishment in the areas of social service, drama, and music. Similar results were reported by Rotter, Langland, and Berger (1971) with second-grade children.

Kogan and Pankove (1972) conducted a five-year longitudinal study of the predictive validity of divergent thinking tests, and they too used extracurricular accomplishments as criteria. Kogan and Pankove found that divergent thinking tests only had adequate long-term predictive validity for the children from a small school system. Kogan and Pankove (1974) extended this longitudinal research by using a sample of both fifth- and tenth-grade children, and by utilizing both academic and extracurricular criteria. Here the only support for the long-term validity of divergent thinking tests involved the tenth-grade children from the small school system, and the musical domain of extracurricular accomplishment. Kogan and Pankove (1974) concluded that divergent thinking may be indicative of the level of ability at the time of testing, but that it is unrelated to future performance. Howieson (1981) reported similar findings from a ten-year longitudinal study with seventh-grade Australian children.

The most exacting assessments of the predictive validity of the divergent thinking test are those of Milgram and Milgram (1976) and Hocevar (1980). Milgram and Milgram utilized a partial-correlation procedure in order to evaluate the unique contribution of divergent thinking (i.e., the variance not shared with intelligence) to the prediction of creative performance. They reported that in their sample of Israeli high-school seniors, divergent thinking significantly contributed to the prediction of extracurricular accomplishment above and beyond the contribution of IQ. Additionally, like earlier research, they demonstrated that divergent thinking only predicts performance in certain domains. For males, the unique variance of divergent thinking scores was significantly correlated with leadership, writing, community service, and fine arts, and for females, with writing and fine arts. Hocevar (1980) regressed fluency and *Concept Mastery Test* scores on the creative performance scores of college undergraduates. Results indicated that fluency was significantly related to performance in crafts, performing arts, and math-science; and the *Concept Mastery Test* scores were significantly related to performance in art and literature.

Overall, previous research in this area suggests that divergent thinking tests have limited criterion-related validity. Hocevar (1980) went as far as to conclude that divergent thinking tests are no more accurate than verbal intelligence in predicting real-world creative performance. There are, however, several reasons why the validity of divergent thinking tests deserves another examination. First, divergent thinking tests have been evaluated primarily with nongifted individuals, and intellectual measures often have idiosyncratic properties at different levels of ability. In fact, divergent thinking in particular is qualitatively and quantitatively different in gifted and nongifted individuals (Runco, 1985; Runco & Albert, 1985). Runco and Albert (1985), for example, reported that gifted children have more reliable and valid originality scores than nongifted children. Therefore, the criterion-related validity of divergent thinking may differ in gifted and nongifted individuals.

The second limitation to previous research on the criterion-related validity of divergent thinking tests is that of the criteria employed. Typically, self-report measures have been used as criteria. These have acceptable psychometric properties, and are generally well-respected (Bull & Davis, 1980). However, only the quantity of creative performance has been considered in the previous evaluations of the validity of divergent thinking tests. This is empirically problematic because the quantity of performance is not necessarily related to the quality of performance (Runco, 1987), and theoretically problematic because the quality of creative performance is probably more important than its quantity in most real-world settings (Simonton, 1984).

The present project was conducted because of these limitations in earlier research. The unique aspects of this study include its comparing gifted and nongifted children, and its comparing the quantity and quality of creative performance as criteria of real-world accomplishment.

## Method

### Participants

Two hundred and twelve intermediate school children participated in this project. Ninety-six of the children were "gifted" according to school district criteria (including IQs in excess of 130) and 116 were nongifted children who shared a "home room" with the gifted children (and had IQs below 130). Boys and girls were nearly equally represented, as were the four intermediate school grades (fifth through eighth grade).

### Tests and Procedure

Three divergent thinking tests from Wallach and Kogan (1965) were used in this project. These were Instances, Uses, and Similarities. Each test had three items, and was scored for ideational fluency, originality, and flexibility. These indices are described in detail by Runco (1985) and Runco and Albert (1985).

A 65-item self-report was used to assess extracurricular creative performance. This questionnaire was similar in format and content to that used by Milgram and Milgram (1976) and Wallach and Wing (1969), but this particular version contained activities that were appropriate for intermediate school children. Seven performance domains were represented: writing (e.g., wrote a short story), music (e.g., composed music), crafts (e.g., designed a wooden craft), art (e.g., painted a picture), science (e.g., conducted an original experiment), performing arts (e.g., choreographed a dance), and public presentation (e.g., won an award for a speech). Each domain had at least six items. An example of the wording is, "How many times have you . . . painted a picture?" The possible responses were (a) Never, (b) Once or twice, (c) Three to five times, and (d) Six or more times. Quantity scores were calculated by finding the average rating for the items in each particular domain, and the quality of creative performance was assessed with a procedure from Milgram and Milgram (1976). More precisely, the children were requested to give detailed information about their most creative activity in each of the seven performance areas. They were asked to describe the activity, explain why they performed that particular activity, and explain to what end it was used. Quality of creative performance was scored using a ten-point system that was developed by Runco (1987) in which high quality ratings are indicative of activities that are unusual, entirely self-motivated, and applied in a noteworthy fashion (e.g., winning a large art show, publishing a poem), and low scores are indicative of popular activities which involve little initiative (e.g., painting-by-numbers).

The experimenter administered the self-report and the divergent thinking tests to the children in their classrooms. The divergent thinking tests were administered with procedures adapted from Wallach and Kogan (1965). Testing involved two hours a day for three consecutive days, with work breaks every hour. Because of the wide age range in the sample of subjects and the research demonstrating that divergent thinking tests are significantly influenced by subjects' ages (Runco, 1986), age was regressed on the predictors and the criteria, and the analyses were conducted on standardized residual scores. In addition to controlling the variance attributable to age, this precluded the possibility that heteroscedasticity was responsible for differences between the gifted and nongifted children and among the various criteria.

## Results

Interitem correlations were calculated to evaluate the reliability of the divergent thinking indices. Results indicated that all three were adequately reliable with alpha coefficients as follows: fluency (.81), originality (.82), and flexibility (.89). To evaluate the reliability of the quantity scores of the creative performance questionnaire, interitem correlations were calculated within each domain of performance. These alpha coefficients were all adequate, with a median of .78 and a range of .74 to .85. The reliability of the quality scores of the creative performance questionnaire was evaluated in terms of interrater agreement. Because of the categorical nature of the scoring system, this was accomplished by calculating the percentage of perfect interrater agreements. This scoring system was reliable with two independent judges assigning identical categories to 77% of the activities.

Pearson correlations were calculated in order to evaluate the relationship of each divergent thinking index and each domain of performance. Table 14-1 presents the correlation coefficients of fluency, originality, and flexibility with the quantity of performance for both groups of subjects. These coefficients have been adjusted for attenuation due to the imperfect reliabilities of the measures (Cohen & Cohen, 1975, p. 63), but the tests of significance are of course based on the unadjusted coefficients. The quality of performance scores were almost entirely unrelated to the divergent thinking test scores, and only the median coefficients will be reported. For the nongifted group, these were .09 for fluency, .10 for originality, and .15 for flexibility, and for the gifted group, .04 for fluency, .08 for originality, and .13 for flexibility.

Canonical correlational procedures were then applied to these data. Canonical procedures supply a multivariate correlation which represents the degree of association between two "variates." One variate is an optimized weighted sum of the predictors, and the other is an optimized weighted sum of the criteria. Additionally, after the multivariate test, the predictors can be regressed on the criterion variate. In the present analyses, these were "hierarchical" regressions, meaning that each predictor was tested on the variance not attributed to predictors already tested, and that predictors were tested in a prescribed sequence. Hierarchical tests must be used when testing the interaction of predictors (Cohen & Cohen, 1975).

The first canonical analysis was conducted using the seven quantity of performance scores as criteria, and seven indices of divergent thinking as predictors. These were, in the hierarchical order, fluency, originality, flexibility, fluency $x$ originality, fluency $x$ flexibility, originality $x$ flexibility, and fluency $x$ originality $x$ flexibility. For the gifted children, the canonical correlation between the divergent thinking variate and the quantity of performance variate was significant ($R_c = .59$, $F$ (49, 365) = 1.71, $p$ <.01). The hierarchical regressions of the predictors indicated that the fluency $x$ flexibility interaction and the fluency $x$ originality $x$ flexibility interaction were significantly related to the quantity of performance variate ($R^2_\Delta = .17$, $F$ (7, 73) = 2.24, $p < .05$, and $R^2_\Delta = .21$, $F$ (7, 71) = 2.70, $p < .05$, respectively). For the nongifted children, the divergent thinking indices were unrelated to the quantity of performance scores, in both the canonical and the hierarchical analyses. The quality of performance was evaluated in the same manner. Results indicated that quality was unrelated to the divergent thinking of both the gifted and the nongifted groups, in the canonical and hierarchical analyses.

Table 14-1

Correlations Between the Divergent Thinking Indices
and the Quantity of Performance Area Scores

| | Writ. | Music | Crafts | Art | Sci. | Perf. Art | Public Pres. |
|---|---|---|---|---|---|---|---|
| **Gifted Children (*n* = 96)** | | | | | | | |
| Fluency | 35** | 03 | 22* | 34** | 20 | 23* | 24* |
| Originality | 35** | –01 | 20* | 32** | 28** | 19 | 27* |
| Flexibility | 36** | 02 | 21* | 28** | 12 | 14 | 27** |
| **Nongifted Children (*n* = 116)** | | | | | | | |
| Fluency | 19 | 13 | 08 | 21* | 11 | –04 | 18 |
| Originality | 11 | 25* | –01 | 17 | 10 | –08 | 15 |
| Flexibility | 19 | 02 | 06 | 16 | 07 | –06 | 10 |

Area of Performance

Note: Coefficients have been adjusted for attenuation (Cohen & Cohen, 1975, p. 63), but tests of significance are based on unadjusted coefficients with *$p <$ .05 and **$p <$ .01. Decimals have been omitted.

## Discussion

These results suggest that divergent thinking tests have criterion-related validity only with gifted subjects. Additionally, even for gifted subjects, divergent thinking seems to be related only to the quantity of performance, and only to performance in particular domains. For the gifted children in the present investigation, divergent thinking was related to the quantity of writing, crafts, art, and public presentation. For the nongifted group, fluency scores were related to art and originality scores were related to music. Keep in mind that heteroscedasticity probably did not contribute to the differences between the two groups and to the differences among the criteria, for all data were standardized before the correlations were calculated.

These findings are very consistent with earlier research on creativity in gifted children (e.g., Albert & Runco, 1986; Runco, 1986; Runco & Albert, 1985) and have several important practical implications. Put briefly, the criterion-related validity of intellectual measures should not be generalized across all levels of ability. Further, the bivariate correlation coefficients suggest that divergent thinking tests are not valid predictors of performance in all domains, even for gifted individuals. That the quantity of creative performance is more predictable than the quality of creative performance suggests that both quantity and quality should be recognized. This is especially important considering how frequently performance measures are employed to measure creativity, with usually only quantity or quality scores taken into account. The orthogonality of performance quantity and quality is also congruent with several comprehensive theories of creativity, in that divergent thinking probably only reflects the ability to generate ideas, while quality performance probably requires much more (see Albert, 1983). High-quality performance probably requires problem-finding abilities, persistence, task-commitment, and intelligence per se, in addition to the capacity for divergent thinking. Divergent thinking is just one component of creativity.

A secondary finding was that the interactions between the divergent thinking indices were significantly related to the quantity of creative performance. Put simply, this suggests that one index alone does not convey all of the information contained in divergent thinking test scores. That the indices of divergent thinking interact is an intuitively attractive idea because a creative individual probably does not have ideational fluency or originality or flexibility; he or she has some of each. Divergent thinking ability involves the capacity to generate ideas (fluency), the capacity to generate unusual associations (originality), and the capacity to shift ideational categories (flexibility).

The interactions between the indices of divergent thinking also demonstrate the usefulness of canonical correlational procedures for validation studies. However, recall that the interactions were tested with a variate, or composite variable, rather than one discrete criterion. One might question the interpretability of this type of criterion. On the other hand, the differences between the groups of subjects and among the criteria were apparent in the bivariate, canonical, and hierarchical analyses.

Each of these results is of course meaningful only if the creative performance questionnaire has external validity. Certainly this questionnaire has the limitations which are inherent in any self-report; and there are other ways to assess real-world creativity. Runco (1984), for example, developed a reliable and valid teachers' evaluation of children's creativity. However, the performance measure used in the present investigation is frequently used in psychological research, is psychometrically sound, and reflects real-world performance rather than merely estimated potential. Bull and Davis (1980) argued that this type of measure is preferable to other measures of creativity because the examinee is very knowledgeable about his or her own accomplishments and activities. This is not to deny that the present findings should be interpreted in light of the measures used. In fact, given the importance of these findings for theory and practical application, a replication with other real-world criteria of creativity should be considered.

## REFERENCES

Albert, R. S. (Ed.). (1983). *Genius and eminence: The social psychology of creativity and exceptional achievement*. New York: Pergamon Press.

Albert, R. S., & Runco, M. A. (1986). Achievement and eminence: A model of exceptionally gifted boys and their families. In R. J. Sternberg and J. E. Davidson (Eds.), *Conceptions of giftedness* (pp. 332-357). New York: Cambridge University Press.

Bull, K. S., & Davis, G. A. (1980). Evaluating creative potential using the statement of past creative activities. *Journal of Creative Behavior, 14,* 249-257.

Cohen, J., & Cohen, P. (1975). *Applied multiple regression/correlational analysis for the behavioral sciences.* Hillsdale, NJ: Erlbaum.

Hocevar, D. (1980). Intelligence, divergent thinking, and creativity. *Intelligence, 4,* 25-40.

Howieson, N. (1981). A longitudinal study of creativity: 1965-1975. *Journal of Creative Behavior, 15,* 117-134.

Kogan, N., & Pankove, E. (1972). Creative ability over a five-year span. *Child Development, 43,* 427-442.

Kogan, N., & Pankove, E. (1974). Long-term predictive validity of divergent thinking tests: Some negative evidence. *Journal of Educational Psychology, 66,* 802-810.

Milgram, R. M., & Milgram, N. A. (1976). Creative thinking and creative performance in Israeli students. *Journal of Educational Psychology, 68,* 255-259.

Rotter, D. M., Langland, L., & Berger, D. (1971). The validity of tests of creative thinking in seven-year old children. *Gifted Child Quarterly, 16,* 273-278.

Runco, M. A. (1984). Teachers' judgments of creativity and social validation of divergent thinking tests. *Perceptual and Motor Skills, 59,* 711-717. [Chapter 5]

Runco, M. A. (1985). Reliability and convergent validity of ideational flexibility in the divergent thinking of gifted, talented, and nongifted children. *Perceptual and Motor Skills, 61,* 1075-1081. [Chapter 11]

Runco, M. A. (1986). Maximal performance on divergent thinking tests by gifted, talented, and nongifted children. *Psychology in the Schools, 23,* 308-315. [Chapter 6]

Runco, M. A. (1987). The generality of creative performance in gifted and nongifted children. *Gifted Child Quarterly, 31,* 121-125.

Runco, M. A., & Albert, R. S. (1985). The reliability and validity of ideational originality in the divergent thinking of academically gifted and nongifted children. *Educational and Psychological Measurement, 45,* 483-501. [Chapter 10]

Simonton, D. K. (1984). *Genius, creativity, and leadership.* Cambridge, MA: Harvard University Press.

Wallach, M. A., & Kogan, N. (1965). *Modes of thinking in young children.* New York: Holt, Rinehart, & Winston.

Wallach, M. A., & Wing, E. W., Jr. (1969). *The talented student.* New York: Holt, Rinehart, & Winston.

## Chapter 15

# The Interaction of IQ
# and Ideational Fluency

### Abstract[*]

The predictive validity of divergent thinking test scores was evaluated with (a) extracurricular creative performance in seven domains—both performance quantity and quality scores—as the criteria, (b) gifted and talented children ($N = 150$), and most importantly, (c) fluency, fluency$^2$, and an IQ $x$ fluency interaction as predictors. Hierarchical regression analyses indicated that fluency has predictive validity; however, this is limited to certain areas of performance (e.g., writing and crafts). The IQ was significantly related to other areas of performance (e.g., science and performing arts), but there was little indication of a quadratic relationship or an IQ $x$ fluency interaction.

---

[*] Adapted from: Runco, M. A. (1986). Predicting children's creative performance. *Psychological Reports, 59*, 1247-1254.

Early investigations of divergent thinking were primarily concerned with "construct validity." As a result, divergent thinking tests have typically been evaluated independently or compared to traditional measures of intelligence (Getzels & Jackson, 1962; Wallach & Wing, 1969). Most research on the predictive validity of divergent thinking tests has also been comparative. Milgram and Milgram (1976), for example, used partial-correlational procedures to compare (a) the predictive validity of ideational fluency controlling for IQ, and (b) the predictive validity of IQ controlling for fluency. Results indicated that divergent thinking test scores accurately predicted real-world accomplishments in several areas (e.g., fine arts, writing) for both males and females.

While it is informative to compare divergent thinking and intelligence tests and to examine their unique variance, contemporary theories of creative achievement suggest that divergent thinking and traditional forms of intelligence do not operate independently in the "real-world." Instead, they probably interact (e.g., Albert, 1975, 1980; Albert & Runco, 1986; Nicholls, 1972; Renzulli, 1978). A realistic evaluation of the predictive validity of divergent thinking tests should therefore consider their interaction as well as their unique contribution.

In the only investigation that evaluated the interaction of divergent thinking and intelligence, Hocevar (1980) found that fluency scores were only marginally related to creative performance, and a fluency $x$ intelligence interaction was unrelated to performance. Still, these results have limited generalizability because they are based on verbal divergent thinking tests, verbal intelligence, nongifted subjects, and a performance criterion that assessed only the quantity of the subjects' accomplishments. Having only nongifted subjects is especially problematic because the psychometric properties of tests administered to one population do not necessarily apply to other populations (Chauncey & Hilton, 1965; Albert & Runco, in press; Wallach, 1977). Divergent thinking tests in particular are more reliable and valid in the gifted than the nongifted population (Guilford, 1968; Mednick, 1962; Runco, 1985, 1986; Runco & Albert, 1985).

Divergent thinking and its interaction with intelligence should therefore be examined further. The present project was conducted to evaluate the predictive validity of divergent thinking fluency—before and after controlling IQ—the fluency $x$ IQ interaction, and fluency$^2$. The unique facets of this project include its employing gifted and nongifted subjects, figural and verbal divergent thinking tests, and performance quality and quantity as criteria.

## Method

### Participants

Fifth- through eighth-grade children from a public intermediate school participated in this project ($N$ = 150). Many of these children were labeled "gifted" by school psychologists based on teacher recommendations and IQs (with IQs above 130). The mean of the IQ was 133 (with a standard deviation of 13) and the range was 98 to 165. Sixty-seven of the participants were boys (44.7%), and 83 were girls (55.3%). There were 28 fifth-graders, 35 sixth-graders, 45 seventh-graders, and 42 eighth-graders. Because this is one aspect of an on-going study of divergent thinking, more detailed descriptions

146

of these children can be found in earlier reports (Runco, 1984, 1986; Runco & Albert, 1985).

## Measures and Procedure

IQs (Stanford-Binet or WISC-R) were obtained from school district records. Five divergent thinking tests (Instances, Uses, Similarities, Pattern Meanings, and Line Meanings) from Wallach and Kogan (1965) were used to estimate divergent thinking. Each of these tests had three items. The divergent thinking tests were administered in the classroom while in groups of about 30. Later the tests were scored for "ideational fluency," which is simply the number of ideas given. A total fluency score was calculated by adding together the 15-item scores. Ideational originality and flexibility were not used because of their strong relationship with fluency and dubious reliability (Runco, 1985; Runco & Albert, 1985).

Creative performance was assessed with a questionnaire which was developed by Runco (1987). This self-report was comparable in format to Hocevar (1980), Milgram and Milgram (1976), and Wallach and Wing (1969). It contained 65 questions from seven extracurricular domains: writing, music, crafts, art, science, performing arts, and public presentation. Each domain of performance had at least six items; and each item had four possible responses (i.e., "Never," "Once or twice," "Three to five times," "Six or more times"). Quantity of performance was calculated by finding the average rating within each domain, and a total quantity score was the sum of the domain scores.

Quality of performance was evaluated as in the research of Milgram and Milgram (1976), Runco (1987), and Skager, Schultz, and Klein (1965). This involved asking the children to describe on the questionnaire their most creative activity in each domain. These responses were then scored by two independent judges using a 10-point scoring system that was developed by Runco (1987). High scores reflect self-motivated and original work; and low scores reflect extrinsically motivated and unoriginal activities.

## Results

The reliability of the quantity scores of the performance measure was evaluated with alpha, an index of interitem consistency. All scales were reliable, with alpha coefficients as follows: writing (.67), music (.79), crafts (.84), art (.69), science (.76), performing arts (.77), and public presentation (.69). Because of the subjective nature of the quality scores, their reliability was evaluated with inter-rater reliability. These too were reliable, with two judges in perfect agreement on 77% of their ratings.

Hierarchical regression analyses were conducted using sex, age, IQ, fluency, IQ x fluency, $IQ^2$, $fluency^2$, sex x IQ, and sex x fluency (in that sequence) as predictors. Results using performance quantity scores as criteria are presented in Table 15-1. The zero-order correlations indicate that fluency was related to six performance areas and the performance total. Additionally, the unique variance of fluency ($R^2_\Delta$) was related to writing and art, and the unique variance of IQ to science, performing art, and writing. None of the quadratic or interaction predictors had significant $R^2_\Delta$ values, and they were therefore omitted from Table 15-1. The degree to which these coefficients are attenuated by the reliabilities of these tests is demonstrated in Table 15-1 with an adjustment from Nunnally (1978) applied to the zero-order coefficients.

A second analysis was conducted to test fluency before IQ, and IQ after fluency, as in Milgram and Milgram (1976). These results are presented in Table 15-2. Here fluency was related to writing, art, science, and performing art. (Sex and age were controlled in this particular set of analyses; but of course the results for sex and age are identical to those found in Table 15-1.)

Table 15-1

Hierarchical Regression with IQ, then Fluency

| | $r$ | $r^a$ | $R$ | $R^2$ | $F$ | $R^2_\Delta$ | $F_\Delta$ |
|---|---|---|---|---|---|---|---|
| Writing Performance | | | | | | | |
| Sex | .008 | .010 | .008 | .000 | 0.01 | .000 | 0.01 |
| Age | .326*** | .398 | .327 | .107 | 6.76*** | .107 | 13.52*** |
| IQ | .314*** | .384 | .442 | .195 | 9.07*** | .089 | 12.32*** |
| Fluency | .280*** | .342 | .471 | .222 | 7.92*** | .027 | 3.78* |
| Music Performance | | | | | | | |
| Sex | .172* | .194 | .172 | .030 | 3.47 | .030 | 3.47 |
| Age | .044 | .050 | .180 | .032 | 1.90 | .003 | 0.35 |
| IQ | −.074 | −.083 | .188 | .035 | 1.37 | .003 | 0.32 |
| Fluency | .018 | .020 | .188 | .035 | 1.02 | .000 | 0.02 |
| Crafts Performance | | | | | | | |
| Sex | .144 | .157 | .144 | .021 | 2.40 | .021 | 2.40 |
| Age | .100 | .109 | .180 | .032 | 1.89 | .012 | 1.37 |
| IQ | .170* | .185 | .259 | .067 | 2.69* | .035 | 4.18* |
| Fluency | .169* | .184 | .285 | .081 | 2.45* | .014 | 1.70 |
| Art Performance | | | | | | | |
| Sex | .108 | .130 | .108 | .012 | 1.33 | .012 | 1.33 |
| Age | −.232** | −.279 | .250 | .063 | 3.78* | .051 | 6.16** |
| IQ | .123 | .148 | .295 | .087 | 3.57* | .025 | 3.01 |
| Fluency | .157* | .189 | .353 | .124 | 3.94** | .037 | 4.71* |

Table 15-1 (Continued)

| | $r$ | $r^a$ | $R$ | $R^2$ | $F$ | $R^2_\Delta$ | $F_\Delta$ |
|---|---|---|---|---|---|---|---|
| Science Performance | | | | | | | |
| Sex | .174 | .200 | .174 | .030 | 3.56 | .030 | 3.56 |
| Age | −.027 | −.031 | .178 | .032 | 1.85 | .001 | 0.16 |
| IQ | .302*** | .346 | .334 | .111 | 4.67** | .080 | 10.03** |
| Fluency | .165* | .189 | .360 | .130 | 4.14** | .019 | 2.36 |
| Performing Arts | | | | | | | |
| Sex | .148 | .169 | .148 | .022 | 2.54 | .022 | 2.54 |
| Age | −.036 | −.041 | .150 | .023 | 1.30 | .001 | 0.08 |
| IQ | .206** | .235 | .277 | .077 | 3.11* | .054 | 6.59** |
| Fluency | .176* | .201 | .316 | .100 | 3.07* | .023 | 2.80 |
| Public Presentation | | | | | | | |
| Sex | .071 | .085 | .071 | .005 | 0.58 | .005 | 0.58 |
| Age | .276*** | .332 | .281 | .079 | 4.85** | .074 | 9.08** |
| IQ | .171* | .206 | .316 | .100 | 4.14** | .021 | 2.57 |
| Fluency | .179* | .215 | .330 | .109 | 3.40** | .009 | 1.17 |
| Performance Total | | | | | | | |
| Sex | .086 | .089 | .086 | .007 | 0.85 | .007 | 0.85 |
| Age | .069 | .072 | .113 | .013 | 0.74 | .005 | 0.63 |
| IQ | .231** | .240 | .267 | .071 | 2.87* | .058 | 7.05** |
| Fluency | .225** | .233 | .320 | .102 | 3.17* | .031 | 3.85* |

[a] Adjusted for reliability of the criterion (Nunnally, 1978)

*$p < .05$ **$p < .01$ ***$p < .001$

Quality of performance was evaluated in a similar fashion, but results indicated that these were largely unrelated to the predictors. The only significant $R^2_\Delta$ coefficients were between fluency and music ($R = .26$, $R^2_\Delta = .05$, $p < .01$) and IQ and science ($R = .25$, $R^2_\Delta = .03$, $p < .05$). There was some indication of a IQ x fluency interaction for crafts performance ($R = .34$, $R^2_\Delta = .10$, $p < .001$); and some indication of a curvilinear relationship between $IQ^2$ and writing ($R = .27$, $R^2_\Delta = .04$, $p < .05$), and $IQ^2$ and performing arts ($R = .24$, $R^2_\Delta = .03$, $p < .05$).

## Discussion

These results indicate that certain areas of extracurricular creative performance are predictable from fluency—both before and after IQ is controlled—and other areas are predictable from IQ. That the IQ predicts certain areas of performance may seem somewhat surprising because of the extracurricular nature of the performance criteria; but similar results have been reported by Kogan and Pankove (1974) in their longitudinal study with nongifted individuals. Of most importance is that both the zero-order and multiple regression coefficients reported here are more supportive of the predictive validity of fluency than might be expected based on earlier reports (e.g., Hocevar 1980; Kogan & Pankove, 1974). This is probably because the subjects in the present investigation included gifted children (Runco, 1985; Runco & Albert, 1985).

The multiple regression analyses indicated that the interaction of IQ and fluency was not significantly related to creative performance. One explanation for this is psychometric. The tests used here may not capture the specific abilities that interact in creative performance. For example, perhaps it is a "problem-finding" component of intelligence that interacts with divergent thinking, and problem-finding ability is not tapped by IQ. A second explanation for the nonsignificant interactions is that the interaction tested may have been incomplete. Perhaps motivation or "task commitment" is necessary for creative performance (Renzulli, 1978; Simonton, 1984), and a three-way interaction would predict real-world performance. Future research could test a motivation $x$ fluency $x$ IQ predictor. A final possibility is that the age of the participants precluded a fluency $x$ IQ interaction. Most interactive theories of achievement are focused on adults. Therefore, the present results do not entirely refute the interactive theories of achievement.

Looking at the differences among the performance areas, it is especially noteworthy that performance in art was predictable from fluency scores, while science was not; and science was predictable from IQ while performance in art was not. This is consistent with Hudson's (1966) view about convergent and divergent thinking in art and science. Of course, given that the participants in this study were children and adolescents, the difference between art and science might at least in part reflect a difference in the tasks themselves (e.g., composing a picture vs. writing music) rather than just differences in what is brought to the tasks by the subjects. In this sense, the art-science difference is also consistent with the research on the influence of stimulus-type on divergent thinking (e.g., Guilford, 1968; Runco & Albert, 1985; Runco & Pezdek, 1984).

The present findings also suggest that the quality of creative performance is not related to fluency or IQ. This point should be emphasized because in the real world, the quality of performance is probably more important than the quantity of performance (Anderson, 1960; Runco, 1987; Simonton, 1984).

Table 15-2

Hierarchical Regression with Fluency, then IQ

| | $r$ | $r^a$ | $R$ | $R^2$ | $F$ | $R^2_\Delta$ | $F_\Delta$ |
|---|---|---|---|---|---|---|---|
| **Writing** | | | | | | | |
| Flcy | .280*** | .342 | .388 | .151 | 6.62*** | .044 | 5.75* |
| IQ | .314*** | .384 | .471 | .222 | 7.92*** | .071 | 10.19** |
| **Music** | | | | | | | |
| Flcy | .018 | .020 | .180 | .033 | 1.25 | .000 | 0.00 |
| IQ | −.074 | −.083 | .188 | .035 | 1.02 | .003 | 0.40 |
| **Crafts** | | | | | | | |
| Flcy | .169* | .184 | .232 | .054 | 2.13 | .022 | 2.56 |
| IQ | .170* | .185 | .285 | .081 | 2.45* | .027 | 3.29 |
| **Art** | | | | | | | |
| Flcy | .157* | .189 | .330 | .109 | 4.57** | .047 | 5.84* |
| IQ | .123 | .148 | .353 | .124 | 3.94** | .015 | 1.93 |
| **Science** | | | | | | | |
| Flcy | .165* | .189 | .253 | .064 | 2.56* | .032 | 3.87* |
| IQ | .302*** | .346 | .360 | .130 | 4.14** | .066 | 8.38** |
| **Performing Arts** | | | | | | | |
| Flcy | .176* | .201 | .239 | .057 | 2.27 | .035 | 4.14* |
| IQ | .206* | .235 | .316 | .100 | 3.07* | .042 | 5.21* |
| **Public Presentation** | | | | | | | |
| Flcy | .179* | .215 | .305 | .093 | 3.84** | .014 | 1.76 |
| IQ | .171* | .206 | .330 | .109 | 3.40** | .016 | 1.98 |
| **Performance Total** | | | | | | | |
| Flcy | .225** | .233 | .242 | .058 | 2.31 | .045 | 5.40* |
| IQ | .231 | .240 | .320 | .102 | 3.17* | .044 | 5.45* |

[a]Adjusted for reliability of the criterion (Nunnally, 1978)

*$p < .05$ **$p < .01$ ***$p < .001$

The criterion measure used in this study was a self-report, and therefore has several inherent problems (e.g., subject memory and honesty). Still, this is a widely used criterion (e.g., Bull & Davis, 1980; Hocevar, 1976, 1980; Holland, 1961; Howieson, 1981; Milgram & Milgram, 1976; Rotter, Langland, & Berger, 1971; Runco, 1987; Skager et al., 1965; Wallach & Wing, 1969), and also has several virtues. It is, for example, easily interpreted given the plethora of earlier research, has very good psychometric qualities, and is a measure of actual performance rather than a measure of potential. Bull and Davis (1975) and Walkup (1971) have argued in favor of this type of measure precisely because it is a self-report, for examinees are well informed about their own past performance. Thus, even though the coefficients reported here are probably lower than would be the case in a sample with a less restricted range of scores (Cohen & Cohen, 1975; Yamamoto, 1965), we can conclude that the fluency index of divergent thinking tests does have predictive validity, but that this validity is applicable only to certain areas of creative performance.

## REFERENCES

Albert, R. S. (1975). Toward a behavioral definition of genius. *American Psychologist, 30,* 140-151.

Albert, R. S. (1980). Genius. In R. H. Woody (Ed.), *The encyclopedia of clinical assessment* (Vol. 2). San Francisco: Jossey-Bass.

Albert, R. S., & Runco, M. A. (1986). Achievement and eminence: A model of exceptionally gifted boys and their families. In R. J. Sternberg and J. E. Davidson (Eds.), *Conceptions of giftedness.* New York: Cambridge University Press.

Anderson, J. E. (1960). The nature of abilities. In E. P. Torrance (Ed.), *Talent and education* (pp. 9-31). Minneapolis: University of Minnesota Press.

Bull, K.S., & Davis, G.A. (1980). Evaluating creative potential using the statement of past creative activities. *Journal of Creative Behavior, 14,* 249-257.

Chauncey, H., & Hilton, T. L. (1965). Are aptitude tests valid for the highly able? *Science, 148,* 1297-1304.

Cohen, J., & Cohen, P. (1975). *Applied multiple regression/correlation analysis for the behavioral sciences.* Hillsdale, NJ: Erlbaum.

Getzels, J. W., & Jackson, P. W. (1962). *Creativity and intelligence: Explorations with gifted students.* New York: Wiley.

Guilford, J. P. (1968). *Intelligence, creativity, and their educational implications.* San Diego, CA: Knapp.

Hocevar, D. (1976). Dimensions of creativity. *Psychological Reports, 39,* 869-870.

Hocevar, D. (1980). Intelligence, divergent thinking, and creativity. *Intelligence, 4,* 25-40.

Holland, J. L. (1961). Creative and academic performance among talented adolescents. *Journal of Educational Psychology, 52,* 136-147.

Howieson, N. (1981). A longitudinal study of creativity: 1965-1975. *Journal of Creative Behavior, 15,* 117-134.

Hudson, L. (1966). *Contrary imaginations.* Baltimore: Penguin.

Kogan, N., & Pankove, E. (1974). Long-term predictive validity of divergent-thinking tests: Some negative evidence. *Journal of Educational Psychology, 66,* 802-810.

Mednick, S. A. (1962). The associative basis for the creative process. *Psychological Review, 69,* 220-232.

Milgram, R. M., & Milgram, N. A. (1976). Creative thinking and creative performance in Israeli students. *Journal of Educational Psychology, 68,* 255-259.

Nicholls, J. G. (1972). Creativity in the person who will never produce anything original and useful: The concept of creativity as a normally distributed trait. *American Psychologist, 27,* 717-727.

Nunnally, J. C. (1978). *Psychometric theory* (2nd ed.). New York: McGraw-Hill.

Renzulli, J. S. (1978). What makes giftedness? Reexamining a definition. *Phi Delta Kappan, 60,* 180-184.

Rotter, D. M., Langland, L., & Berger, D. (1971). The validity of tests of creative thinking in seven-year-old children. *Gifted Child Quarterly, 16*, 273-278.

Runco, M. A. (1984). Teachers' judgments of creativity and social validation of divergent thinking tests. *Perceptual and Motor Skills, 59*, 711-717. [Chapter 5]

Runco, M. A. (1985). The reliability and convergent validity of ideational flexibility as a function of academic achievement. *Perceptual and Motor Skills, 61*, 1075-1081. [Chapter 11]

Runco, M. A. (1986). Divergent thinking and creative performance in gifted and nongifted children. *Educational and Psychological Measurement, 46*. [Chapter 14]

Runco, M. A. (1987). The generality of creative performance in gifted and nongifted children. *Gifted Child Quarterly, 31*, 121-125. [Chapter 13]

Runco, M. A., & Albert, R. S. (1985). The reliability and validity of ideational originality in the divergent thinking of academically gifted and nongifted children. *Educational and Psychological Measurement, 45*, 483-501. [Chapter 10]

Runco, M. A., & Pezdek, K. (1984). The effect of television and radio on children's creativity. *Human Communications Research, 11*, 109-120. [Chapter 4]

Simonton, D. K. (1984). *Genius, creativity, and leadership*. Cambridge, MA: Harvard University Press.

Skager, R. W., Schultz, C. B., & Klein, S. P. (1965). Quality and quantity of accomplishment as measures of creativity. *Journal of Educational Psychology, 56*, 31-39.

Walkup, L. E. (1971). Detecting creativity: Some practical approaches. *Journal of Creative Behavior, 5*, 88-93.

Wallach, M. A. (1977). Tests tell us little about talent. In I. L. Janis (Ed.), *Current trends in psychology* (pp. 237-243). Los Altos, CA: William Kaufmann.

Wallach, M. A., & Kogan, N. (1965). *Modes of thinking in young children*. New York: Holt, Rinehart & Winston.

Wallach, M. A., & Wing, C. W., Jr. (1969). *The talented student*. New York: Holt, Rinehart, & Winston.

Yamamoto, K. (1965). Effects of restriction of range and test unreliability on correlation between measures of intelligence and creative thinking. *British Journal of Educational Psychology, 35*, 300-305.

Creativity is not easily described, nor easily measured. However, Guilford (1977, 1984) offers a convincing argument for the use of divergent thinking tests as estimates of creative potential. Guilford (1977) suggests that there are 30 separate "divergent production" abilities which ostensibly reflect five "informational contents" (i.e., auditory, behavioral, semantic, symbolic, and visual) and six "products" associated with each content. More recently, Guilford (1984) discusses three second-order factors, namely semantic, symbolic, and visual, and one third-order factor. Although there are numerous criticisms of Guilford's structure of intellect model and methodology (e.g., Carroll, 1968; Horn, 1970; Undeim & Horn, 1977; Vernon, 1979), divergent thinking tests have generally satisfactory psychometric qualities, and are probably the most commonly used measure of creative potential.

Responses to divergent thinking tests are usually scored in terms of "fluency" (the number of distinct ideas), "originality" (the number of unusual or unique ideas), and "flexibility" (the number of categories or themes in the responses). Unfortunately, there are three areas of research that suggest that these indices lack discriminant validity. Hocevar (1979a), for example, reviewed the studies that allowed comparisons of within-test coefficients (e.g., fluency from the Instances test correlated with flexibility from the same test) and within-index coefficients (e.g., fluency from the Instances test correlated with fluency from the Similarities test). Hocevar found that within-test coefficients were generally larger than the within-index coefficients, and therefore the divergent thinking indices lacked discriminant validity in terms of multitrait-multimethod criteria (Campbell & Fiske, 1959).

The second line of relevant research is the partial-correlational work of Hocevar (1979b, 1979c) and Runco and Albert (1985). Hocevar (1979b), for instance, administered three verbal divergent thinking tests to a sample of undergraduates; and after these were scored for fluency and originality, he evaluated the reliability and validity coefficients with partial-correlational procedures. Results indicated that originality was only spuriously reliable and valid. More specifically, after partialing the variance that was shared with fluency, originality had reliability and validity coefficients of approximately zero. Hocevar (1979c) demonstrated that flexibility was also only spuriously reliable and valid.

The third line of research on this issue is factor-analytic. Plass, Michael, and Michael (1974), for example, administered seven divergent thinking tests to sixth-grade children. Each test was scored for fluency, originality, flexibility, and elaboration. Analyses indicated that there were clear factors for the separate tests, but not for the separate indices. Harvey, Hoffmeister, Coates, and White (1970) factor analyzed the divergent thinking of teachers and staff members of a suburban school district. Here the divergent thinking tests were scored for fluency, originality, and flexibility. Four factors were extracted. Two of these factors were test-specific, each loaded on the flexibility and fluency indices of particular divergent thinking tests. The third factor was loaded on three of the fluency scores and three of the flexibility scores. The fourth factor was loaded on four originality indices. Harvey et al. (1970) concluded that "fluency and flexibility should be treated as one dimension instead of two, as practiced by Torrance, and both the Unusual Uses and Unusual Questions test should be eliminated . . ." (p. 366). Similar factor analytic results were reported by Kazelskis (1972).

The case against the discriminant validity of fluency, originality, and flexibility is thus quite strong. However, all of this research has focused on the divergent thinking of nongifted individuals, and there is reason to believe that these findings do not apply to gifted individuals. Dewing (1970) and Runco and Albert (1985), for instance, demonstrated that the ideation of gifted individuals differs both quantitatively and qualitatively from that of nongifted individuals. Put briefly, gifted individuals seem to generate more ideas and have more reliable divergent thinking test scores. Furthermore, Guilford (1968) offers a cogent theoretical explanation for the differences between gifted and nongifted individuals. Hence gifted individual's fluency, originality, and flexibility scores may have more discriminant validity than those of the nongifted individuals reported earlier. The purpose of the present investigation is to test this proposition by evaluating gifted children's ideational fluency, originality, and flexibility scores with a multitrait-multimethod matrix and a principal components analysis.

## Method

### Subjects

Ninety-seven gifted children from an intermediate school in Southern California participated in this study. These children were "gifted" according to school district criteria, namely IQs (mean of 141, with a range of 130 to 165) and teacher nominations. The teacher nominations were derived from the Teacher Indicator of Potential, a standardized measure which reflects motivation, attitude, and ability (Piper, 1974). There were 42 boys and 55 girls; and 21 of the children were in the fifth grade, 14 were in the sixth grade, 30 were in the seventh grade, and 32 were in the eighth grade.

### Measures and Procedures

Four divergent thinking tests from Wallach and Kogan (1965) were administered to the children in their classrooms. To evaluate differences between "informational contents" (Guilford, 1968), two of these involved verbal stimuli (Instances and Uses), and two involved figural stimuli (Pattern Meanings and Line Meanings). Each test was scored for fluency, originality, and flexibility, as prescribed by Torrance (1974). Fluency was simply the number of distinct ideas; originality was a weighted sum of statistically infrequent ideas; and flexibility was the number of different ideational themes or categories.

### Results

Table 16-1 presents the means and standard errors of the dependent measures.

A comparison of the within-test and within-index correlations indicated that the separate ideational indices lacked discriminant validity in terms of multitrait-multimethod criteria (Campbell & Fiske, 1959). More precisely, the within-test coefficients were larger than the within-index coefficients. Table 16-2 presents the average within-test and within-index coefficients.

Table 16-1

Means and Standard Errors of the Dependent Measures

|  | Boys (n = 42) | | Girls (n = 55) | |
|---|---|---|---|---|
|  | M | SE | M | SE |
| Fluency |  |  |  |  |
| Instances | 19.9 | 1.7 | 20.8 | 1.7 |
| Uses | 8.2 | 0.8 | 7.0 | 0.6 |
| Patterns | 4.0 | 0.4 | 3.8 | 0.5 |
| Lines | 4.7 | 0.4 | 4.9 | 0.5 |
| Originality |  |  |  |  |
| Instances | 12.2 | 2.0 | 11.3 | 1.7 |
| Uses | 10.1 | 1.9 | 6.6 | 1.1 |
| Patterns | 5.8 | 0.8 | 5.7 | 1.1 |
| Lines | 6.4 | 0.8 | 7.0 | 1.0 |
| Flexibility |  |  |  |  |
| Instances | 23.3 | 1.0 | 23.5 | 0.9 |
| Uses | 14.3 | 0.9 | 13.6 | 0.8 |
| Patterns | 9.6 | 0.8 | 9.1 | 0.8 |
| Lines | 11.2 | 0.7 | 11.5 | 0.8 |
| IQ | 143 | 1.5 | 139 | 0.9 |

A principal components analysis was also conducted. Because each of these tests and each of these indices is a facet of divergent thinking, and to facilitate an interpretation in the light of previous research, an oblique factor rotation was used. Three factors were extracted (having eigenvalues in excess of 1.0). These accounted for 88% of the total variance and are presented in Table 16-3. The first factor accounted for 72% of the solution variance and was essentially a figural divergent thinking factor. The second factor accounted for 16% of the solution variance and was an Instances factor, although it did have positive loadings on fluency and flexibility from Line Meanings and flexibility from Uses. The third factor accounted for 12% of the solution variance and was also a verbal factor, but had large loadings only on the Uses test. Because these are oblique factors, it is helpful to know that the two verbal factors were moderately correlated ($r = .44$), and the Instances factor was correlated with the figural factor ($r = .48$) and with the Uses factor ($r = .46$).

Table 16-2

Average Within-Test and Within-Index Correlations ($N = 97$)

| Within-Test | | Within-Index | |
|---|---|---|---|
| Instances | .899 | Fluency | .531 |
| Uses | .898 | Originality | .558 |
| Patterns | .952 | Flexibility | .526 |
| Lines | .945 | | |
| Mean | .924 | Mean | .538 |

## Discussion

These results are relatively consistent with earlier investigations on divergent thinking in nongifted samples, and it appears that originality and flexibility are presently not sound and useful indices of divergent thinking and creativity. Put simply, they are redundant with fluency. The correlations are similar to those reported by Hocevar (1979a) and indicate that the divergent thinking indices lack discriminant validity in terms of multitrait-multimethod criteria. Additionally, the factor pattern in Table 16-3 is similar to factor analyses with nongifted individuals (e.g., Harvey et al., 1970) in that there are primarily test-specific factors and no index-specific factors.

It is possible that the lack of discriminant validity reflects a problem of operationalization rather than a problem with the constructs. Hocevar and Michael (1979) and Harrington, Block, and Block (1983), for instance, suggest that divergent thinking tests should be scored in a manner other than the traditional fluency, originality, and flexibility scheme. Hocevar and Michael (1979) recommend using ratio-scores (originality divided by fluency); and Harrington et al. (1983) suggest that controlling for obvious responses (responses imposed by the immediate environment) improves the validity of ideational fluency. Hocevar and Michael (1979) and Harrington et al. (1983) have included only nongifted subjects in their research, and therefore these new scoring techniques should be tested with the divergent thinking of gifted individuals. Of most relevance is that the inadequate discriminant validity of the ideational indices might reflect their present operational definitions; and if this is the case, their discriminant validity might be improved through redefinition.

Table 16-3

Rotated Factor Pattern

| | Factor I | Factor II | Factor III |
|---|---|---|---|
| Fluency | | | |
| Instances | −.03 | .96 | .04 |
| Uses | −.02 | .10 | .96 |
| Patterns | .97 | −.16 | .07 |
| Lines | .74 | .25 | .05 |
| | | | |
| Originality | | | |
| Instances | .06 | .80 | .16 |
| Uses | .07 | −.13 | .97 |
| Patterns | .90 | −.11 | .13 |
| Lines | .74 | .16 | .12 |
| | | | |
| Flexibility | | | |
| Instances | .08 | .90 | −.06 |
| Uses | .06 | .33 | .63 |
| Patterns | .97 | −.03 | −.16 |
| Lines | .71 | .27 | −.01 |

That the verbal and figural tests were clearly distinct is an important finding of the present study. It is important theoretically because verbal and figural stimuli presumably constitute different "informational contents" (Guilford, 1968) and are not equally open to divergent thinking strategies. Butcher (1972) claims that the verbal-nonverbal distinction is problematic in that there should be a general divergent thinking factor. Guilford (1984), on the other hand, does not predict a general factor at this level of analysis, although he does present evidence for a general third-order divergent thinking factor.

The verbal-nonverbal distinction is also important in an applied sense. More specifically, the findings from this project and those of Dacey, Madaus, and Allen (1969), Dewing (1970), Fee (1968), Moran, Milgram, Sawyers, and Fu (1983), Roid (1984), and Runco and Albert (1985) suggest that the particular type of stimulus in a divergent thinking task influences the quantity and the quality of an individual's ideation. In general, nonverbal tasks elicit fewer responses, but these responses are more reliable and valid than those of verbal stimuli (Runco & Albert, 1985). Runco and Albert propose that this is due to the unfamiliarity of the nonverbal stimuli. Unfamiliar tasks are presumably solved with spontaneous ideational strategies, whereas familiar stimuli might elicit rote ideation or preconceived associations. Further research should investigate this in greater depth, especially given the difficulties in assessing creative potential (Treffinger, Renzulli, & Feldhusen, 1971) and the popularity of divergent thinking tests.

Several qualifications about the findings from the present investigation should be mentioned. For example, Sternberg (1980) discusses the limitations of factor theories of general intelligence; and these limitations certainly also apply to the factor analytic research on divergent thinking. Sternberg argues that factor-based theories are not useful in education and training, and his recommendation is to supplement our factor theories with componential theories and delineate the intellect into operational and manageable units, or "components." Perhaps future research could isolate the components of divergent thinking.

Another important qualification is that this project relied on a school district's definition of "giftedness." Only IQ and teacher nominations were used as criteria, and although many schools rely on these same criteria, there are other important aspects of giftedness (e.g., Albert & Runco, 1986; Renzulli, 1978). In fact, the possibility still exists that the divergent thinking test indices have discriminant validity in individuals who are gifted in terms of criteria other than IQ and teacher nominations.

Finally, the findings of this and earlier investigations on the validity of ideational indices do not indicate that divergent thinking tests are unreliable estimates of creativity. Rather, they suggest that as presently operationalized, fluency alone is probably sufficient to index divergent thinking ability. Divergent thinking tests have predictive validity (Runco, 1984, 1986; Wallach & Wing, 1969) and are independent of other forms of intelligence (Runco & Pezdek, 1984; Wallach & Kogan, 1965). Further, they are involved in many conceptions of "giftedness" (e.g., Albert & Runco, 1986; Renzulli, 1978), and are generally informative measures of one component of creativity.

## REFERENCES

Albert, R. S., & Runco, M. A. (1986). Achievement of eminence: A model of exceptionally gifted boys and their families. In R.J. Sternberg & J.E. Davison (Eds.), *Conceptions of giftedness* (pp. 332-357). New York: Cambridge University Press.

Butcher, H. J. (1972). Divergent thinking and creativity. In W. D. Wall & V. P. Varma (Eds.), *Advances in educational psychology* (pp. 83-95). London: London University Press.

Campbell, D. T., & Fiske, D. W. (1959). Convergent and discriminant validation by the multitrait-multimethod matrix. *Psychological Bulletin, 56,* 81-105.

Carroll, J. B. (1968). Review of "The nature of human intelligence." *American Educational Research Journal, 5,* 249-256.

Dacey, J., Madaus, G. F., & Allen, A. (1969). The relationship of creativity and intelligence in Irish adolescents. *British Journal of Educational Psychology, 39,* 261-266.

Dewing, K. (1970). The reliability and validity of selected tests of creative thinking in a sample of seventh-grade West Australian children. *British Journal of Educational Psychology, 40,* 35-42.

Fee, F. (1968). An alternative to Ward's factor analysis of Wallach and Kogan's "creativity" correlations. *British Journal of Educational Psychology, 38,* 319-321.

Guilford, J. P. (1968). *Intelligence, creativity, and their educational implications.* San Diego, CA: Knapp.

Guilford, J. P. (1977). *Way beyond the IQ.* Buffalo, NY: Creative Education Foundation.

Guilford, J. P. (1984). Varieties of divergent production. *Journal of Creative Behavior, 18,* 1-10.

Harrington, D. M., Block, J., & Block, J. H. (1983). Predicting creativity in preadolescence from divergent thinking in early childhood. *Journal of Personality and Social Psychology, 45,* 609-623.

Harvey, O. J., Hoffmeister, J. K., Coates, C., & White, B. J. (1970). A partial evaluation of Torrance's test of creativity. *American Educational Research Journal, 7,* 359-372.

Hocevar, D. (1979a, April). *Multitrait-multimethod analyses of tests of divergent thinking.* Paper presented at the meeting of the Western Psychological Association in San Diego, California.

Hocevar, D. (1979b). Ideational fluency as a confounding factor in the measurement of originality. *Journal of Educational Psychology, 71,* 191-196.

Hocevar, D. (1979c). The unidimensional nature of creative thinking in fifth-grade children. *Child Study Journal, 9,* 273-278.

Hocevar, D., & Michael, W. B. (1979). The effects of scoring formulas on the discriminant validity tests of divergent thinking. *Educational and Psychological Measurement, 39,* 917-921.

Horn, J. L. (1970). Review of J. P. Guilford's "The nature of human intelligence." *Psychometrica, 35,* 273-277.

Kazelskis, R. (1972). The convergent, divergent, and factorial validity of the Torrance Figural Test of Creativity. *Southern Journal of Educational Research, 6,* 123-129.

Moran, J. D., Milgram, R. M., Sawyers, J. K., & Fu, V. R. (1983). Stimulus specificity in the measurement of original thinking in preschool children. *The Journal of Psychology, 114,* 99-105.

Piper, J. (1974). *The teacher indicator of potential scale.* Redwood City, CA: Gifted Resource Center.

Plass, H., Michael, J., & Michael, W. (1974). The factorial validity of the *Torrance tests of creative thinking* for a sample of 111 sixth grade children. *Educational and Psychological Measurement, 34,* 413-414.

Renzulli, J. S. (1978). What makes giftedness? Reexamining a definition. *Phi Delta Kappan, 60,* 180-184.

Roid, G. H. (1984). Construct validity of the figural, symbolic, and semantic dimensions of the structure-of-intellect learning abilities test. *Educational and Psychological Measurement, 44,* 692-702.

Runco, M. A. (1984). Teachers' judgments of creativity and social validation of divergent thinking tests. *Perceptual and Motor Skills, 59,* 711-717. [Chapter 5]

Runco, M.A. (1986). Predicting children's creative performance. *Psychological Reports, 59,* 1247-1254. [Chapter 15]

Runco, M. A., & Albert, R. S. (1985). The reliability and validity of ideational originality in the divergent thinking of academically gifted and nongifted children. *Educational and Psychological Measurement, 45,* 483-501. [Chapter 10]

Runco, M. A., & Pezdek, K. (1984). The effect of television and radio on children's creativity. *Human Communications Research, 11,* 109-120. [Chapter 4]

Sternberg, R. J. (1980). Factor theories of intelligence are all right almost. *Educational Researcher, 9,* 6-13, 18.

Torrance, E. P. (1974). *Torrance tests of creative thinking.* Bensenville, IL: Scholastic Testing Services.

Treffinger, D. J., Renzulli, J. S., & Feldhusen, J. F. (1971). Problems in the assessment of creative thinking. *Journal of Creative Behavior, 5,* 104-112.

Undeim, J. O., & Horn, J. L. (1977). Critical evaluation of Guilford's structure-of-intellect theory. *Intelligence, 1,* 65-81.

Vernon, P. E. (1979). *Intelligence: Heredity and environment.* San Francisco: Freeman.

Wallach, M. A., & Kogan, N. (1965). *Modes of thinking in young children.* New York: Holt, Rinehart, & Winston.

Wallach, M. A., & Wing, C. W., Jr. (1969). *The talented student.* New York: Holt, Rinehart, & Winston.

For the past quarter of a century the predominant view concerning the relationship between creativity and intelligence has been the "threshold theory." This theory predicts that measures of intelligence and creativity are related, but only up to a moderate level of intelligence (e.g., Albert & Elliott, 1973; Anderson, 1960; Barron, 1969; MacKinnon, 1962; Torrance, 1962). Barron and Torrance have been relatively precise in their estimate of the cutoff: IQ of 120. Above that, intelligence and creativity are ostensibly independent. The popularity of this view is probably due as much to its convincing logic as the empirical support. Put briefly, the argument is that a moderate level of intelligence is necessary for an individual to recognize that a meaningful problem exists, to select and integrate the relevant information, and to generate an applicable and perhaps original solution.

A sizable body of empirical research has reported that creativity and intelligence are related in some sort of curvilinear fashion. However, very little empirical work has systematically investigated the threshold theory per se, especially recently (cf. Barron & Harrington, 1981). More importantly, the research that has been conducted specifically to test the threshold theory contains evidence supporting the threshold, and evidence against the threshold. Guilford and Christensen (1973), for instance, administered five divergent thinking (DT) tests to children from two elementary schools. Lorge-Thorndike IQs were available for the children from one school, and derived from an achievement test for the other. The average correlation between IQ and DT was .25 (with a range of .07 to .43). Guilford and Christensen also generated scatterplots and concluded that "the higher the IQ, the more likely we are to find at least some individuals with high creative potential" (p. 251). Other support for the threshold view is given by Guilford and Hoepfner (1966), Richards (1976), and Schubert (1973).

There are, on the other hand, several investigations which report findings contrary to the threshold theory. Runco and Pezdek (1984) tested linear, quadratic, and cubic relationships between three DT indices and verbal achievement scores, and reported that all were small and nonsignificant. Mednick and Andrews (1967) used the *Remote Associates Test* (RAT) to estimate creative potential and the *Scholastic Aptitude Test* (SAT) to estimate intelligence in a sample of college freshmen. They reported an overall correlation of .43 between the RAT and SAT verbal scale and .20 between the RAT and SAT math scale. The correlations were largest in the lowest SAT group, but the differences between the coefficients of the low and high SAT groups were negligible. Further evidence contrary to the threshold view is given by Ripple and May (1962).

Note the methodological differences among the studies. The most important is probably that the various studies used different intellectual tests. Several studies used *Lorge-Thorndike IQ* tests to estimate intelligence or the *Otis Quick Scoring Mental Ability Test*; others have employed achievement tests or military aptitude tests. For creative potential, several studies used divergent thinking tests scored in a variety of manners, and other studies estimated creativity with the RAT or their own tests for creativity. Another important methological difference is that of the subject samples. Widely different and incomparable populations have been sampled, which raises the question of the generality of the findings. Moreover, frequently there is the problem of a restricted range of scores (Yamamoto, 1965). Finally, the higher levels of ability are not sufficiently represented in the earlier research, and measures of ability seem to perform idiosyncratically at the higher levels (e.g., Chauncey & Hilton, 1965; Runco & Albert, 1985; Stanley, 1977).

Hence the inconsistencies in earlier research on the threshold theory may have resulted from the different measures employed and the incomparable samples of subjects. The present study was conducted to test the threshold hypothesis with a heterogeneous sample of subjects, including both gifted and nongifted children, and several measures of creativity and intelligence.

## Method

### Subjects

Children from a public intermediate school participated in this project ($N$ = 228). Forty-three percent were "gifted," with IQs of 130 or higher and outstanding scores on the Teacher Indicator of Potential (Piper, 1974), and 57% were nongifted subjects from the same classes. There were 46 fifth-graders, 57 sixth-graders, 57 seventh-graders, and 68 eighth-graders. Boys and girls were approximately equally represented (44% and 56% of the sample, respectively).

### Measures and Procedure

*California Achievement Test* (CAT) scores and IQs (Stanford-Binet or WISC-R) were obtained from school district records. An achievement composite was calculated by transforming the reading, language, and mathematics CAT scores into z-scores, and adding them together. The z-scores were calculated within each grade to preclude age differences in the CAT composite.

Creativity was estimated with five DT tests from the Wallach and Kogan (1965) battery (Instances, Pattern Meanings, Similarities, Uses, and Line Meanings). Each test contained three items and was administered in the classrooms as one part of a large project on creativity and giftedness (Albert & Runco, 1986; Runco, 1984, 1987; Runco & Albert, 1985). The DT tests were scored for ideational fluency (the number of distinct responses), originality (the number of statistically infrequent responses), and flexibility (the number of categories or themes in the responses). Verbal and figural tests were treated separately because of their empirical independence (Runco & Albert, 1985; Wallach & Kogan, 1965).

## Results

The reliability of the creativity tests was evaluated with coefficient $\alpha$. Results indicated that the tests were highly reliable with $\alpha$ coefficients as follows: verbal fluency (.85), verbal originality (.82), verbal flexibility (.86), figural fluency (.90), figural originality (.89), and figural flexibility (.87). The CAT composite and IQ were marginally correlated ($r$ = .21, $p <$ .01).

To test for age and gender effects on the DT scores, a multivariate analysis of variance was conducted using grade and gender as between-subjects factors and the six DT indices as the dependent measures. The results indicated that the DT scores of the four grades were significantly different, with two orthogonal canonical functions ($R_C$ = .45, $F$ (18, 628) = 4.58, $p$ < .001, and $R_C$ = .32, $F$ (10, 446) = 2.83, $p$ < .01). All six univariate tests of the individual DT indices reflected a significant difference, with older subjects having higher scores. The two genders did not differ, nor was the interaction significant. The data for the two genders were therefore pooled. Because of the grade effect, age (in months) was covaried from the DT scores, and the subsequent analyses were conducted with the residuals.

## Group Differences

The threshold hypothesis was first tested by calculating correlations between creativity test scores and IQs within four IQ levels: 98-120 (mean of 113), 121-130 (mean of 125), 131-145 (mean of 136), and 146-165 (mean of 152). To take test reliability into account and allow the comparison of the coefficients across groups, these coefficients were adjusted for possible attenuation and range restriction (Bobko, 1983). For this adjustment, the variance of the entire sample was used as an estimate of unrestricted range, and thus the adjusted within-group coefficients are not biased by restricted variance. Tests of significance are of course based on the unadjusted coefficients. The first analysis indicated that the only significant coefficients were those between IQ and verbal fluency ($r$ = .25, p < .05, $r'$ = .22) and IQ and verbal flexibility ($r$ = .27, $p$ < .05, $r'$ = .27) in the IQ 131-145 group. All other coefficients were nonsignificant. The average coefficients were: IQ 98-120 ($r$ = .02 and $r'$ = .05); IQ 121-130 ($r$ = .12 and $r'$ = .13); IQ 131-145 ($r$ = .15 and $r'$ = .15); and IQ 146-165 ($r$ = −.12 and $r'$ = −.08). The next evaluation of the threshold hypothesis involved correlations between the creativity measures and the IQ within CAT Quartiles (with Quartile One having the lowest CAT scores, and Quartile Four the highest). Here again, there were very few significant correlations. In the low CAT Quartile, IQ was significantly related to verbal fluency ($r$ = .40, $p$ < .05, $r'$ = .58) and verbal originality ($r$ = .52, p < .01, $r'$ = .75); and in the high CAT Quartile, IQ was significantly correlated with verbal flexibility ($r$ = .32, $p$ < .05, $r'$ = .30) and figural fluency ($r$ = .28, $p$ < .05, $r'$ = .23) The average coefficients across DT indices were: Quartile One ($r$ = .26 and $r'$ = .40), Quartile Two ($r$ = −.03 and $r'$ = −.04), Quartile Three ($r$ = −.07 and $r'$ = −.10), and Quartile Four ($r$ = .26 and $r'$ = .21).

The final bivariate test of the threshold hypothesis involved correlating the creativity measures with the CAT composite within the four IQ levels, and within the CAT Quartiles. The unadjusted and adjusted coefficients are presented in Tables 17-1 and 17-2.

Table 17-1

Pearson and Adjusted[a] (in parentheses) Correlations between
Achievement[b] and the Creativity Measures[c] within IQ Levels

IQ Level

| Measures | 98-120 (n = 24) | | 121-130 (n = 30) | | 131-145 (n = 68) | | 146-165 (n = 28) | |
|---|---|---|---|---|---|---|---|---|
| **Verbal** | | | | | | | | |
| Fluency | 43* | (51) | 58*** | (62) | 34** | (33) | 56** | (58) |
| Originality | 36 | (69) | 52** | (45) | 27* | (27) | 50** | (48) |
| Flexibility | 58** | (65) | 57** | (63) | 28* | (28) | 63*** | (59) |
| **Figural** | | | | | | | | |
| Fluency | 38 | (48) | 16 | (18) | 17 | (19) | 60** | (45) |
| Originality | 48** | (66) | 15 | (19) | 13 | (17) | 65*** | (42) |
| Flexibility | 39 | (45) | 15 | (16) | 15 | (15) | 56** | (47) |

[a]adjusted for attenuation and range restriction (Bobko, 1983)

[b]*California Achievement Test* composite

[c]Decimals have been omitted from the coefficients, with *$p < .05$, **$p < .01$, and ***$p < .001$.

## Multivariate Analyses

The relationship between creativity and intelligence was also tested with canonical and multiple regression procedures, and the data from all subjects. This allowed another check of our hypothesis using an unrestricted variance; and the multivariate tests minimize the possibility of Type I errors by calculating very few tests of significance. A canonical correlation was conducted to find an optimized composite—or "variate"—of the six divergent thinking indices, and "hierarchical" regression analyses were conducted to test linear (IQ or CAT), quadratic ($IQ^2$ or $CAT^2$), and cubic ($IQ^3$ or $CAT^3$) curvilinear relationships (Cohen & Cohen, 1975). The results of the analysis using the IQ predictors indicated that divergent thinking and IQ were entirely unrelated, while the analysis with the CAT predictors indicated that there were significant linear ($F (6, 216) = 8.72$, $p < .001$), quadratic ($F (6, 215) = 2.46$, $p < .05$), and cubic trends ($F (6, 214) = 2.23$, $p < .05$) in the DT-CAT distribution.

Table 17-2

Pearson and Adjusted[a] (in parentheses) Correlations between
Achievement[b] and the Creativity Measures[c] within CAT Levels

CAT Level[b]

| Measures | Quartile One (n = 57) | | Quartile Two (n = 57) | | Quartile Three (n = 57) | | Quartile Four (n = 57) | |
|---|---|---|---|---|---|---|---|---|
| Verbal | | | | | | | | |
| Fluency | 07 | (11) | 08 | (10) | 20 | (24) | 47*** | (41) |
| Originality | −11 | (−19) | 04 | (07) | −09 | (−11) | 39*** | (30) |
| Flexibility | 12 | (16) | 10 | (12) | 20 | (36) | 41** | (38) |
| Figural | | | | | | | | |
| Fluency | −11 | (18) | −08 | (−08) | 24 | (28) | 29* | (23) |
| Originality | −05 | (−11) | −06 | (08) | 15 | (24) | 31* | (23) |
| Flexibility | −12 | (−18) | −07 | (−07) | 28* | (32) | 25 | (22) |

[a]adjusted for attenuation and range restriction (Bobko, 1983)

[b]*California Achievement Test* (CAT) composite

[c]Decimals have been omitted from the coefficients, with $*p < .05$, $**p < .01$, and $***p < .001$.

## Discussion

These results indicate that the relationship between creativity and intelligence is very much a function of the particular measures employed and heterogeneity of the subjects sampled. For example, when IQ was used to estimate intelligence, there was very little indication of any relationship between IQ and creativity. In contrast, when the CAT was used as the estimate of intelligence, there was a strong relationship between creativity and intelligence. Additionally, the coefficients were large and significant in the high ability groups (IQ > 145 and Quartile Four), and this essentially refutes the threshold theory.

One explanation for the differences between the two measures of intelligence is that IQ and achievement tests reflect different intellectual processes. Typically, the IQ is defined as a predictive measure of general intellectual ability, while achievement tests are believed to reflect specific learning experiences (Anastasi, 1982). On the other hand, over the years a number of studies have reported that achievement test scores and IQs are highly correlated, and many theorists argue that the distinction between them is misleading (Humphreys, 1974; Sternberg, 1982). On the basis of the present results, we believe that academic achievement and IQ relate to creativity in significantly different ways, and that the distinction between them is a crucial one. Scores of one should not be used as substitutes for the other because the two very well might reflect different underlying cognitive processes.

Stanley (1977) argued that achievement and IQ tests sample intellectual ability in significantly different ways, and the difference between the two types of measures might be due in part to their requiring different test-taking skills rather than thinking skills per se. This could explain the moderate correlation between them and their dissimilar relationships with creativity. Further research should be conducted to delineate the processes tapped by these tests, perhaps using "componential analyses" (Sternberg, 1981). The IQ and CAT might both rely on the same cognitive components but use different strategic components, or "metacomponents."

Recall that the potential problems with range restriction were avoided by adjusting the bivariate coefficients and by conducting the canonical correlation. The adjusted coefficients suggest that heteroscedasticity was partly responsible for the group differences; however, even the adjusted coefficients offered no support for the threshold theory. Type I errors were unlikely because the direction and pattern of the results would not be altered if the probability levels were modified to take the number of coefficients into account. Moreover, the multivariate analyses demonstrated the curvilinear relationship without the potential problems of statistical probability. For now, it appears that the traditional view of the threshold of intelligence necessary for creativity is at least partly a psychometric artifact.

## REFERENCES

Albert, R. S., & Elliott, R. C. (1973). Creative ability and the handling of personal and social conflict among bright sixth graders. *Social Behavior and Personality, 1,* 169-181.

Albert, R. S., & Runco, M. A. (1986). Achievement and eminence: A model of exceptionally gifted boys and their families. In R.J. Sternberg & J.E. Davidson (Eds.), *Conceptions of giftedness* (pp. 332-357). New York: Cambridge University Press.

Anastasi, A. (1982). *Psychological testing* (5th ed.). New York: Macmillan.

Anderson, J. E. (1960). The nature of abilities. In E. P. Torrance (Ed.), *Talent and education* (pp. 9-31). Minneapolis: University of Minnesota Press.

Barron, F. (1969). *Creative person, creative process.* New York: Holt, Rinehart, & Winston.

Barron, F., & Harrington, D. M. (1981). Creativity, intelligence, and personality. *Annual Review of Psychology, 32,* 439-476.

Bobko, P. (1983). An analysis of correlations corrected for attenuation and range restriction. *Journal of Applied Psychology, 68,* 584-589.

Chauncey, H., & Hilton, T. L. (1965). Are aptitude tests valid for the highly able? *Science, 148,* 1297-1304.

Cohen, J., & Cohen, P. (1975). *Applied multiple regression/correlation analysis for the behavioral sciences.* Hillsdale, NJ: Erlbaum.

Guilford, J. P., & Christensen, P. R. (1973). The one-way relation between creative potential and IQ. *Journal of Creative Behavior, 7,* 247-252.

Guilford, J. P., & Hoepfner, R. (1966). Creative potential is related to measures of IQ and verbal comprehension. *Indian Journal of Psychology, 41,* 7-16.

Humphreys, L. G. (1974). The misleading distinction between aptitude and achievement tests. In D. R. Green (Ed.), *The aptitude-achievement distinction.* Monterey, CA: CTB/Mc-Graw-Hill.

MacKinnon, D. W. (1962). The nature and nurture of creative talent. *American Psychologist, 17,* 484-495.

Mednick, M. T., & Andrews, F. M. (1967). Creative thinking and level of intelligence. *Journal of Creative Behavior, 1,* 428-431.

Piper, J. (1974). *The teacher indicator of potential scale.* Redwood City, CA: Gifted Resource Center.

Richards, R. L. (1976). A comparison of selected Guilford and Wallach-Kogan creative thinking tests in conjunction with measures of intelligence. *Journal of Creative Behavior, 10,* 151-164.

Ripple, R. E., & May, F. (1962). Caution in comparing creativity and IQ. *Psychological Reports, 10,* 229-230.

Runco, M. A. (1984). Teachers' judgments of creativity and social validation of divergent thinking tests. *Perceptual and Motor Skills, 59,* 711-719. [Chapter 5]

Runco, M. A. (1987). The generality of creative performance in gifted and nongifted children. *Gifted Child Quarterly, 31,* 121-125. [Chapter 13]

Runco, M. A., & Albert, R. S. (1985). The reliability and validity of ideational originality in the divergent thinking of academically gifted and nongifted children. *Educational and Psychological Measurement, 45,* 483-501. [Chapter 10]

Runco, M. A., & Pezdek, K. (1984). The effect of television and radio on children's creativity. *Human Communications Research, 11,* 109-120. [Chapter 4]

Schubert, D. S. P. (1973). Intelligence as necessary but not sufficient for creativity. *Journal of Genetic Psychology, 122,* 45-47.

Stanley, J. C. (1977). The predictive value of the SAT for brilliant seventh- and eighth-graders. *College Board Review, 106,* 2-8.

Sternberg, R. J. (1981). A componential theory of intellectual giftedness. *Gifted Child Quarterly, 26,* 157-161.

Sternberg, R.J . (1982). Lies we live by: Misapplication of tests in identifying the gifted. *Gifted Child Quarterly, 26,* 157-161.

Torrance, E. P. (1962). *Guiding creative talent.* Englewood Cliffs, NJ: Prentice-Hall.

Wallach, M. A., & Kogan, N. (1965). *Modes of thinking in young children.* New York: Holt, Rinehart, & Winston.

Yamamoto, K. (1965). Effects of restriction of range and test unreliability on correlation between measures of intelligence and creative thinking. *British Journal of Educational Psychology, 25,* 300-305.

Chapter 18

# Associative Hierarchies

## Abstract[*]

Previous research on the ideational process indicates that original ideas increase in frequency as an examinee works through an open-ended task. The present investigation evaluated ideational flexibility in order to determine if ideas also become more varied and diverse. Additionally, the relationship of intelligence (the IQ) with order effects of both originality and flexibility was investigated. A verbal and a figural divergent thinking test were administered to 80 school children. The midpoint of each individual's ideational set was found, and the flexibility and originality scores of each half of the set were compared. Results indicated that flexibility and originality scores were higher in the second half than the first half of the ideational set, but there were significant differences between high- and low-originality subjects, and differences between the verbal and the figural tests. The order effect was unrelated to the IQ scores of the subjects. Suggestions are made to integrate ideational flexibility into existing theories of divergent ideation.

[*] Adapted from Runco, M. A. (1986). Flexibility and originality in children's divergent thinking. *Journal of Psychology, 120,* 345-352. Reprinted with permission of the Helen Dwight Reid Educational Foundation. Published by Heldref Publications, 4000 Albemarle Street, N.W., Washington, D.C. 20016. Copyright 1986.

Ideational processes and patterns have been investigated for many years. Mednick, Mednick, and Jung (1964), for example, evaluated the responses given by undergraduates to a variety of verbal stimuli. Their findings indicated that nouns elicited more responses than adjectives, more responses were elicited by common words than uncommon words, and creative individuals (i.e., those scoring high on the *Remote Associates Test*) gave more responses than less creative individuals. More recent research has turned to divergent thinking tests to study ideational processes and patterns.

Divergent thinking tests contain open-ended problems (e.g., "How are a potato and a carrot alike?"), and are theoretically and empirically related to creativity (Guilford, 1968; Runco, 1985). Divergent thinking ability is not equivalent to creative ability, but it is indicative of the potential for creative performance. Hence, evaluating the ideational patterns that are elicited by divergent thinking tests ostensibly helps us understand one component of the creative process. An example of this research is that of Christensen, Guilford, and Wilson (1957). They evaluated the temporal qualities of ideational responses using Guilford's Plot Titles and Brick Uses tests. Their methodology involved comparing the fluency and originality scores of each two-minute interval of a ten minute test, with originality defined in terms of "cleverness, remoteness of association, and uncommonness of association" (p. 82). Results indicated that ideational productivity (fluency) was relatively constant throughout the test, while the remoteness and uncommonness dimensions of originality increased as a function of time. Ward (1969) conducted a similar investigation with seven- and eight-year-old children; and his findings were largely consistent with those of Christensen et al. (1957). He added that children with high fluency scores generated responses more quickly than children with low fluency scores, while high- and low-fluency children did not differ from one another in their originality scores or the rate at which they stopped generating common responses and started generating uncommon responses.

Milgram and Rabkin (1980) evaluated ideational patterns by comparing the first one-half of each individual's ideational set to the second half. This procedure has a notable advantage over the method of Christensen et al. (1957) and Ward (1969) because subjects are not evaluated with the same temporal intervals. In other words, response rate is not assumed to be constant across subjects. Milgram and Rabkin compared 4th, 7th, and 12th graders, and high- and low-originality subjects; and results indicated that the number of uncommon ideas was significantly higher in the second half of the ideational set than the first-half, while the number of common or "popular" ideas was significantly lower. There were also differences between the various grade levels and between the high-and low-originality subjects, with the "order effect" more apparent in the high-originality and older subjects. Similar results were reported by Phillips and Torrance (1977), although they reported differences between verbal and figural tests.

In addition to offering an interesting description of the divergent thinking process, these investigations help us to understand individual differences in ideation (e.g., high-fluency and high-originality individuals vs. low-fluency and low-originality individuals). Unfortunately, previous research on ideational patterns has focused entirely on the number and originality of the ideas. No research has been conducted to evaluate the pattern of "ideational flexibility."

Ideational flexibility is defined as the tendency to generate a hetero-geneous pool of responses, or to utilize a variety of categories and themes when producing ideas. It is a very important facet of divergent thinking, and conveys information that is not conveyed by fluency or originality (Guilford, 1968; Runco, 1985, 1986a; Torrance, 1974). Flexibility is important because it discriminates between gifted and nongifted children better than fluency or originality scores (Runco, 1985). Additionally, flexibility scores are necessary for divergent thinking tests to have predictive validity with real-world criteria (Runco, in press-a). And on a practical level, flexibility comes into play when scoring originality, for a truly original idea is statistically and thematically unique. Flexibility is, then, an interesting and important facet of divergent ideation, and one objective of the present project is to evaluate the ideational pattern of flexibility.

A second objective of this project is to determine whether or not conventional expressions of intelligence (i.e., the IQ) influence ideational patterns. Previous studies have reported significant differences between creative and noncreative individuals, but no studies have been conducted to evaluate ideational patterns as a function of intelligence. We know that creativity and intelligence are related at some levels of ability (Runco & Albert, 1984; Schubert, 1973; Yamamoto, 1964), and this suggests that intelligence might influence the ideational patterns of some individuals. The second objective of the present investigation is to evaluate the influence of intelligence on ideational patterns.

## Method

### Subjects and Procedure

The participants in this project are involved in an ongoing longitudinal study of giftedness (summarized by Albert & Runco, 1986). The present investigation involves 80 children, with 15 fifth-graders, 20 sixth-graders, 21 seventh-graders, and 24 eighth-graders. Forty percent of the sample was male and 60% was female. All of the children received the Uses and Pattern-Meanings divergent thinking tests (Wallach & Kogan, 1965) while in their classrooms. Each test had three items, and they were administered with the procedures from Wallach and Kogan (1965). IQs were obtained from school district records. The mean IQ was 129, with a standard deviation of 12.7.

### Scoring and Indices

The method of Milgram and Rabkin (1980) was used to test the primary hypothesis of this investigation by comparing the first half of the ideational set with the second half. This method involves finding the midpoint of each individual's ideational set and calculating originality and flexibility scores for each half of the set.

Originality was defined and scored as the number of unique ideas, and flexibility was defined as the number of thematic changes in an individual's response set. The categories and basic methodology for scoring flexibility are described by Runco (1985). The number of changes was used rather than the absolute number of categories in order to keep the two halves of the ideational set on equal ground. Similarly, because a large portion of the sample of subjects would be expected to generate an uneven number of ideas, and as a result have an uneven number of ideas in each half of their ideational set, the originality and flexibility scores were divided by the fluency score of that half to create ratio scores. Ratio scores have demonstrated their utility in Hocevar and Michael (1979), and were used in all subsequent analyses.

## Results

The first analysis was conducted to check the reliability of the divergent thinking scores. Cronbach's a was used, and results indicated that all indices were reliable. The a coefficients were as follows: fluency (.86), flexibility (.79), and originality (.86).

The primary hypothesis of this project was tested by comparing the divergent thinking test scores of the first half of the ideational set with those in the second half. To make the results of this project interpretable in the light of Milgram and Rabkin (1980), these comparisons (t-tests for dependent samples) were conducted separately in two groups of subjects. These were high- and low-originality groups, with a median split of the originality score (from the test that was being compared) used for defining the groups. Means and standard errors of each divergent thinking test, each index, and each group are presented in Table 18-1.

For the Uses test in the high-originality group, flexibility scores in the second half of the ideational set were significantly higher than those in the first half (t (39) = 6.10, p < .001). Flexibility scores from the Pattern Meanings test were also higher in the second half than the first half for the high-originality group (t (39) = 9.24, p < .001). Similarly, the originality scores of the second half of the ideational set were higher than those in the first half for Uses and Pattern Meanings in the high-originality group (t (39) = 6.00 and 4.25, both p < .001).

For the low-originality group, the second half of the ideational set had higher flexibility and originality scores than the first half in the Pattern Meanings test (t (39) = 2.84, p < .01, and t (39) = 2.84, p < .01). However, the difference between the two halves was not significantly different in this group for flexibility or originality from the Uses test.

Another set of analyses was conducted to test the possibility that the order effects were moderated by IQ scores or age. An "analysis of partialed variance" was used to this end (Cohen & Cohen, 1975, Chap. 9). This involves regressing the scores of the first half of the ideational set and then age or IQ on the scores of the second half. The critical result is the proportion of the variance accounted for by age or IQ that is associated with the difference between the two halves of the ideational set.

Table 18-1

Means and Standard Errors (in parentheses) of the Divergent Thinking Indices for each Half of the Ideational Set

|  | First Half | | Second Half | |
|---|---|---|---|---|
| **Low-Originality Group** (*n* = 40) | | | | |
| Uses | | | | |
|     Originality | .099 | (.01) | .141 | (.02) |
|     Flexibility | .570 | (.13) | .862 | (.08) |
| Patterns | | | | |
|     Originality | .259 | (.03) | .474** | (.05) |
|     Flexibility | .418 | (.04) | .918*** | (.02) |
| **High-Originality Group** (*n* = 40) | | | | |
| Uses | | | | |
|     Originality | .251 | (.02) | .427*** | (.02) |
|     Flexibility | .539 | (.02) | .789*** | (.03) |
| Patterns | | | | |
|     Originality | .567 | (.03) | .783*** | (.04) |
|     Flexibility | .395 | (.04) | .897*** | (.03) |

Note: Asterisks indicate a significant difference between the two halves, with **$p < .01$ and ***$p < .001$.

      Results indicated that the order effects of flexibility and originality scores were not significantly influenced by age or IQ. For example, on the Uses test, 3.3% of the variance accounted for by the difference between the two halves was attributed to IQ, and 0.5% to age. For originality scores on the Uses test, 4.8% of the variance of the difference was related to IQ, and 3.9% was related to age. Similar regression analyses indicated that these percentages were smaller for the Pattern Meanings test, and that the quadratic contribution of IQ (testing IQ2) was not significant for Uses or Pattern-Meanings.

## Discussion

      These results confirm that there are significant differences between the ideas given in the first half of an ideational set and those given in the second half. Indeed, there appears to be an order effect for both flexibility and originality scores, with each being higher in the second half of the ideational set. Of particular interest here is the order effect for flexibility, for previous research has demonstrated that flexibility is a crucial facet of divergent thinking (Runco, 1985, 1986a). Looking at the flexibility scores of the participants of the present investigation, we see that ideation becomes more varied and diversified in the second half of the ideational set as compared to the first half. Clearly a theory of divergent ideation should take flexibility and the progressive diversity of ideas into account.

This theory should also acknowledge individual differences, for the high- and low-originality examinees seemed to be using different ideational processes. These differences were apparent in the mean scores (see Table 18-1), and in the order effect of the responses to the Uses test. The order effect is important here because previous research has reported that original individuals produce more ideas, and do so more reliably than unoriginal individuals; but the present findings make a step towards describing the processes that create these differences. Put briefly, the findings of the present investigation offer a process explanation for the individual differences found in divergent thinking test performance.

Although ideation is clearly a "cognitive" process, the possibility exists that extracognitive ability contributed to the order effects and to the differences between the high- and low-originality examinees. For example, the examinees may have been using more effort and applying more strategy to their ideation in the second half of the tasks. Runco (1986b) demonstrated that strategy is very important in divergent thinking, and the subjects in the present study could have been intentionally searching for appropriate associations and responses after the reservoir of obvious ideas was depleted.

Note here that the order effects for originality and flexibility were independent of age and the IQ. In a sense, the independence from the IQ gives flexibility a type of discriminant validity. However, the subjects in the present investigation were all in the moderate or high levels of IQ, and there is therefore the potential problem of restricted range. Restricted range does not explain why the order effect was independent of age, for there were fifth-, sixth-, seventh-, and eighth-graders in the sample of subjects. This was also unexpected because Milgram and Rabkin (1980) reported that there were age differences in ideational order effects, and age was found to correlate specifically with flexibility by Runco and Pezdek (1984). Still, the previous research had younger children represented in their samples.

Probably more important is that Milgram and Rabkin (1980) and Runco and Pezdek (1984) used stimuli unlike those in the present study. The data in Table 18-1 indicate that ideation is influenced by stimulus characteristics. Put simply, the Uses and Pattern-Meanings tests seemed to elicit qualitatively and quantitatively different ideation. This is congruent with earlier findings on the effects of different stimuli on divergent thinking (Moran, Milgram, Sawyers, & Fu, 1983; Sawyers, Moran, Fu, & Milgram, 1983; Phillips & Torrance, 1977; Runco & Albert, 1985). Runco and Albert suggest that differences between verbal and figural stimuli result from the two being differentially accessible to ideational associations. They described the ideation elicited by verbal tasks as rote and preconceived, while the ideation of figural tasks was described as effortful and spontaneous. Mednick's (1962) associative theory also applies here for the verbal stimuli were probably more familiar to the subjects than the ambiguous figural stimuli. Sawyers et al. (1983) offer empirical support for the relevance of stimulus familiarity.

Future research might use explicit instructions to "be creative" (Runco, 1986b) in order to evaluate further the role of strategy in ideational patterns. Future research could also further evaluate order effects elicited by different stimuli and developmental trends in ideational patterns. Runco and Pezdek (1984) discuss the influence of audio, visual, and audiovisual stimuli on divergent thinking, and Moran et al. (1983) investigated divergent thinking elicited by three-dimensional stimuli. The developmental issue is an interesting one, for there are several views of the development of divergent thinking ability (see Albert & Runco, 1986), and an analysis focused on the actual ideational process—like that of the present investigation—could be used to test existing theories.

## REFERENCES

Albert, R. S., & Runco, M. A. (1986). The achievement of eminence: A model of exceptionally gifted boys and their families. In R. J. Sternberg & J. E. Davidson (Eds.), *Conceptions of giftedness* (pp. 332-357). New York: Cambridge University Press.

Christensen, P. R., Guilford, J. P., & Wilson, R. C. (1957). Relations of creative responses to working time and instructions. *Journal of Experimental Psychology, 53*, 82-87.

Cohen, J., & Cohen, P. (1975). *Applied multiple regression/correlation analysis for the behavioral sciences.* Hillsdale, NJ: Erlbaum.

Guilford, J. P. (1968). *Creativity, intelligence, and their educational implications.* San Diego, CA: Knapp.

Hocevar, D., & Michael, W. B. (1979). The effects of scoring formulas on the discriminant validity of tests of divergent thinking. *Educational and Psychological Measurement, 39*, 917-921.

Mednick, S. A. (1962). The associative basic of the creative process. *Psychological Review,* 69, 220-232.

Mednick, M. T., Mednick. S. A., & Jung, C. I. (1964). Continual association as a function of level of creativity and type of verbal stimulus. *Journal of Abnormal and Social Psychology, 69*, 511-515.

Milgram, R. M., & Rabkin, L. (1980). Developmental test of Mednick's associative hierarchies of original thinking. *Developmental Psychology, 16*, 157-158.

Moran, J. D., Milgram, R. M., Sawyers, J. K., & Fu, V. R. (1983). Stimulus specificity in the measurement of original thinking in preschool children. *Journal of Psychology, 4,* 114, 99-105.

Phillips, V. K., & Torrance, E. P. (1977). Levels of originality at earlier and later stages of creativity test tasks. *Journal of Creative Behavior, 11,* 147. (Abstract)

Runco, M. A. (1985). Reliability and validity of ideational flexibility as a function of academic achievement. *Perceptual and Motor Skills, 61,* 1075-1081. [Chapter 11]

Runco, M. A. (1986a). Divergent thinking and creative performance in gifted and nongifted children. *Educational and Psychological Measurement, 46,* 375-384. [Chapter 14]

Runco, M. A. (1986b). Maximal performance on divergent thinking tests by gifted, talented, and nongifted children. *Psychology in the Schools, 23*, 308-315. [Chapter 6]

Runco, M. A., & Albert, R. S. (1985). The originality and convergent validity of ideational originality in academically gifted and nongifted children. *Educational and Psychological Measurement, 45*, 483-501. [Chapter 10]

Runco, M. A., & Albert, R. S. (1986). The threshold theory regarding creativity and intelligence: An empirical test with gifted and nongifted children. *Creative Child and Adult Quarterly, 11*, 212-220. [Chapter 17]

Runco, M. A., & Pezdek, K. (1984). The effect of television and radio on children's creativity. *Human Communications Research, 11*, 109-120. [Chapter 4]

Sawyers, J. K., Moran, J. D., Fu, V. R., & Milgram, R. M. (1983). Familiar versus unfamiliar stimulus items in measurement of original thinking in young children. *Perceptual and Motor Skills, 57*, 51-55.

Schubert, D. S. P. (1973). Independence of intelligence and creativity only at upper levels. *Journal of Genetic Psychology, 122*, 45-47.

Torrance, E. P. (1974). *Torrance tests of creative thinking.* Lexington, MA: Personnel Press.

Wallach, M. A., & Kogan, N. (1965). *Modes of thinking in young children.* New York: Holt, Rinehart, & Winston.

Ward, W. C. (1969). Rate and uniqueness in children's creative responding. *Child Development, 40*, 869-878.

Yamamoto, K. (1964). The threshold of intelligence in academic achievement of highly creative students. *Journal of Experimental Education, 32*, 401-405.

## Section V

# Overview and Conclusions

The research presented in this volume suggests that divergent thinking tests are very useful, but care must be taken in their administration, scoring, and interpretation. The research also suggests that ideational skills may not be normally distributed in the population, for the divergent thinking of gifted children is more reliable than the divergent thinking of nongifted children. The two chapters in Section V present an overview, with (a) the argument that ideational tests are meaningful and objective measures of the potential for creative thinking; (b) directions for future research; and (c) practical implications of the research presented in this volume.

# DIVERGENT THINKING

Creativity has been of interest to many individuals for many years. This may be in part because creativity plays an important role in many fields and endeavors. Its role in art, science, and technology is well recognized, but creativity is also important in business, teaching, mathematics, the physical sciences, and many everyday activities. However, not everyone has been appreciative of the research on creativity. One recurring criticism of the research on creativity is that it lacks objectivity.

Early explanations of the creative process were merely subjective descriptions, and a concern for objectivity was certainly warranted. An example of an early view is given by Wallas (1926). He suggested that the creative process involves four stages: preparation, incubation, illumination, and verification. Unfortunately these stages were only supported with evidence from subjective reports. Introspection was often used, and this is not an adequately objective technique (cf. Nisbett & Wilson, 1977).

There are more recent views of the creative process that rely on subjective accounts, and several of these seem to have uncovered reliable aspects of creativity (Gruber, 1981; John-Steiner, 1985; Runco & Bahleda, 1986). There are also more objective approaches to the study of creativity. One of the first was that of Guilford (1950, 1968). Guilford presented a structure of intellect (SOI) model, and one of its catchy dimensions was called "divergent production." This idea led to the concept of divergent thinking. Divergent thinking is the process used by most of us when we are faced with open-ended tasks.

How do you answer the question, "Name all of the things you can think of that are strong"? You think divergently, and give numerous ideas. Responses to these tasks are scored for ideational fluency, flexibility, originality, and sometimes elaboration (see Chapter 12).

Guilford's was an attractive theory, and especially so back in the 1950s because Sputnik was overhead and the U.S. started to recognize the need to emphasize creativity in the schools. However, the concept of divergent thinking was soon attacked because (a) Guilford used a questionable factor analytic technique to isolate this facet of his SOI model, and (b) the empirical evidence did not support the predictive validity of divergent thinking test scores. In this sense, divergent thinking was also dismissed due to a lack of objectivity. Still, divergent thinking tests are probably the most common test of children's creativity.

There are other examples of attempts to define and study creativity, but many lack convincing, objective evidence. Instead of reviewing each of these, I would like to suggest that we look very carefully at the recent work on divergent thinking tests. I believe that our technology of testing has improved dramatically, and that divergent thinking tests can be used to estimate the potential for creative thinking. Note the emphasis on "estimate" and "potential." It would be foolish to claim that divergent thinking tests are perfect measures of significant real-world creative performance. Actual creative performance is still unpredictable in the psychometric sense; and the best predictor is probably past performance. Past performance is, however, not a completely satisfactory predictor, for if you create on one occasion, there is no guarantee that you will behave creatively in the future. The situational and motivational factors that are necessary for creativity may change with time. Also, data on past performance are not always available or reliable. We cannot, for instance, rely on the past performance of children. On the other hand, divergent thinking tests seem to be useful with children.

The argument is, then, that we reconsider divergent thinking tests as *estimates* of the *potential* for creative performance. One reason that these tests should be reconsidered is that their predictive validity is not as poor as we thought 10 and 15 years ago. If you take the three primary indices of divergent thinking (fluency, flexibility, and originality) into account, as Guilford and others suggested, and use their interaction terms in a predictive validity equation, these tests have much better validity than reported in early investigations. Multiple regression and canonical correlational techniques have been used to this end, with predictive validity coefficients of approximately .60 (Chapter 14). Early work on divergent thinking tests did not use these multivariate techniques.

Divergent thinking tests can also be used in a more comprehensive manner than they have previously been used. By comprehensive, I mean use them as more than tests of ideational skill. Usually they are used to find out how well an examinee generates ideas; but creativity is much more than that. It also involves finding worthwhile problems; applying and testing initial ideas and solutions that are generated; and often modifying the original ideas to make them more applicable and fitting. Open-ended divergent thinking tests can be used to assess both problem discovery and problem solving; and when both are taken into account, fluency scores do have much improved predictive validity (Chapter 8).

A third area of relevant research is that which tests associative patterns. This area of research goes back to Mednick (1962), but is just recently gaining popularity as a method to determine if original ideas flow regularly and evenly, or in some sort of formation. A very simple experimental technique for examining ideational patterns—one the reader may chose to try—involves counting an examinee's responses to an open-ended task, and finding the half-way point. If the examinee gives 20 items to the question, "Name all of the things you can think of that are strong," two sets of 10 ideas can be compared in terms of the number of original ideas, and the flexibility of the ideas. Results from several independent projects using this technique suggest that original ideas come later in a set of responses, but ideas are no more flexible and varied in the second half compared to the first (Chapter 18).

What is most important is (a) that ideas can be counted in a reliable and objective fashion; and (b) ideas can be used as an indication of how people generate solutions to solve problems. In fact, the notion that ideas come late in the ideational process may explain the utility of brainstorming. It is also consistent with my thesis in that we can use associative hierarchies as an objective technique to investigate an important cognitive process—namely, the ideational process.

The final evidence I will describe comes from an area of research where "explicit instructions" are given to examinees when they take divergent thinking tests in order to control their "task perception" (Chapter 6 and 7). This is an important area of work because it demonstrates that metacognitive and strategic skills are used when an examinee is faced with a divergent thinking task. People do not just generate ideas in some haphazard fashion, and divergent thinking is not just a matter of ideational fluency. Examinees seem to first make a decision about what type of idea is most suited to the problem at hand (a variety of ideas? only bizarre and unusual ideas? a large number of ideas, regardless of their quality?), and then they generate ideas that seem suitable. This componential view has been supported by the research on instructional effects in divergent thinking, and is consistent with my thesis in that it suggests that creative performance actually requires several skills. Moreover, divergent thinking tests can be used to separate the different components of the creative process; and both strategic and cognitive components can be measured in a reliable and objective fashion.

There are, then, several lines of research that suggest that divergent thinking tests provide meaningful and objective data about processes that contribute to an individual's creative performance. Put differently, as I did earlier, divergent thinking tests are useful estimates of the potential for creative performance. Fortunately for those of us who still are interested in future research, there remains a number of important questions and avenues left to explore (Chapter 20). I am particularly interested in finding a way to operationalize the motivation for creative performance. The motivation to create, if operationalized, could then be used in combination with divergent thinking abilities in a predictive equation. I am also interested in the role of evaluative skill in creative ideation. I suspect that when faced with an open-ended task, examinees generate many ideas, and select and retain the best using some evaluative skill. Research on motivation and evaluative skill is underway. And I suspect that here again, divergent thinking tests will help us to understand the creative process.

## REFERENCES

Gruber, H. E. (1981). *Darwin on man.* Chicago: University of Chicago Press.

Guilford, J. P. (1950). Creativity. *American Psychologist, 5,* 444-454.

Guilford, J. P. (1968). *Creativity, intelligence, and their educational implications.* San Diego, CA: Knapp.

John-Steiner, V. (1985). *Notebooks of the mind.* Albuquerque, NM: University of New Mexico Press.

Mednick, S. A. (1962). The associative basis for creative process. *Psychological Review, 69,* 220-232.

Nisbett, R. E., & Wilson, T. D. (1977). Telling more than we know: Verbal reports on mental processes. *Psychological Bulletin, 84,* 231-254.

Runco, M. A., & Bahleda, M. D. (1986). Implicit theories of artistic, scientific, and everyday creativity. *Journal of Creative Behavior, 20,* 93-98.

Wallas, G. (1926). *The art of thought.* New York: Harcourt Brace.

Chapter 20

# Future Research and Practical Suggestions

There can be little doubt that we are making progress towards the understanding of ideational processes and children's creativity. Indeed, a technology of ideational assessment seems to be evolving. There are, however, a number of important questions that still need to be addressed with empirical research. This chapter presents a short discussion of the practical implications of the research presented in this volume. This is followed by an outline of directions for future research.

## Practical Implications

There are a number of practical implications of the recent research on divergent thinking (Runco, 1985). A short discussion of these is presented below. They include: (a) the use of particular topics or stimuli to facilitate divergent thinking; (b) the recognition of the influence of the setting, teacher, and feedback; and (c) the importance of recognizing both the quantity and the quality of ideas. Each of these can be used in the classroom.

## Tasks and Stimuli

The thinking of children at all levels of ability is significantly influenced by the type of opportunities they are given. Students, for example, are frequently constrained by their assignments. Looking specifically at divergent thinking, it appears that unfamiliar stimuli elicit more original ideas than familiar stimuli. Further, unfamiliar stimuli seem to elicit original ideas more consistently and reliably than familiar stimuli. To give a fairly extreme example, abstract figural stimuli (like those in the Line Meanings and Pattern Meanings tasks of Wallach and Kogan [1965]) elicit many more original ideas than verbal divergent thinking tasks (e.g. "name all the things you can think of that are round"). This difference has been explained in terms of the ideational strategies required by the two types of stimuli (Chapter 10). The figural tasks probably allow the student to look to new, spontaneous ideational paths. Workaday topics that involve commonplace and familiar questions should be avoided. A teacher may want to avoid the standard assignment, "How I spent my summer vacation," and give their students a chance to think divergently with, "How I circled the globe in a day," or "What I saw when I was one inch tall."

## Setting, Teacher, and Feedback

Many aspects of the classroom environment influence students' divergent thinking and creativity. The room itself may be a factor, for some children in cue-rich settings seem to generate more than those in cue-poor settings (see Chapter 9). Unfortunately, the ideas that are generated in a cue-rich setting are often unoriginal. Because we want the student to use their heads rather than relying on the classroom for ideas, the trick is to have a rich environment that does not impose ideas on the student. Note the connection between the classroom environment and the potential influence of familiar stimuli on divergent thinking.

The teacher him- or herself is also extremely important. First and most directly, the teacher is a powerful model. If we want creative students, we should provide creative teachers. But not only will creative teachers demonstrate divergent thinking: Creative teachers are more likely than less creative teachers to look for, value, appreciate, and reinforce creativity in their students. The reinforcement of divergent and creative thinking is crucial, for too often teachers inadvertently "shape" convergent thinking in their students by only giving attention and other reinforcers to students with the correct answer. This is as it should be for some tasks, but when it is time to write creatively, one should respond in a positive way to divergent ideas. This can be difficult when one is trying to conduct a smooth, organized class, and when one has a particular curriculum or game plan. Similarly, it can be difficult because we do not always grasp the relevance of an idea—especially remote ideas, and original ideas. The valuation of divergent thinking can be very difficult in the classroom. This brings us to our last point of discussion, namely—What is a creative idea

### Recognizing Creative Ideas

The research on divergent thinking also suggests guidelines for recognizing creative ideas. There are, for example, both theoretical and empirical reasons to consider the quantity and the quality of students' ideas. The quantity of ideas is fairly easy to determine, even in a task like writing a short story. Like most divergent thinking tasks, one can count the number of distinct ideas and use of this as an estimate of ideational fluency. The quality of ideas is slightly more difficult to determine, but can be accomplished by counting the uniqueness of ideas (relative to the universe or pool of ideas given by the entire class) and taking this as an estimate of originality. The diversity or flexibility of ideas should also be recognized, and this can be accomplished by checking the number of ideational themes used in a student's story, essay, or other set of ideas (Chapter 7).

Hence there are operational definitions of ideational quantity and quality. And fluency, originality, and flexibility are all important for divergent thinking. In fact, divergent thinking tests have the highest predictive validity (e.g., are associated with creative writing) when all three of these dimensions are taken into account (Chapter 9). Still, operational theories are not always easy to use. Research in progress is being conducted to determine how accurately parents and teachers recognize original ideas given by children.

Consider the question, "Now that I know what to look for in students' ideas, how do I encourage divergent thinking?" The answer is simple—tell them what you are looking for! Give them explicit instructions on ideational originality and flexibility; tell them to give a wide range of varied ideas, and to think of things that no one else will think of. Explicit instructions have been used very successfully with children and adolescents (Chapters 6 and 7).

## Future Research

1. Comparisons should be made of the divergent thinking of individuals who are talented in specific areas. This is particularly true given the differences between mathematically gifted adolescents and high IQ adolescents (e.g., Chapter 1), and given the individual differences in art, science, crafts, music, and other domains (e.g., Chapters 13, 14, and 15).

2. Further research is needed on the influence of television and the differential effects of audio (radio) and video (television). Effects resulting from long-term exposure are especially important. All research to date has focused on short-term exposure (Chapter 4). In real-world settings, exposure to television is long-term.

3. Parental judgments of creativity should be studied with the social validation of divergent thinking tests (see Chapter 5). Runco (1989) developed a reliable socially valid measure of parental ratings of children's creativity, but its validity is yet to be assessed.

4. An analysis of the interaction of a problem finding (Chapter 8), divergent thinking, and evaluative skill is needed (and is presently being conducted). Current theory suggests that the creative process involves several stages or components, including the identification and definition of a worthwhile problem, the generation of possible ideas and solutions, and the evaluation, selection, and modification of those ideas. The interaction of the components is particularly important, for the skills may be distinct, but work together in creative performance.

5. Empirical research is needed to determine whether or not each component of the process mentioned above can be enhanced. Previous enhancements have focused on the generation of ideas. In a sense, the maximal performance paradigm (Chapters 6 and 7) dealt with the selective component, but the focus was an immediate performance rather than enduring and generalized effects.

6. Research is needed to examine the actual contents of children's divergent thinking. Sex differences and age trends would be especially revealing. Perhaps the categories used for evaluating the flexibility of ideas (Chapters 11 and 18) could be adapted and used to this end. Alternatively, more general categories could be used to test contents reflecting affiliation or achievement, as a test of ostensible sex differences in children's play.

7. More sensitive and controlled analyses of "environmental cues" are needed (see Chapter 9). Still to be examined are intra-individual and intra-test patterns. These would be very helpful

for the understanding of the associative process (Chapter 18), as well as metacognitive strategy.

8. Additional research is needed on the predictive validity of divergent thinking tests. Interaction terms should be included in all analyses (Chapters 14 and 15) and further efforts should be made to use measures of real-world performance as criteria. Validation is an ongoing process. A test does not have or lack validity; certain applications of a test are valid or invalid. Many applications of ideational tests have yet to be examined.

9. Meta-analyses should be conducted on the discriminant validity of divergent thinking tests. The relationship between creativity and intelligence is still being debated; and a meta-analysis could bring together all earlier research on this issue.

## Final Comments

Educators can continue to use divergent thinking tests with some confidence, cognizant that they estimate the potential for creative ideation. This position is supported by empirical research. Similarly, each of the suggestions outlined immediately above—using the classroom setting, unfamiliar stimuli, modeling and reinforcing divergent thinking, and giving explicit instructions to "be creative"—has empirical support. These suggestions should be tried in various combinations. In fact, they may work best if used simultaneously rather than separately. However, for maximal efficacy, we need to remind ourselves that students (particularly young children) come in a wide variety of shapes and sizes; and not all of the aforementioned suggestions will be effective with all students. Too often, psychological research deals with "the average child," and a truly average child is hard to find!

## REFERENCES

Runco, M. A. (1985, November). *Creative writing and divergent thinking*. Presented at the meeting of the Hawaii Council of Teachers of English, Honolulu, HI.

Runco, M. A. (1989). Parents' and teachers' ratings of the creativity of children. *Journal of Social Behavior and Personality, 4*, 73-83.

Wallach, M. A., & Kogan, N. (1965). *Modes of thinking in young children*. New York: Holt, Rinehart, & Winston.

# The Author

Mark A. Runco, PhD, earned a BA from Claremont Men's College (1979), and an MA and PhD from the Claremont Graduate School (1984). He has worked with several populations of exceptional children, including autistic and exceptionally gifted children. After earning his PhD, he taught psychology at the University of Hawaii, Hilo (1983-1987). At present, he is an associate professor at California State University, Fullerton, and director of the Creativity Research Center of Southern California. He is also editor of the *Creativity Research Journal.* Dr. Runco's current research is extending the investigations reported in this volume. He is, for example, examining cognitive and metacognitive components of children's creativity, children's art, and parents' and teachers' views of creativity.

# Author Index

# Subject Index